The Rockies
in First Person

The Rockies in First Person

*A Critical Study of
Recent American Memoirs
from the Region*

Ron McFarland

McFarland & Company, Inc., Publishers
Jefferson, North Carolina, and London

LIBRARY OF CONGRESS CATALOGUING-IN-PUBLICATION DATA

McFarland, Ronald E.
　　The Rockies in first person : a critical study of recent American memoirs from the region / Ron McFarland.
　　　　p.　　cm.
　　Includes bibliographical references and index.

　　ISBN 978-0-7864-3717-7
　　softcover : 50# alkaline paper ∞

　　1. Rocky Mountains Region — Biography.　2. Authors, American — 20th century — Biography.　3. Rocky Mountains Region — Social conditions.　4. Rocky Mountains Region — Economic conditions.　5. Autobiography.　I. Title.
　　F721.M46　2008
　　920.00978 — dc22　　　　　　　　　　　　　　　　2008016242

British Library cataloguing data are available

©2008 Ron McFarland. All rights reserved

No part of this book may be reproduced or transmitted in any form or by any means, electronic or mechanical, including photocopying or recording, or by any information storage and retrieval system, without permission in writing from the publisher.

Cover photograph ©2008 Shutterstock

Manufactured in the United States of America

McFarland & Company, Inc., Publishers
　Box 611, Jefferson, North Carolina 28640
　　www.mcfarlandpub.com

For Georgia Tiffany

What I remember is less trustworth than the story I tell about it.
— Mary Clearman Blew, *All But the Waltz* (1991)

Acknowledgments

I am grateful to the University of Idaho, where I have now taught for nearly four decades, which helped support this project with a sabbatical leave. On campus I have appreciated the advice and encouragement of two superb writers of memoir or life narratives, Mary Clearman Blew and Kim Barnes. Beyond the walls, I learned a great deal from my experience writing entries for the *Dictionary of Literary Biography* series, *Twentieth-Century Western American Writers* under the able and sometimes inspiring editorship of Professor Richard H. Cracroft of Brigham Young University. Tara Penry, and before her, James Maguire and Wayne Chatterton, at Boise State University's Western Writers Series have also aided and abetted my inquiries into contemporary writers from these parts, and dropping back in time, I owe a large debt to my publishers at Confluence Press, M.K. Browning and James R. Hepworth. Working with editor Rick Newby of Montana writing the entry on literature for the Rocky Mountain region of the Greenwood Press's *Encyclopedias of American Regional Cultures* series proved an invaluable experience. When I've needed an outsider reviewer for this or other projects over the years, I have often called on my former colleague here, now retired from the English department at BYU, Stephen Tanner, who informed me it was not "Church of *the* Latter-Day Saints" (the "the" was extraneous). Back in the summer and fall of twenty-aught-three, when this project was just a vague notion rattling about my brain, I taught a couple of graduate classes dealing with the major texts of this study, so particular thanks to the following: Amber Atkins, Jennifer Anderson, Kim

Crimmins, Anne Ernest, Cindy Hollenbeck, Marcia Kmetz, Rick Kmetz, Gaye LeGresley, Nate Lowe, Beth Matuska, Sean Prentiss, Chris Ritter, Patrick Rolland, Nikol Watson, Kent Williams, and Lindsay Wilson. They were all part of the inspiration and the incentive (whether they enjoyed those courses or not). And of course I cannot forget my greatest debt of gratitude, to my wife Georgia Tiffany, who read every word of this manuscript, ferreted out nearly all of the be-verbs, wrote DYN ("do you need") on various occasions, and clipped about fifty pages of "stuff" from the text.

Table of Contents

Acknowledgments	vii
Preface	1
ONE. The Genre of the Self	11
TWO. The Context of Northern Rockies Memoir	29
THREE. Ivan Doig and Mark Spragg: Fathers and Sons in Place	55
FOUR. Mary Clearman Blew's and Teresa Jordan's Western Family Albums	77
FIVE. Coming to Womanhood with Kim Barnes and Judy Blunt	100
SIX. The Indian Lives of Sidner J. Larson and Janet Campbell Hale	124
SEVEN. The Ecomemoirs of William Kittredge and Terry Tempest Williams	152
Conclusions and Speculations	176
Chapter Notes	185
Works Consulted	195
Index	203

Initial numbers indicate the specific or general locale of all or most of the life narrative commented upon herein; the number with capital A indicates the current residence or residences of the writer, with the exception of Sidner Larson, who currently teaches at Iowa State University in Ames, Iowa.

1, 1A Ivan Doig
2, 2A Mark Spragg
3, 3A Mary Clearman Blew
4, 4A (2) Teresa Jordan
5, 5A Kim Barnes
6, 6A Judy Blunt
7 Sidner Larson
8 Janet Campbell Hale
9, 9A William Kittredge
10, 10 (2) Terry Tempest Williams

Preface

Plutarch's renowned *Lives of the Noble Grecians and Romans*, more commonly known as *Plutarch's Lives*, serves as the loose paradigm for this book. Arthur Hugh Clough reminds readers in his 1864 introduction to the revised version of John Dryden's translation of the classic, which served as a source for Shakespeare's Roman plays, that Plutarch (46–120 C.E.) was "a moralist rather than an historian."[1] I do not approach these memoirs from the perspective of a moralist, but from that of a historian and literary critic with some scholarly aspirations. My method, has been at least generally similar to that of Plutarch: Life A (for example, Alexander the Great); Life B (for example, Julius Caesar); brief comparison of Life A with Life B. While attempting no moralizing, like Plutarch I have performed as something of a biographer as well as a commentator.

With each pair of memoirists I have taken a different angle: Doig and Spragg I approach as father-son life narratives; Blew and Jordan reflect mostly on their families and ranch life; Barnes and Blunt are gendered memoirs that concern coming of age and leaving the rural for an urban setting; Larson and Hale write ethnic (American Indian) memoirs; Kittredge and Williams speak to the environment, although in different ways. Each chapter includes reflections on other life narratives that are similar in various ways to the pair under scrutiny. When, as with Doig, Blew, and Barnes, the writers have written memoirs in addition to the ones singled out for analysis, I have taken those into account in passing.

The first chapter of this book addresses the bewildering array of *topoi*, topics or themes, which have evolved over the past century on the subject of life narrative or autobiography. These concern everything from the nature of memory and the problem of nostalgia to the definitions of memoir, the term that has become most widely employed over the past twenty or so years, and on to the tension between truth and fiction that appears to haunt the increasingly popular genre. I do not mean to imply that enthusiasm over life narrative writing has cropped up just suddenly; in the opening sentence of her essay on postmodernism and the autobiographical subject, Betty Bergland writes, "Between 1945 and 1980 more than five thousand autobiographies were published in the United States."[2] My aim here has been simply to inform or remind readers of the dialogue that is currently underway. In her recently published biography of her schoolteacher Aunt Imogene, Mary Clearman Blew observes that she was trying to "understand my aunt's life, and through her to understand my own."[3] In effect, Blew suggests that her biography, which draws heavily on her aunt's diaries from World War II, is also autobiographical in very significant ways: "I thought that I could trace Imogene's road through heartbreak and disappointment to independence and acceptance, and that I could convince myself that I was following the same road" (8–9).

"All writing is collaborative" (11), Blew notes, and that which involves memory would appear to be exceptionally so. This book, like her earlier memoirs, *All But the Waltz* and *Balsamroot*, involves the merging of the writer's memories, meditations, and reflections with those of her subjects (or characters) as revealed in letters, diaries, interviews, photographs, and such resources as historical texts and newspapers. "After all," Blew writes at the start of the first chapter, "memory occupies no space. Memory lives in its own small realm of bone and brain, and it worries, not about some measureless past which somehow exists behind us, but about the frayed edges of a dimensionless map whose markings of roads and rivers and events are overlaid, like a series of transparencies, upon the shifting present" (15). Through memory the past resists being past. Or at the very least, the past resists being passed over. Although the context is quite different, T. S. Eliot's familiar observations are apposite: "the historical sense involves a perception, not only of the pastness of the past, but of its presence."[4] Apposite, too, is Eliot's observation that "the past should be altered by the present as much as the present is directed by the past" (50). Perhaps the word "should" in this passage deserves particular attention in light of ongoing disputation on the reliability of memory and of fact itself when rendered by, or embodied in, language.

The second chapter provides a survey of earlier life narratives from the northern Rockies* along with some investigation into the nature and importance of regional memoir. The chapter does not offer a complete map of the subject, but I have attempted to analyze the nature of life narrative writing from the region and to demonstrate its variety. It is difficult to ascertain the literary significance of these memoirs, in part because the term "literary" has itself come under critical scrutiny in recent decades with the rise of interest in literary theory. Certainly the canon has been opened up (if not outright exploded) as a result of the controversy, and that enlargement is welcome, but the theoretical dialogue would demand more attention than would prove germane to this study. At the end of that chapter, however, I have outlined some bases or principles by which one might evaluate the life narratives encountered throughout the book. These are, at least to some extent, inevitably and confessedly (and happily) subjective.

Initially I supposed a tradition of Western life narrative might exist from which most of the writers would proceed; that is, in querying the writers whose work is the focus of the following chapters, I presumed most of them would be familiar with, and thus influenced by, one or several of such classics of the northern Rockies as Andrew Garcia's *Tough Trip through Paradise (1878–1879)* (1967), James Willard Schultz's *My Life as an Indian* (1907), Mary Hallock Foote's *A Victorian Gentlewoman in the Far West* (1972), Elinore Pruitt Stewart's *Letters of a Woman Homesteader* (1914), and Anne Ellis's *The Life of an Ordinary Woman* (1929). Moreover, I supposed all of those who wrote their memoirs after 1978 would acknowledge some debt to Ivan Doig's *This House of Sky*. While several writers did express admiration for Doig's memoir, few if any mentioned the earlier life narratives that are the focus of my second chapter, "The Context of Northern Rockies Memoir." Doig mentions having been influenced somewhat by Mari Sandoz's *Old Jules* (1935), Wallace Stegner's *Wolf Willow* (1962), A. B. Guthrie, Jr.'s *The Blue Hen's Chick* (1965), and Nannie Alderson's *A Bride Goes West* (1942). It could be argued, of course, that the influence of such texts is indirect, but that appears rarely to have been the case, although one exception might be such an influence by *Letters of a Woman Homesteader* on William Kittredge via Annick Smith's film *Heartland* (1979), which was based on Stewart's letters. Kittredge wrote some scenes

---

*Throughout the text I have intentionally written "northern" in this context with a lower case n, partly in order to distinguish the phrase as I am applying it from what geographers and geologists refer to as the Northern Rockies, which they locate in British Columbia, Alberta, Idaho, and Montana.

and dialogue for the movie. Mary Clearman Blew has evinced exceptional theoretical interest in and perspective on the subject of life narratives from the region.

Other writers of life narrative from the northern Rockies vary considerably in their awareness of regional memoir. Although she had not read extensively in the genre before writing *In the Wilderness*, Kim Barnes went to school to Blew and Kittredge, who helped her realize how personal narrative can be crafted into story, and she credits Terry Tempest Williams for giving her "permission to push the emotional envelope," to "break through traditional Western cynicism and take emotional risks that seem non–Western."[5] If there is a Montana connection (writers in the region sometimes speak only half jokingly of the "Montana Mafia"), Judy Blunt would be one of the newest recruits. In a personal communication, however, Blunt points out that she cannot remember having ever read a memoir before coming to the University of Montana in 1986. The story of her discovery as a writer goes back to a journalism class she took from Professor William Bevis, for whom she wrote "Breaking Clean," the title essay of her book. But what influenced her memoir, she reports, was "growing up in a community of storytellers."[6] In the course on Western women's memoir she taught at the University of Montana in the fall of 2004 Blunt's reading list included Ellis's *The Life of an Ordinary Woman*, MacLane's *The Story of Mary MacLane*, Hale's *Bloodlines*, Margaret Bell's *When Montana and I Were Young*, and Barnes's *In the Wilderness*. Sidner Larson traces the influences on his memoir to two rather divergent texts, neither of which are from the northern Rockies: Tobias Wolff's *This Boy's Life* and N. Scott Momaday's *The Way to Rainy Mountain*. Larson includes Hale's *Bloodlines* in his course on Native-American women writers. Janet Campbell Hale had read Momaday's memoir but did not feel particularly drawn to it. What she read as she was writing *Bloodlines* was not memoirs or autobiographies, but "a lot of 'Best Essays of.'"[7]

Mark Spragg recalls having read no memoirs before he wrote *Where Rivers Change Direction*, but fellow Wyomingite Jeffe Kennedy reports that she wanted her book, *Wyoming Trucks, True Love, and the Weather Channel* (2004) "to be like JoAnn Beard's *The Boys of My Youth* [1999] or any essays by Barbara Kingsolver or Steven J. Gould."[8] She says she was "strongly influenced" by members of her writing group who had recently published memoirs, notably Julene Bair's *One Degree West* (2000) and Karol Griffin's *Skin Deep* (2003). She also mentions her admiration for Terry Tempest Williams's *Refuge* (1991), Michael Ondaatje's *Running in the*

Family (1982), Teresa Jordan's *Riding the White Horse Home* (1993), and Anne Patchett's *Truth & Beauty* (2004). Teresa Jordan admires Blew's *All But the Waltz* (1991), but felt more strongly influenced by Gretel Ehrlich's *The Solace of Open Spaces* (1985) and such earlier memoirs as Nannie Alderson's *A Bride Goes West*. Most writers of life narrative are likely to agree with Kennedy that they read very widely and "love many more books than fall into the Memoir pigeonhole."

In asking the writers what life narratives might have influenced their work and what memoirs they admired, I anticipated that some might not respond to those queries for various reasons, including an understandable desire to assert their independence or autonomy. My notion that most of these writers from the northern Rockies would be at least generally aware of the life narrative writing that preceded theirs was only about 30 percent accurate, but from their responses it is clear that most of those writers have subsequently become well read in memoirs from the region, often in the process of teaching literature courses like those of Judy Blunt and Sidner Larson, mentioned above, or running workshops in creative nonfiction. I also anticipated a rather broad but predictable range of reference to such memoirs as Mary Karr's *The Liars Club* (1995), about a third of which takes place in Colorado, and *Cherry* (2001), Frank McCourt's *Angela's Ashes* (1996) and *'Tis* (2000), Jill Ker Conway's *The Road from Coorain* (1991), Annie Dillard's 1975 Pulitzer Prize–winning *Pilgrim at Tinker Creek* and *An American Childhood* (1987), Geoffrey Wolff's *The Duke of Deception* (1979), Russell Baker's 1983 Pulitzer Prize–winning *Growing Up* (1982), Chris Offutt's *The Same River Twice* (1993) — the list seems almost endless. Perhaps writers would refer to such classics as *The Autobiography of Malcolm X*, Gertrude Stein's *Autobiography of Alice B. Toklas*, Richard Wright's *Black Boy*, James Baldwin's *Notes of a Native Son*, Mark Twain's *Life on the Mississippi*, Benjamin Franklin's *Autobiography*, Edmond Gosse's *Father and Son*, Rousseau's or St. Augustine's *Confessions* — that list, too, seems almost endless. In short, I brought to my project the delusions of an English professor. For various reasons, I was not especially disappointed to be disabused of those delusions.

My intent has been to deal only with memoirs representing those states that I think share similar demographic, ecological, and socioeconomic characteristics. The five states of Utah, Colorado, Wyoming, Montana, and Idaho are all of the "hinterlands" — they have no coastal identity, despite the fact that Idaho is generally included with Oregon and Washington (and often almost as an afterthought, Alaska) as the Pacific

Northwest (in fact, the Idaho panhandle adheres to Pacific time, while the remainder of the state is on Mountain time). These five states are built on dry and irrigated farming, mining, ranching, and at least some timber harvest. Increasingly, their economy has turned toward tourism. They feature hot, dry summers with low rainfall (about eleven to fifteen inches annually) and cold, windy winters (ski areas, some of them world-class resorts, are located in each of the states). The five states total only a little over nine million in population, although the populations of Idaho, Utah, and Colorado increased by some 30 percent between 1990 and 2000. The largest Consolidated Metropolitan Statistical Areas, as recognized by the U.S. Census Bureau, are Denver-Boulder-Greeley, at nearly 2.6 million, and Salt Lake City–Ogden at a little over 1.2 million. The largest cities in the other three states, according to the 2000 census, are much smaller: Boise, Idaho, about 186,000; Billings, Montana, a little under 90,000; Cheyenne, Wyoming, about 53,000. With a total population of slightly under 490,000, Wyoming is the least populated of the fifty states. All of the states feature sizable public lands in the form of national parks and forests and lands under the control of the Bureau of Land Management (nearly 70% of Idaho is federally owned). All five states also include some land appropriated for Indian reservations. The most populous state, Colorado, is regarded as the most progressive politically; the other four states are extremely conservative. The northern Rockies states are rural, although increasingly less so than some of their denizens might wish to think: more than half of Colorado's and Utah's populations live in the Consolidated Metropolitan Areas indicated above.

My colleague Mary Clearman Blew reminded me that this preface should address the question as to what distinguishes these life narratives from the northern Rockies. I wish my response could be more definitive. But landscape itself constitutes a complex subject, a "texture of intimacy," as Annie Dillard calls it in *Pilgram at Tinker Creek*: "Landscape consists in the multiple, overlapping intricacies and forms that exist in a given space at a moment in time."[9] Perhaps it all comes down to the sense of place, the writer's embrace of the landscape, or what Julia Watson refers to as "anxiety of place."[10] Krista Comer calls landscape "the single most telling signature of western identity,"[11] and she offers a sharp critique of traditional, masculinist treatment of the subject in Western writing, culture, and social commentary. She proposes the West as a "discursive space—*a sociocultural landscape*—in which competing worldviews and politics are laid out and fought over" (21). In the postmodern West, Comer argues, the "male-gendered spatial metaphors and logics" (28) are under attack by "female regionalists," who "find unexpected possibility in western urban imaginaries. Urban spatial fields, that is, offer writers something of a quirky feminist opportunity" (65). While Comer mostly limits her observations to women writers, the sometimes convoluted agenda, if there is one, of postmodernism also applies to contemporary men writing from the West. Consider, for example, Spokane–Coeur d'Alene poet and fiction writer Sherman Alexie's shift, both literally and in his writing, from the interior Northwest, where he grew up and where his first books of poetry and prose were set, to Seattle. Most of the writers I reflect upon hereafter grew up in, or later came to grips with, an outdoors world they find both beautiful and harsh. They appreciate, but sometimes lament, their solitude and lack of what I would call "literary discourse." Their present residence, usually after leaving home for college, even when it is in small cities often requires difficult adjustments as they feel themselves detached not only from their families, but also from their lives on farms or ranches or in the woods. They tend to recognize, too, that the rural world of their childhood, even if it goes back only thirty or so years, hardly more than a generation, has been irrevocably altered, presumably, as in most memoirs, for the worse. Most of these writers, either overtly or more subtly, are conflicted between nostalgia for their former places and lives and resentment over false myths or paradigms of living (Sir Francis Bacon would have called them Idols).

Comer speaks of the "profound mistrust of the urban that resides in the deep heart of western discourse" (63), and for many who live in the northern Rockies that translates into suspicion or outright aversion to anything Californian. Part of Comer's agenda is to reassert California's importance to Western regional literature and culture. Even Californians who relocate to the region sometimes find themselves repudiating what they appear to regard as their former postmodern lives. New regionalists, Comer observes, often compose their narratives as an "*antidote* to the postmodern" (3). Increasingly, the interior Northwest has become a place or places of withdrawal, retreat, or retirement. Ironically, of course, as increasing numbers seek refuge in the prime lands of the northern Rockies (wooded mountains, lakes, trout streams), they compromise the very solitude they seek. And significantly, what was formerly lamented as "isolation" and "distance" has been transformed into blissful solitude and aesthetic distance. Like most writers today, the memoirists I'm writing about are connected to the Internet. Perhaps the major source of their "anxiety of place" has to do with their awareness not only that the past they remember and, generally speaking, love is lost, but also that the present in which they dwell is threatened with obliteration. I employ the word "dwell" with specific intent; its etymological root is in the Anglo-Saxon *dwellan*, which means to lead or go astray, or to hinder. Only in the Middle English does the word acquire the contrary notion "to abide" in contexts like that of Chaucer's Nun's Priest, who tells us "I may nat dwelle" (tarry, linger), and as early as the thirteenth century, by extension, "to stay" or "to establish permanent residence." Not one of the ten writers whose works I have examined currently dwells in the place where she or he locates her or his narration.

Is there an attitude or tone of voice that characterizes the region? "In all this open space," Gretel Ehrlich writes, "values crystallize quickly. People are strong on scruples but tenderhearted about quirky behavior."[12] There probably *is* such a thing as "Northern Rockies Hospitality," but if so, it is quite different from the fabled warmth of "Southern Hospitality." In her introduction to *The Story of Mary MacLane* Julia Watson cites one of MacLane's columns from the *Butte Evening News* in 1910: "Since I've been gone from it I realize that the people in Butte are all abnormal in that they form no real intimacies. They are as shy as wild seafowl with each other, and absolutely deadlocked in iron-bound personal isolation. [...] [T]hey are not, they seemingly can't be, intimate with each other" (xx). Gretel Ehrlich: "The solitude in which westerners live makes them quiet. [...] Sentence structure is shortened to the skin and bones of a thought" (6); "What's behind this laconic style is shyness. [...] The silence is profound. Instead of talking, we seem to share one eye" (7). Volubility, loquaciousness, effusiveness of any sort appears to come from outside the region, from the Midwest or the Northeast, maybe from California. Or perhaps this frugal Western style is more apparent than actual. Kim Barnes mentions a conversation with Lisa Norris, who won the Willa Cather Fiction Prize for her stories in *Toy Guns* (2000), to the effect that even when Westerners "write from a position of emotional vulnerability, their voices are strong and under control" (personal communication). Certainly the spare and understated voice is changing. Ehrlich could be speaking for all of the northern Rockies when she describes Wyoming's politics as "strongly conservative, but with a populist twist" (12), but that, too, is likely to change as what Krista Comer calls "the fast and furious world of contemporary transnational capitalism" (236) imposes on the spaces of the New West.

"Remember to get weather in your god damned book," Hemingway wrote in a letter to John Dos Passos in 1932, "weather is very important."[13] Beautiful, sunny days exist throughout the five states of the northern Rockies (Wyoming, Montana, Utah, Idaho, Colorado), but such days are rarely the subject of much text in the memoirs. To the extent we are aware of weather conditions in memoirs from the northern Rockies, they tend to be harsh; such weather, whether in Wyoming or Maine, makes for better stories. In an interview for Powells Books in Portland, Oregon, Judy Blunt reports that the blizzard of December 1964 she describes in *Breaking Clean* is a "composite" drawn from her own childhood memories and from those of her father and other ranchers she interviewed.[14] Implicitly, her own recollections were insufficient to the icy peril the story demanded. Terry Tempest Williams's *Refuge* is constructed on a catastrophic flood that becomes symbolic as the memoir unwinds. Writers like Rick Bass and Pete Fromm, Ivan Doig and Edward Abbey, Gretel Ehrlich and Janet Campbell Hale hurl wind and snow or heat and aridity at the reader throughout their texts. And if the texture of northern Rockies life narratives is a function of geology, geography, and climatology, it is also definitive by what it is not: wet and humid, for example, or coastal. If the region were one huge state, its flower would be the *Artemisia tridentata*, sagebrush. Certain species of hardwood found in its cities (maple, oak, elm) would not qualify for the state tree, but white or ponderosa pine, western larch (tamarack), cottonwood, or aspen would be good bets. The state bird would be that worthy scavenger, the ubiquitous magpie, and the state animal would be, of course, the coyote. The state human would not be African American or Asian American, or Hispanic, but it might be Ute, Crow, Blackfeet, Northern Cheyenne, Arapaho, Gros Ventre, Coeur d'Alene, or Nez Perce. Or Anglo American, if one were to go only by the percentages.

When I began to write the first complete draft of this book, the 70th Annual Lewiston Roundup was underway about 35 miles to the south, complete with bucking broncos, bull-dogging, and rodeo queens; a bicyclist had successfully fended off a grizzly in the Tetons near Jackson, Wyoming; President George W. Bush was holding back on his controversial proposal to allow road building on some 58 million acres of wilderness; the Denver Broncos were about to host the Kansas City Chiefs at Mile High Stadium; the previous week a battered salmon zipped between my feet while I was fishing for rainbow trout on Lolo Creek, near where the starving Lewis and Clark expedition first met the Nez Perce on my birthday, September 22, in 1805. My collection of personal essays,

Confessions of a Night Librarian & Other Things, does not much concern Idaho, where I have lived for the past 35 years, but Florida, where I grew up during the 1950s and 1960s. If I were to leave Idaho and the northern Rockies, however, I might compose a memoir drawn from a very different nostalgia.

Chapter One

The Genre of the Self

Long neglected by serious students of literature, scholars, and theoreticians, autobiographical writing since the 1970s has now been written, discussed, and theorized nearly to death. It has been proposed that autobiography transcends issues of genre, at least so far as it pertains to literature, that the province of autobiography may need to be broadened to encompass history, philosophy, psychology, anthropology, sociology, perhaps even biology.[1] Whether focusing on autobiography's often slighted step-child, memoir, will simplify or complicate the issues remains to be seen, but because most of the writers whose work I will be examining identify what they have written as "memoir," I will inquire into its nature: what *is* "memoir," as distinct from "autobiography"? Has memoir successfully established itself as a literary genre or subgenre, or is memoir simply light-weight autobiography? And will it last? While Mary Clearman Blew, herself the author of two memoirs, reflects on the 1990s as "the memoir decade" and appears rather eager to get on with other kinds of writing it thrives.[2] To Kathleen Boardman's query about the future of memoir writing and reading, particularly in the West, Blew responded by citing her friend and fellow memoirist Kim Barnes, whose agent advised her, "'Oh, don't do memoir. It's so nineties.'"[3]

Something of the confusion inherent in the nature of the beast is implicit in how libraries classify life narratives via the Library of Congress system. The ten books on which this study is based are classified as follows: Doig's *This House of Sky*, Spragg's *Where Rivers Change Direction*,

Blew's *All But the Waltz*, Kittredge's *Hole in the Sky* are under F for "United States local history" (four of the northern Rockies states are listed between the 720s and the 780s; Utah is 821–825); Kittredge's book, along with Barnes's *In the Wilderness*, is also under PS for "American literature"; Blunt's *Breaking Clean* and Jordan's *Riding the White Horse Home* are classified as CT, "general biography"; Larson's *Catch Colt* and Hale's *Bloodlines* are under E99, "American Indians"; Williams's *Refuge* may be found under both QH, "natural history," or RC, "internal medicine." One might wonder why such life narratives as Mary Karr's *The Liar's Club*, Tobias Wolff's *This Boy's Life*, Annie Dillard's *An American Childhood*, and Russell Baker's *Growing Up*, along with such regional memoirs as John Rember's *Traplines* and those of Kim Barnes, are classified as "American Literature," while the others are not. South Dakota memoirist Linda Hasselstrom's *Windbreak: A Woman Rancher on the Northern Plains* (1987), a year on a cattle ranch composed in diary form, is classified PS; her more recent memoir, *Feels Like Far: A Rancher's Life on the Great Plains* (1999), is classified F. A survey of the Pulitzer Prizes awarded in the category of Biography and Autobiography turns up some suggestive finds. In the first eight years of awards made in that category, 1917–1924, four awards were made in each, the first in autobiography going to Henry Adams's *The Education of Henry Adams* in 1919. In the next fifty-seven years, however, only two autobiographies or memoirs won a Pulitzer. In 1983 Russell Baker won the prize for *Growing Up*, and three memoirs were won during the 1990s, the most recent prize-winner being Katherine Graham's *Personal History* in 1998.

The issue I am taking up in this book is not whether autobiographical writing in its bewildering multiplicity of shapes and visages will survive (Sidonie Smith and Julia Watson describe 52 "genres of life narrative" in *Reading Autobiography*[4]), but more specifically whether the kind known as "memoir" will in some way prevail and whether regional memoir, specifically that of the West, will sustain its fad-like popularity. One is tempted simply to say "yes" to the former and "not likely" to the latter. For better or worse, however, the subject of life narrative is fraught with manifold complexities, with conflicting ideas and issues that range from the depths of ontology and epistemology to the veneers of rhetoric and semantics. So perhaps, then, it is "for better," as such discourse in academic circles tends to be self-perpetuating. My intent here is not to make original contributions to that theoretical discourse (certainly not to the metaphysical aspects thereof) so much as it is to summarize it and to outline what I think are some of its salient features, what Renaissance rhetoricians called *topoi* or commonplaces, topics, premises, and ideas to think and talk about.

First comes the old Aristotelian impulse to define: What is autobiography, and what is memoir, presuming memoir is not (as it often seems to be in common usage) simply a synonym? Scholars tend not to be satisfied with simple dictionary definitions; as Jerome Bruner notes, "Autobiography is altogether too familiar a form to be taken at face value."[5] A common practice is to break the word into its etymological parts: auto (self), bio (life), graphy (writing). One of the most frequently cited recent definitions is that of the French linguist Philippe Lejeune: "Retrospective prose narrative written by a real person concerning his own existence, where the focus is his individual life, in particular the story of his personality."[6] Lejeune comments explicitly on the implications of his careful definition, and in a book dating from 1975 he outlines in some detail what he calls the "autobiographical pact," a direct or implied contract with the reader concerning "the identity ('identicalness') of the *name* (author-narrator-protagonist). The autobiographical pact is the affirmation in the text of this identity, referring back in the final analysis to the *name* of the author on the cover" (14). Predictably, both Lejeune's definition and his concept of the pact have been much debated over the past thirty years. At about the same time Lejeune's studies were being published, Elizabeth W. Bruss, in *Autobiographical Acts* (1976), offered what she calls three "rules" that might be used to define such texts: (1) the dual role of the autobiographer as both source of the text and its subject matter; (2) the claim as to the "truth-value of what the autobiographer reports," along with the corollary that "the audience is expected to accept these reports as true, and is free to 'check up' on them or attempt to discredit them"; (3) whether or not what is reported can be authenticated, "the autobiographer purports to believe in what he asserts."[7] Although Bruss submits that "[a]ny and all of these rules may be and occasionally are broken," what she proposes does not differ much from Lejeune's notion of a pact or implied contract that concerns the "responsibilities of the author" and the "rights of the readers."

Robert Folkenflik traces the initial appearance of the word "autobiography" in any language to 1786 (an English text), and he reflects on the arrival of the term in German usage while observing that the French "got along happily with *les mémoires*."[8] "Of course," he notes, "autobiography existed before the term came into being, just as one could catch a disease before it was diagnosed or named" (7). Folkenflik's rather playful analogy could be taken as a warning against the perils of theorizing. Paul de Man begins his essay, "Autobiography as De-facement," in similar metaphoric fashion: "The theory of autobiography is plagued by a recurrent series of questions and approaches that are not simply false, in the sense that they are aberrant, but that are confining, in that they take for granted assumptions about autobiographical discourse that are in fact highly problematic."[9] While Georges Gusdorf begins his 1956 essay, "Conditions and Limits of Autobiography," rather triumphantly ("Autobiography is a solidly established literary genre"[10]), de Man suggests that one of the problems plaguing the theory of autobiography is "the attempt to treat autobiography as if it were a literary genre among others." De Man goes on to say that beside such genres as tragedy and epic poetry, "autobiography always looks slightly disreputable and self-indulgent in a way that may be symptomatic of its incompatibility with the monumental dignity of aesthetic values" (919). Disease, diagnosed, plagued, aberrant, symptomatic — the metaphoric web implies that autobiography is not a healthy genre.

De Man argues that "autobiography lends itself poorly to generic definition," and he finds "the distinction between fiction and autobiography" to be "undecidable" (921). He concludes that autobiography is not so much a genre or mode as it is "a figure of reading or of understanding." Northrup Frye makes very little of autobiography in his *Anatomy of Criticism* (1957), perhaps because serious dialogue on the subject was twenty years up the road. "Autobiography," Frye notes in passing, "is another form which merges with the novel by a series of insensible gradations. Most autobiographers are inspired by a creative, and therefore fictional, impulse to select only those events and experiences in the writer's life that go to build up an integrated pattern."[11]

Frye's conflation of autobiography with fiction and de Man's consignment of the genre to the realm of the "undecidable," if not downright indecipherable, are not unique. In fact, it is more the rule than the exception. The classic study of autobiography is that of Georg Misch, which first appeared in 1907 with a third, two-volume edition in 1949 and 1950 translated as *A History of Autobiography in Antiquity*. A philosopher, Misch writes of the "limitless variety of autobiographical writing" and of its "Protean character": "In itself it is a representation of life that is committed to no definite form. [...] Hardly any form is alien to it."[12] Under the chameleonic umbrella of autobiography, as it applies to literature, we may include diaries, letters, journals (like those kept by explorers, conquistadors, and pioneers), confessions, certain poems (for example, Wordsworth's

Prelude, but not Milton's *Paradise Lost*, setting aside such moments as III, 13–55), personal essays (Montaigne, yes; Bacon, for the most part, no), memoirs, and autobiographies, to the extent that they are considered distinct from memoirs. In effect, the basis of autobiography is in "the fundamental — and enigmatical — psychological phenomenon which we call consciousness of self or self-awareness. [...] In a certain sense the history of autobiography is a history of human self-awareness" (8). The first sentence in C. G. Jung's prologue to his autobiography, *Memories, Dreams, Reflections*, reads, "My life is a story of the self-realization of the unconscious." In writing what he calls his "personal myth," Jung adds, "An autobiography is so difficult to write because we possess no standards, no objective foundation, from which to judge ourselves."[13]

Misch attempts to distinguish memoir from autobiography in a paragraph that begins, "Man's relation to the world may be conceived actively or passively." From this, Misch observes, comes the distinction between the two types of autobiographical writing, using "memoirs," he notes parenthetically, "with the personal connotation that has become current since the nineteenth century":

> In memoirs that relation is passive in so far as the writers of memoirs (although like the autobiographers, and even more exclusively, they use the form of the first-personal narrative) introduce themselves in the main as merely observers of the events and activities of which they write, and if they join the active participants it is only in minor parts [20].

Lejeune pointedly excludes the memoir from his rigorous definition of autobiography on grounds that many writers of what they call memoir would reject: that the "subject treated" is not the writer's "individual life, [the] story of a [his/her] personality" (4). Francis R. Hart concurs, and perhaps goes a step farther: "Memoir is not a kind of autobiography, but, like confession and apology, a kind of autobiographical intention."[14]

More recently, William Zinsser, who begins his book, "This is the age of the memoir," has described memoir as "some portion of a life": "Unlike autobiography, which moves in a dutiful line from birth to fame, omitting nothing significant, memoir assumes the life and ignores most of it."[15] In her important study of collaboration in Western literature, Linda K. Karell argues that "Unlike formal autobiography [...] the autobiographical genre of memoir makes no claim to seamless representation *or factual recall*" (my italics).[16] Vivian Gornick offers the following carefully constructed definition of memoir, having largely effaced the term "autobiography" from her book: "A memoir is a work of sustained narrative prose controlled by an idea of the self under obligation to lift from the raw material of life a tale that will shape experience, transform event, deliver wisdom."[17] Nothing in Gornick's definition commits the memoirist to the production of a fully elaborated portrait of his or her life, or to matters of fact; rather, the salient terms are the noun "tale" and the verbs "shape" and "transform."

In Zinsser's anthology Annie Dillard writes, "The best memoirs [...] forge their own forms," and she refers to her book, *An American Childhood* (1987), as neither autobiography nor "memoirs" (with stress on the plural): "I wouldn't dream of writing my memoirs; I'm only forty years old. Or my autobiography; any chronology of my days would make very dull reading." Dillard defines memoir rather loosely as "any account, usually in the first person, of incidents that happened a while ago."[18] In a bibliographical note on Russell Baker's *Growing Up* (1982), Dillard observes, "Most of the best memoirs, like this vivid and genial one, refrain from examining the self at all" (211). William Gass, in an essay wherein he argues that "An honest autobiography is as amazing a miracle as a doubled sex, and every bit as big a freak of nature," describes memoir as "usually the recollection of another place or personality, and its primary focus is outward."[19] Smith and Watson concur: "the memoir directs attention more toward the lives and actions of others than to the narrator" (198).

Reflecting on how memory appears to reach out toward imagination, and therefore moves into invention, Patricia Hampl defines memoir as "the intersection of narration and reflection, of storytelling and essay writing." She adds: "The first commandment of fiction — Show, Don't Tell — is not part of the memoirist's faith. Memoirists must show *and* tell."[20] Elsewhere, when Hampl asks herself why she has abandoned the novel and "consorted with a flabby genre," she concludes that the "truth memoir has to offer is not neatly opposite from fiction's truth," and she pledges her allegiance to "the mongrel nature of the genre" (202, 205). Question: Does memoir tend to behave more like fiction than does autobiography? That is, does memoir somehow have greater license to be fictive? Novelists have written memoirs (Henry James, Ernest Hemingway), and memoirists have written novels (Kim Barnes, Mark Spragg). Are we to suppose they make no distinction when they turn from one genre to the other? Wallace Stegner makes no distinction between memoir and autobiography in his declaration of their inseparability from fiction: "The guts of any significant fiction — or autobiography — is an anguished question." He concludes: "Autobiography and fiction are variant means to the same end."[21]

Clearly such discourse about memoir is distinct from traditional views of the subject as expressed in James Goodwin's *Autobiography: The Self Made Text*, although he begins in words reminiscent of Dillard and Gass: "In the memoir form there is typically an extensive concern with actions and experiences other than those of the writer."[22] Goodwin describes memoir as "the narrative mode in which the individual uses the incidents of an active public life as a guide to understanding the culture or political tenor of the times," the "leading assumption" of such a memoirist being that "the public record of an individual life is likely to be interesting and useful to both contemporaries and succeeding generations." This restricted definition of the term would obviously fit the ubiquitous presidential memoirs, along with those of other public figures, from generals like Ulysses S. Grant to corporate tycoons like Lee Iacocca and star athletes like Michael Jordan. The memoirs to be examined hereafter, however, concern private lives and personal experiences that rarely touch on public events. In that respect, *Company Aytch*, the Civil War memoir of Sam Watkins, who served with the First Tennessee Cavalry, is closer to those that Goodwin describes than are the ones I will be inquiring into. Moreover, while most of the memoirists whose works I will deal with are now at least fairly well known as writers, it would not be quite accurate to describe them as "literary memoirs" in the sense of, for example, Gertrude Stein's *The Autobiography of Alice B. Toklas* or Ernest Hemingway's *A Moveable Feast*. Stein and Hemingway had established reputations as writers prior to writing their memoirs, which are of interest partly (perhaps largely) because they concern the writer's life. They are the nonfictional counterparts of the *Künstlerroman*, the classic modernist example of which is James Joyce's *A Portrait of the Artist as a Young Man*. Even though Ivan Doig, as a case in point, is now widely known as a novelist, his memoir, *This House of Sky: Landscapes of a Western Mind*, which appeared in 1978, was his first book. In fact, most of the writers to be considered here began with memoir.

Nothing about the subject of memoir is "given." The problem facing students of autobiographical discourse (the term may be broadly construed to cover a painter's self-portraits, film, and recorded conversation as well as writing, despite the presumed limitation of "graphy") begins with the self, the "autos." Controversy swirls over the question of whether an autonomous self exists as opposed to a socially constructed self. Paul John Eakin devotes a substantial part of his study, *How Our Lives Become*

Stories (1999), to examining the nature of the self and the "relational self," the self as defined by relations with others, which he considers "the most prominent form of life writing in the United States today."[23] To what extent is the self composed of language? Does self manipulate language, or does language manipulate self? And where or how does the life, the outer and inner life-as-lived, the "bios," figure in? Is the person/writer who lived that life necessarily (or even at all likely) to be the best or most reliable portrayer of it? What is the nature of the author's authority? Students of first-person narration in fiction are taught early on to interrogate the speaker. To what extent are Huckleberry Finn or Holden Caulfield or Sister in Eudora Welty's "Why I Live at the P.O." or *any* first-person speaker in a story by Poe reliable? Surely a critical thinker should proceed with caution when it comes to autobiographical discourse of any kind. Georges Gusdorf asserts, "in autobiography the truth of facts is subordinate to the truth of the man" (43). Mary Clearman Blew comments on the "conflicting claims of the exact truth of the story and its emotional truth."[24] And Andrew Hudgins writes approvingly of eight "loving lies" an autobiographer tells "with hope and good intentions," concluding, "The autobiographer dances on the shifting middle ground between fact and fiction, reportage and imagination, actuality and art."[25] Thomas Larson cites Hudgins's essay in his book *The Memoir and the Memoirist* (2007), but while he indicates that the truth is both factual and emotional, he asserts, "The truth — not the fiction and not the imagination — matters if you're going to write memoir."[26]

In effect, the autobiographer and the memoirist dance on the same ballroom floor, but they are not necessarily easy partners. Paul John Eakin indicates in the first line of his preface "This is a book about autobiography" (ix), and he tends to distinguish between memoir, in which "the story of the self [...] is subordinated to the story of some other for whom the self serves as privileged witness," and "relational autobiography," in which "the story of the self is not ancillary to the story of the other" (58). Thomas Larson appears even more adamant about the generic distinction, and he obviously prefers the memoir: "To write memoir is to be selective; to write autobiography is to be indiscriminate" (2). Autobiography Larson decries as the genre of the "great-person-turned-writer," and he describes the tone as "self-justifying" (11); autobiography, he asserts, "is a male genre" (12), and its "central tenet — wisdom gained through many years — is much too grandiose for the memoirist" (16). Larson concludes, "Autobiography is written by the public person who tells the birth-to-death story of [his or] her persona. By contrast, memoir allows the authentic self to lift the mask and tell the story of how mask and self have been intertwined" (129). Sidonie Smith and Julia Watson's preference for the term "life narratives" at least skirts the semantic and etymological problems of the word "autobiography," even as it allows for such unwritten forms of expression as painting, film, and video and audio recording.

In a brief essay reprinted in an anthology entitled *The Fourth Genre*, Fern Kupfer begins, "It is the authority of the truth — the idea of truth, anyway — that makes the memoir attractive to readers."[27] Kupfer acknowledges, however, that we "need to give memoir writers permission to lie," provided "the reconstructed version of the story does not deceive the reader in its search for the aesthetic truth." She offers three acceptable kinds of lie: (1) "little white lies" that result from blurred memory as to relatively small details (was the coat blue or red?); (2) a much larger category that includes "composite characterization, compression of time, omission of unnecessary detail" (the first of these three is surely the most problematic); and (3) the sort of "conjecture" she describes as "'the gift of perhaps'" (for example, *perhaps* when my thrice great uncle was wounded at the Battle of Lookout Mountain in 1863 he asked himself ...). Suspecting that "the past arrives at memory's door already out of focus," Thomas Larson reflects on "clarifying the blur" (107), and he admonishes that "Fiction's falsification is entirely different from that of a memoirist" (108). To "preserve that not-knowing, that tentativeness," Larson observes, "is vital to the memoir's story" (189).

It is curious that serious students and scholars of autobiography appear to be so committed to the project of distinguishing autobiography from memoir, often with a condescending wink at the latter. While confessions are generally listed along with memoirs among such subspecies as diaries, letters, and journals, most scholarly studies of autobiography nearly apotheosize Augustine's *Confessions*, which are the culmination of Misch's volumes and the point of departure for such tomes as historian Karl Joachim Weintraub's *The Value of the Individual: Self and Circumstance in Autobiography* (1978) and William C. Spengemann's *Forms of Autobiography: Episodes in the History of a Literary Genre* (1980). Scholars often propose that genuine autobiography, setting Augustine aside, is a "modern" genre beginning with the Renaissance concept of the individual and individuality; others contend that the real flowering does not begin till the Romantic era. Suzanne Nalbantian declares Rousseau's *Confessions* (1782) to be "the first autobiography to contain an historical self-consciousness of the genre itself."²⁸ Spengemann laments in his introduction that "the more the genre gets written about, the less agreement there seems to be on what it properly includes."²⁹ As the preceding has suggested the "self-biographical mode" has increasingly tended "to assume fictive forms in the modern era," largely "in response to changing ideas about the nature of the self" (xiii). Spengemann outlines three fundamental "forms" in his study: historical autobiography, evolved between the Middle Ages and the Enlightenment, inclusive of Benvenuto Cellini, presumably, and Benjamin Franklin (self-recollection); philosophical autobiography, evolved during the pre–Romantic and Romantic era, inclusive of Jean-Jacques Rousseau and William Wordsworth (self-exploration); and poetic autobiography, inclusive of Charles Dickens's *David Copperfield* and, perhaps less convincingly, Nathaniel Hawthorne's *The Scarlet Letter* (poetic self-expression) (32). Although his approach may seem overly contrived at times (he locates the paradigm for all three forms in Augustine's *Confessions*), it is useful. With respect to twentieth-century autobiography (notably that of such writers as Yeats, Proust, and Plath), Spengemann suggests what seems to me to be potentially another "form": poetic self-invention. That, I think, is what often happens in what we now call "memoir."

Various kinds of life narrative constitute the bulk of what is today being published as "creative nonfiction" and "literary nonfiction," and these designations have won only gradual, and often grudging, acceptance. Somewhat playfully, various writers have suggested calling it "faction." Although, as Robert Frost suggests in "Mowing," it may be true that "The fact is the sweetest dream that labor knows," serious students and writers of the new genre are understandably suspicious of fact.

The fact seems no sweet dream to Jill Ker Conway, who poses a rhetorical question in the opening sentence of *When Memory Speaks: Reflections on Autobiography* (1998): "Why is autobiography the most popular form of fiction for modern readers?"³⁰ "Thirty Years ago," Vivian Gornick writes, "people who thought they had a story to tell sat down to write a novel. Today they sit down to write a memoir" (89). Gornick suggests that one reason for the recent surge in memoir has to do with "a state of reading" that has "grown oppressive," and she argues that the urge to "tell a tale rich in context, alive to situation, shot through with event and perspective" has been "suppressed," but cannot be eradicated. While Barrett J. Mandel concedes that autobiographers use techniques of fiction, he maintains it "is not fiction" while at the same time asserting, "It would also be misleading to label autobiography nonfiction."³¹ Thomas Larson's observations on the gap that separates the novel from the memoir seem pertinent here: "a novel emphasizes the emotional truth of a character while a memoir emphasizes the emotional truth of the author" (104). "We deprive memoir of its singular character," Larson adds, "if we lump it into fiction simply because we know that any personal narrative has irremediable fictional traits" (108). Autobiography, declares Robert Folkenflik, "may be truthful or mendacious, for factuality is not crucial to its autobiographical interest, despite some critics' neo–Romantic insistence on sincerity."[32] Is the issue merely semantic? Smith and Watson observe that "While autobiographical narratives may contain 'facts,' they are not factual history about a particular time, person, or event," but "offer subjective 'truth' rather than 'fact'" (10).

Perhaps the supreme irony of the genre, if its ambiguous identity is not supremely ironic enough, is the fact that this most personal and individualistic of modes (forms, acts, intentions, impulses) should achieve its greatest popularity and acquire its most intense critical scrutiny at this historical moment of global, collective, mass-produced, commodified, corporate-cultural-social totalitarianism. At the moment that *avant garde* intellectuals are preaching everything from the death of the author to the nonexistence of the autonomous self, autobiographers and memoirists seem defiant. Or are they in some ways desperate? Does the current celebration of the self amount to some sort of triumph, or is it reactionary? Do texts of this sort inevitably retain some germ of nostalgia for a mythic golden age (we were more self-reliant then, the earth was less polluted then)? If the latter is in fact the case, if such texts are covertly reactionary, perhaps especially those texts that celebrate a particular region, are they truly healthy? William Kittredge grieves over his lost childhood in the opening pages of *Hole in the Sky* (1992): "I would like to reclaim the ease and clarity with which I was able to think about what I was and what I wanted."[33] Mark Spragg recognizes his boyhood on a dude ranch in western Wyoming as "an anachronism."[34] To what extent are these memoirs from the northern Rockies laments for a lost past? Perhaps all memoirs and autobiographies are, at least to some degree, laments. Do such laments serve any purpose other than expression of regret? Perhaps all memoirs and autobiographies are also cautionary tales. They may also offer some sort of healing for the readers as much as for the writers.

The "I" of autobiography wishes to put his or her best foot forward, unless, of course, it would be more effective to put his or her *worst* foot forward. The classic success story might not sell nearly as well as the story of rise and fall, or as the story of one's wretched, traumatized life. As will be apparent, a reader cannot even be confident that the focus of a text identified as "autobiography" or "memoir" is really on the self at all, as opposed to a social or political issue (or psychological, economic, philosophical, religious, historical, environmental, or combinatory for that matter). At what point do autobiographers or memoirists yield to other impulses? And if they plunge into another mode, does the book become something else? In *Wind in the Rock*, for example, Utah naturalist Ann Zwinger alternates between the personal and the scientific:

> [W]hen one walks alone in this country one takes on a new responsibility for self.[35]

> Behind me the sun shatters on the canyon rim, obliterating its outline, like some baroque apotheosis of light [26].

> I sleep in stop motion, watching the light change. At moonrise, as on many other nights in the canyon, almost simultaneously a draft of wind sighs downcanyon [28].

In the preceding passages the writing is metaphorically charged and downright poetic. But consider these passages:

> A small black snail leaves a narrower, smoother groove. The alkaline water provides the calcium carbonate necessary for shell building [29].

> Large herbivores are the first to go in a deteriorating ecosystem because of their needs for greater space, food, and cover [32].

> Available plants, among dozens that were utilized, were piñon, wild grasses (especially rice grass), saltbush, prickly pear, yucca, sego lily, wild onions, and scrub oak [33].

When she writes as a naturalist, Zwinger occasionally even drops into the passive voice. Is the appropriate genre of this book simply "natural history" or "description and travel," or, at least potentially, "memoir"?

Smith and Watson propose the subgenre of "ecobiography" (194) for books like Terry Tempest Williams's *Refuge*, and that designation might apply as well to several of Zwinger's books. Like Janet Varner Gunn, I do not wish to "control" so much as to "respond" to the "strangeness" of autobiographical writing.[36] James Olney goes so far as to create a neologism, "periautography," which would mean "'writing about or around the self,'" and he recommends this word for "its *in*definition and lack of generic rigor."[37]

If readers were to come to Zwinger's books primarily for her lifestory or because they were attracted to the personality recorded therein, those readers might appropriately classify the books as "memoir," and perhaps as "natural history," too (the Library of Congress designation for the book is GH, "natural history"). But such readers are not likely to become fans of her writing. In Zwinger's writing, the self is subordinated to the natural world. Her personable, often poetic style renders the empirical observations more familiar and readable than a strictly denotative treatise on the history, geology, flora, and fauna of the southeastern Utah canyonlands, but her focus is on the landscape. Zwinger does create herself as a character in the book, but only in a very limited sense. The book is not so much about herself and her attitudes or feelings as it is a record of her exact observations. After all, one might argue, she includes not only her own illustrations (complete with scientific names of the species), but offers endnotes and an index as well—hardly the stuff of memoir. Janet Gunn's study of what she calls the "autobiographical situation" concentrates on "the cultural act of a self reading" (8). Barrett Mandel reminds us that in autobiography, as in other literary genres, the work "is completed by the satisfied reader" (54). Regardless of what might be considered the "autobiographical intention," the reader is a collaborator who plays a vital part in determining whether any given book is a memoir. I doubt that readers who prefer memoir would experience much satisfaction from Zwinger's books, despite their occasional moments of personal reflection or meditation.

If Zwinger's books constitute one end of the spectrum, perhaps Norman Maclean's *A River Runs through It* constitutes the other. The title novella and its companion piece, *USFS 1919: The Range, the Cook, and a Hole in the Sky* (setting aside the story, "Logging and Pimping and 'Your Pal, Jim'") were published as fiction at Maclean's insistence, even though precious little of a fictive nature occurs in these "true stories."[38] Maclean's fictional gestures are comprised mostly of the compacting of events that occurred over several summers into a single summer and the relocation of his brother Paul's murder from Chicago to Helena (surely allowable prevarications as per Hudgins and Kupfer, above). Numerous memoirs have contained more fictional elements, in fact more out-and-out lies, than Maclean's novellas. (Gusdorf observes in passing that Chateaubriand's *Voyage en Amérique* is filled with "the recollection of landscapes that he never saw" [43].) In writing about Maclean and teaching his book, I have conformed in my approach to his statement in the acknowledgments that "It's primarily fiction all right" (xi). But if readers or scholars were to insist that it be reclassified as memoir, I would have a hard time disputing them. Perhaps if Maclean had written those novellas during "the memoir decade" of the Nineties, he would have de-fictionalized some of the text and offered them to the world in a different guise.

Some books that appear, at least initially, to possess all of the traits of memoir or autobiography end up becoming something else. Both of Montana writer Annick Smith's books, *Homestead* (1995) and *In This We Are Native* (2001), begin as memoir. Perhaps as much as three-quarters of the essays that comprise *Homestead*, starting with the title essay, pertain to Smith's story of the 163-acre homestead she and her husband David Smith and their four sons built on the Big Blackfoot River in 1964 and of his death from a heart attack in 1974, when he was just 41 years old, and to related autobiographical matters. The second essay, "Generations," concerns her Hungarian Jewish parents who immigrated to Chicago, but although her husband David reappears in the next several essays, they tend to move in other directions. The third essay, for example, "Better than Myth," deals with what might be called, as she phrases it, "the texture of Montana life."[39] Later essays in the book, including "Wallowa," "Fishing the Tundra," and "Andalusia, Again," clearly enter the realm of travel journalism. On the other hand, Sidonie Smith and Julie Watson include "travel narrative" as a sub-species of "life narrative" among their 52 genres (207). Similarly, in her more recent book, *In This We Are Native*, Annick Smith revisits the memoir of her life with David Smith and introduces her relationship with William Kittredge for the first ninety or so pages before branching into nature writing with essays like "Gleaning Wild Gardens" and travel writing like "Falling into the Canyon." The longest single essay in the volume is "Big Bluestem," a fine piece of nature or environmental writing (Smith and Watson's "ecobiography") that is set in the Tallgrass Prairie Reserve in Oklahoma. Curiously, the last three essays, which include a memoir on her father's death, return to the mode of autobiography or memoir, that is, of life narrative, so the book is something of a hybrid.

Because the fictional aspects of creative nonfiction have become so pronounced, it seems to me that much recent autobiographical writing has tended to behave like either novels or short story collections, depending on whether the text is conceived as a book structured around a more-or-less unified plot or as a collection of related essays. Laura Marcus, among others, has observed that modern autobiography "emerged alongside, though independently of, the eighteenth-century novel, but its development from the late eighteenth century onwards involved a borrowing of novelistic techniques" (237). Pete Fromm's *Indian Creek Chronicles* (1993), for example, is built much like a short novel of twenty numbered chapters that retell his experiences in the Selway wilderness area of the Idaho panhandle during the winter of 1978-79, when he was a naïve twenty-year-old undergraduate at the University of Montana. Gretel Ehrlich's *The Solace of Open Spaces* (1985), however, is composed of a dozen essays, individually titled, that deal with her introduction to life in Wyoming. Although the narrative mode dominates (as opposed to the expository), her essays vary considerably in what might be called their story-likeness. Like Fromm's memoir, Mary Clearman Blew's *Balsamroot* (1994) is built like a novel with numbered but untitled chapters, while her *All But the Waltz* (1991) is a collection of individually titled essays.

The tension that exists in most memoirs between the poles of fact and fiction may be connected with the writers' use of two elements that occur almost inevitably in their prose: photographs and dreams. Most writers of memoir use *both* photographs (or snapshots), presumably to help establish their credibility, and dreams (or reveries), presumably to establish a kind of intimacy. The mix of photographs and dreams dramatizes the movement between the outer and the inner in their writing. The dreams or nightmares, some of which may strike readers as invented or improbable (more likely *created* out of the desire to probe the subconscious than actually *dreamed*), add a texture to the memoir that transcends Kupfer's "gift of perhaps." The writer presents the dream, or its more conscious cousin the reverie, as having actually occurred. But even if the reader accepts the actual fact of the dream, it arises by its nature from the realm of the imagination and adds to the memoir some of the riches of fiction. The photograph, on the other hand, can be and in some cases actually is offered up in evidence. The eleven essays of Mary Clearman Blew's *All But the Waltz* (1991), subtitled "A Memoir of Five Generations in the Life of a Montana Family," are accompanied by a dozen photographs or snapshots and a map. These combine to assert the claims of verifiable reality, of fact.

Because my study concerns autobiographical writing from a particular region, five states of the Rocky Mountain West (Wyoming, Colorado, Utah, Montana, and Idaho), it focuses on how various writers deal with a particular place, and in that respect, as with regional fiction, place itself potentially becomes, as per the going cliché, a character. But even place is problematic in the memoir. Does the writer attempt simply to set forth this or that place accurately and denotatively? Does the writer glamorize or poeticize place (perhaps via personification)? Do we encounter what some call "gendered" landscape? That is, to introduce the issue in passing, to what extent is landscape presented as a place of physical challenge and pragmatic value (male), and to what extent is it perceived as a place of self-realization or self-fulfillment and beauty (female)? Are these conventional gendered ideologies valid, or perhaps, as some ecofeminist critics are now insisting, overly simplified? Because the interior West, the hinterlands, are noted for harsh winters and dry summers, the writer may be inclined to romanticize the severity. In that case, it will not do simply to state flatly that it is windy in Wyoming, that sagebrush litters most of Montana, or that Colorado is dusty. What do the writers and readers of memoir want more, assuming that one quality must inevitably be subordinate — accuracy or vividness?

Surely, most writers would argue they can provide both accuracy *and* animation in their work, but just as surely there remains a tension between the two. Perhaps the best writing derives from that tension, the sometimes perilous balance between the thing itself and that thing as appareled in language. Here are two statements concerning sagebrush from memoirs written more than fifty years apart. Both statements have impact on the reader particular to their nature: "Sagebrush covers 58,000 square miles of Wyoming." "Miles and miles of wilderness, and not a sign of habitation: no tree, no green, only the gray of pungent sagebrush."[40] The first statement, from Gretel Ehrlich's *The Solace of Open Spaces* (1985), is about as denotative as writing gets, no matter what the genre, and it is probably accurate (the total land area of Wyoming is nearly 97,000 square miles). The second statement, from Annie Pike Greenwood's *We Sagebrush Folks* (1934), records an early impression of her new home in southern Idaho, where she moved with her husband in 1906 to begin farming. It, too, is essentially denotative, but it is also, in a manner of speaking, "poetic." What makes Greenwood's sentence poetic is not so much the spare amount of imagery as the ear, the alliterative play of green and gray, for example, and the long assonantal [ay] sounds of habit*a*tion/g*ray*/s*a*gebrush. One might concede the accuracy of Ehrlich's statement while preferring the affective power of Greenwood's statement because of its potentially greater emotional impact on the reader. Note that I have hedged my bets here with such words as "might" and "potentially." Reader-response or affective criticism is strewn with pitfalls, not the least of which is the assumption that all readers are affected similarly by a given passage. For certain readers, perhaps, Ehrlich's statistic will set their calculator hearts racing, while Greenwood's more descriptive sentence will not resonate at all, but will come off as mere decoration. Sidonie Smith and Julia Watson insist on the crucial role of the reader: "autobiographical truth [...] is an intersubjective exchange between narrator and reader aimed at producing a shared understanding of the meaning of life" (13).

One of the most recent book-length studies of autobiography, Richard Freadman's *Threads of Life: Autobiography and the Will* (2001), presents the central metaphor of "the self as a weaver who is possessed of certain innate powers to shape and create," but this "self-as-weaver" has the power to shape his or her life "only within certain limitations."[41] Those limitations would involve, for example, genetics, economics, history, and environment. Freadman presents the autobiographer as "a weaver at a second remove, shaping an account of the life that he or she has played a significant part in shaping." In the face of a world in which the force of an individual's will appears puny and in defiance of thinkers who would dismiss the concept of will altogether, Freadman argues for a will that is "real and at least partially free." Autobiography and memoir come down to a series of statements and reflections: this happened to me; I experienced, thought, read, dreamed, or felt this; I did, said, or caused this to happen (including the text before us). While noting that the issue is "far more complicated," Smith and Watson observe that "traditional autobiography has been read as a narrative of agency, evidence that subjects can act freely" (42). As we read autobiographies and memoirs, we will find ourselves asking, inevitably, why the writers wrote them. "So," a colleague remarked when I told him about this undertaking, "you're going to write a book about people who care more about themselves than they care about anyone else." Well, yes, I might have said, but in the act of writing, they express their care for those other people; moreover, other selves often figure more largely in the memoir than the writer's self. Whatever else life-writing offers beyond the dramatically conceived and shaped life of the writer will vary with his or her intentions: confession, apology, defiance, surrender, warnings, advice. Much of what the writer intends is implicit in how he or she presents the self: hero or victor, victim, naïf, witness/observer, teacher, moralist, villain.

One reason memoir has become so attractive may be the intuition that we have no other worlds to explore: the self is the last frontier. "Memoir's voice," according to Thomas Larson, "carries a likeableness, in a way the cold irony of postmodern literature does not" (185). But the self is a perilous place. "Pure autobiographies are written by neurotics who are fascinated with their own ego," Friedrich Schlegel wrote some two hundred years ago.[42] Annie Dillard warns against hoping to preserve memories in writing the memoir: "You can't put together a memoir without cannibalizing your own life for parts" (156). My daughter Jennifer was singularly unimpressed when she heard I was going to write this book: "What if all the sudden these self-asphyxiating people would sober up and realize there's someone more important than they are?" The prospect of mining the self without the fictional guise of story or novel strikes some readers as offensive. "To have written an autobiography," William Gass insists, "is already to have made yourself a monster" (45). He adds, "I know of nothing more difficult than knowing who you are, and then having the courage to share the reasons for the catastrophe of your character with the world" (50).

A final reflection on the distinctions between autobiography and memoir is in order. Two factors recur in commentaries by those who attempt to distinguish between the subgenres: (1) memoir examines only a portion of the writer's life (Hemingway's essays in *A Moveable Feast*, for example, concerns his five years in Paris between 1921 and 1926); (2) memoir tends to subordinate the narrator's life to that of others (Geoffrey Wolff's *The Duke of Deception* [1986] is so clearly focused on his father's life that some might argue that it should be classified as biography). Relatively few so-called memoirs fit both categories; a good number of memoirs, perhaps so-called by editors or publishers, have more in common with traditional autobiography than they do with memoir; a good number of so-called autobiographies have more in common with memoir as defined above than they do with traditional autobiography.

Chapter Two

The Context of Northern Rockies Memoir

Place and Myth in Life Narrative

In *Reading Autobiography* Sidonie Smith and Julia Watson suggest the geographical site of life narrative has rarely been studied by critics, who are inclined to regard such a site as a backdrop rather than a place or landscape that "shapes the contexts of both autobiographical subjectivity and the kinds of stories that can be told."[1] Such a narrative, according to Smith and Watson, "can be described as a dense and multilayered intersection of the temporal and the geographic" (74). Perhaps the first such narratives written in English about the Rocky Mountains can be found in the journals of Lewis and Clark that date from the expedition of the Corps of Discovery some two hundred years ago. The observations of Spanish explorers like Pedro de Castañeda (1510?–1554?) preceded the journals of Lewis and Clark, and before that and through it all were the oral myths and legends of various native tribes, including the "coup tales" that scholars who write about Native American autobiography regard as coming closest in spirit to Euro-American life narrative. Both Meriwether Lewis and William Clark spliced personal observations with straightforward documentary, as did such subsequent explorers as Zebulon Pike and John C. Frémont. These result in "autobiographical moments," and for modern readers, those moments of "intersubjective truth" (13), to employ Smith and Watson's term, tend to be more vivid than the raw scientific or anthropological information or efforts at unadorned, objective, factual representation.

Similar autobiographical moments occur in most of the journals of exploration and in such texts as Warren Angus Ferris's diary (1830–1836) published as *Life in the Rocky Mountains*,* Osborne Russell's *Journal of a Trapper* (1834–1843), the Mormon trail journals of Thomas Bullock (1846–1847) published as *Kingdom in the West*, George Frederick Ruxton's adventures published in 1848 as *Life in the Far West*, Horace Greeley's often delightfully condescending *An Overland Journey from New York to San Francisco in the Summer of 1859*, the 1864 trail journal of Julius Merrill published as *Bound for Idaho*, and Mark Twain's *Roughing It* (1872). For some Utahans two texts of particular interest from the pioneering period are the trail diary of Eliza Roxcy Snow (1804–1887), who was secretly married to the Mormon leader Joseph Smith in 1842 and to Brigham Young after Smith's death, and the diaries of John D. Lee (1848–1876), who was involved in the infamous Mountain Meadows Massacre of 1857.

The preceding amounts to a nearly random list of titles that contain "life narrative" moments. To represent the range of early memoir from the northern Rockies, however, I will focus on four books: Andrew Garcia's *Tough Trip through Paradise* (1878–1879), first published in 1967 and reprinted in 2003; James Willard Schultz's *My Life as an Indian*, first published in 1907 and reprinted in 1997; Anne Ellis's *The Life of an Ordinary Woman*, first published in 1929 and reprinted in 1990; Annie Pike Greenwood's *We Sagebrush Folks*, first published in 1934 and reprinted in 1988. Perhaps none of these titles is well known outside the West, but each has some claim to whatever literary stature attaches to the genre of memoir. The dates of the original publication or recent reprinting of these books suggest both the revival of interest in regional writing from the northern Rockies and the current enthusiasm for memoir in general.

All of the books are products of what James C. Work calls in his anthology, *Prose and Poetry of the American West* (1990), "The Mythopoeic Period (1833–89)" and "The Neomythic Period (1890–1914)."[2] What Work calls "The Emergence Period (1540–1832)" includes selections from Native American myths, Pedro de Castañeda's account of his explorations with

---

*Printed serially in the *Western Literary Messenger (1843–1844)*, Life in the Rockies was published in 1940 and reprinted in 1984 but is currently out of print. It holds the best claim to literary quality of all the life narratives written by early trappers in the northern Rockies.*

Coronado, Lewis and Clark's journals, and the journals of trapper and Indian fighter Jedediah Smith. Texts from the Mythopoeic Period concern pioneering and early settlement. The period covers the era of fur trapping and buffalo hunting on a large and ultimately ruinous scale, encounters and conflicts with Indians, the spread of the cattle industry, gold and silver strikes, the opening of the Oregon Trail, the Homestead Act of 1862, and the coming of the railroads: Indian, mountain man, trader, soldier, cowboy, farmer, miner, pioneer-settler, shopkeeper, railroad worker. The Dawes Severalty Act of 1887, which led to assimilation and nearly obliterated tribal culture, offered Indians land (80 acres for an individual or 160 acres for a family) for renunciation of their tribal holdings. The romantic myths of the Old West that have become a major target for recent regional memoirists were being established during the Mythopoeic Period. They were written up primarily during the Neomythic period, after the dust had settled, which is to say sometime after 1893, the year that historian Frederick Jackson Turner promulgated his "frontier thesis" reflecting on the closing of the frontier.

Events of the Neomythic Period, which I would expand about fifteen years past what Work suggests, up to the stock market crash of 1929, are less dramatic than those of the Mythopoeic, at least on a regional scale. They include the Carey Act of 1894, which opened additional land to homesteading; the expansion of national parks (Yellowstone had been created in 1872) to include Mesa Verde (1906), Glacier (1910), Rocky Mountain (1915), and Zion and Grand Canyon (both in 1919); depressions and labor unrest during the 1890s and 1920s (the International Workers of the World was founded in 1905 and was active in mines throughout the Rockies); the Spanish-American War of 1898 and the subsequent Philippines Insurrection; U.S. entry into World War I; the influenza epidemic of 1918–1919; and Wyoming's election of the first woman governor in the United States (1925). Population of the five states in the northern Rockies at least doubled in each state between 1890 and 1920 (from 412,198 to 939,629 in Colorado, for instance), and in states like Idaho and Montana the population quadrupled or better (Idaho grew from 84,385 to 431,866 in that thirty-year period). Meanwhile, Denver, the major metropolis of the Rockies, grew from 106,713 in 1890 to 256,491 in 1920; Salt Lake City expanded from 44,843 (1890) to 118,110 (1920); and Boise exploded from a mere 2,311 (1890) by a multiple of nearly ten to 21,393 (1920).

The notion that the region remained, and remains today, underpopulated and rural is as much a part of the mythic West as the premise that it was, and is, patriarchal and androcentric, essentially and somehow inescapably (or irredeemably) male. Perhaps the salient aspect of memoir from the Rockies is its rural character, but as the population figures indicate, a life outside of town on the sagebrush plains or in the snowy mountains was becoming the exception in the region well before World War II. Do myths by their nature tend to transcend facts and actualities, or is it perhaps more accurate to say that myths tend to oversimplify and to glamorize? An important feature of recent memoir from the region has been a nearly universal effort to counter the old myths, either to debunk them or to correct or somehow amend them. In memoirs written during the past twenty years, women's voices have been prominent, and if there is a trend in these, it has to do with leaving the rural, isolated confines of the ranch.

Presumably, though, the myth was male, and it featured the adventurous loner, the rugged individualist, whether trapper, cowboy, or gold miner. He might be an abused orphan, or a failed businessman, or a veteran of the Union or Confederate army. He possessed (usually) a good heart, a generous nature, a natural inclination to respect women and be kind to children. He was good with dogs and horses. The mythic Western male was self-reliant beyond Emerson's wildest dreams. He could do things with his hands, whether it was pack a mule, lasso and break a wild stallion, build a cabin, shoot an elk, skin out a buffalo, or survive in the wilds on roots and berries and on animals he caught in traps of his own contrivance. Such men valued solitude and a very few friends, appreciated in inverse ratio to the frequency of their encounters. Such men rejected cities and towns, for they valued and needed space, and they did not mind enduring hard weather, wind, and drought in order to sustain their independence and freedom.

While this myth may be partly valid, as Susan Armitage, among others, has observed, "Ordinary lives are the true story of the West, for men as well as for women."[3] Certainly that undesignated personnel who lived ordinary lives included women, and it encompassed the great majority of the population of the towns that popped up seemingly overnight. Writing as recently as 1987, Sidonie Smith decries the scarcity of reference to women in the critical and theoretical commentary on autobiography, but what follows demonstrates that the foremothers of recent memoirists wrote not so much from the margins as from the center of life in the Rockies.[4] Moreover, by 1900 a quarter to one-half of the residents in the five Rocky Mountain states lived in towns of 2,500 or more population, figures that compare closely to those of most other states of the union at that time.

Most writers of recent life narratives from the northern Rockies have themselves emigrated from the woods and mountains, farms and ranches where they grew up, and that trend is likely to increase as those sites become places of recreation rather than, except for a privileged few, homes. These writers tend, however, to reflect primarily on their rural background and upbringing in their memoirs. Krista Comer, noting that the "canonical landscapes of western literature" have made "the rural wild an implicit yardstick by which one measures the one, best West,"[5] insists "a reckoning with the urban, not simply a repudiation of it, is surely inevitable" (63). Among recent memoirs from the region, Terry Tempest Williams's *Refuge* (1991) might be considered urban, although most of the events occur "in nature," outside of Salt Lake City. Other than that, the only urban memoir of significance from the northern Rockies appears to be Kim Barnes's *Hungry for the World* (2000), which takes place in Lewiston, Idaho. The "reckoning," in effect, has been slow in coming.

Whatever one comes to regard as "the story of the West" (here, the northern Rockies) ought to be explicit in its memoirs. It is not as simple a formula as this jingle: Old West, New West, False West, True West. It would be all too convenient if the jingle were valid. Neither is it true that all of the old myth was flawed nor that all of the new myth is accurate. In all likelihood the new (increasingly urban) myths we are writing and talking about only *seem* righteous because we are so close to them: they are the myths *we* are trying to create. Brainstorming the mythology of the Old West, one might produce a randomly ordered list that looks something like this: individualism (usually "rugged"), independence, freedom, power, courage, violence, racism, ownership, romance of place, wide-open spaces (the don't-fence-me-in motif), spectacular (as opposed to subtle) landscape, distance, wind, water. The list is obviously incomplete; however, in various ways one might prefix each item with the phrase, "the story of the West is the story of _____." Wallace Stegner suggests "water," or the lack of it, "aridity."[6] The "defining story" of the West, William Kittredge writes, was "'the Western,'" which he describes as "a morality play about the invasion and conquest of the wilderness and native savagery. [...] It is a story which details the triumph of European people and their laws (read civility and community) in a conflict with both wild indifferent nature and bad men, some of them native, who are driven by the forces of lust and greed."[7] The Western is about "solving problems with violence," Kittredge writes: "Westerns, while they are basically about reestablishing community, embody a sexist, racist, imperialist story of conquest and takeover" (xvi, xvii). Moreover, as Linda K. Karell observes, "The image of the lone individual dominating a western landscape partakes in a romanticized nostalgia — more a vision of a desired past than of an actual one."[8] Unlike the fiction, life narratives from the northern Rockies offer portraits of people establishing community in the actual past.

The Male Worlds of Andrew Garcia and James Willard Schultz

Andrew Garcia's memoir, *Tough Trip through Paradise*, both is and is not in sync with the ideology of the Western as Kittredge defines it. Born around 1854 near El Paso (uncertain of the exact date, he says he was 23 at the time of the events he describes, which occur in the summer of 1878), Garcia worked as a herder and packer for the Second Cavalry at Fort Ellis (near Bozeman, Montana) before he decided to try his luck as a trapper and trader among the Indians around the Musselshell River near the Judith Mountains. Garcia operates in a world of mixed races, of "breeds" and "Injuns," and the concept of political correctness has no application to his memoir. He depicts himself as a "wooly Texan from Spanish America," and he frequently exhibits pride in his Hispanic heritage.[9] He also prides himself in never drinking whiskey, which gives him particular advantage over his first business partner, the dipsomaniacal Beaver Tom, whose story takes up almost the first third of the book.

The life narratives of trappers like Warren Angus Ferris and Osborne Russell, who sojourned in the Rockies between 1830 and the early 1840s, depict an odd balance of amicable relations with some tribes (Flatheads and Shoshones) and bloody confrontation with others (most notably the Blackfeet). Avoiding confrontation, the trader Garcia treats Indians with a blend of admiration and respect and of condescension and outright racism. For example, even though he calls himself "The Squaw Kid" on several occasions, he lashes out early in his memoir in mock indignation against "vulgar" people who refer to Indian women as "squaws," offering that "highly educated highbrows of the plains like Beaver Tom and I called them lady Injuns" (60). Implicitly, Garcia is comically self-aware of his own racist and sexist biases. Readers of the twenty-first century, however, may feel offended and may be inclined to level charges of both racism and sexism. Garcia frequently depicts himself as a man with a divided conscience, an inner voice of "good" that battles with "bad," and one of the victories of the "good" voice is his decision to marry the Nez Perce In-who-lise (also Kot-kot-hi-hih, or White Feather — he calls her Susie), complete with Catholic priest and ring fashioned from a ten dollar gold piece. Garcia's memoir ends with her death at the hands of the Blackfeet.

Ten years thereafter, as his editor Bennett H. Stein informs us in the introduction, Garcia would part from his life as an Indian and marry a white woman by whom he was to have four sons. He took up ranching and growing fruit, and he worked as a guide and outfitter. When he died in 1943, nearly ninety years old, Garcia left behind a manuscript of several thousand pages, handwritten and typed, which Stein discovered in 1948, edited, and had published in 1967. Stein presents the work as "unvarnished recollection" written over some twenty years, beginning when Garcia was in his sixties (the year 1930 is mentioned several times in the text, by which year Garcia would have been well into his seventies).[10] Whether *any* life narrative may be said to be "unvarnished" is debatable, as is Garcia's professed love of the "dusky darlings" with whom he claims to be enamored throughout. His life among the Indians lasted about nine years.

Garcia, as Stein notes, was "a completely unschooled writer" (xv), and in places his memoir, even as cut and edited, tends to ramble. James Willard Schultz (1859–1947), on the other hand, although the memoir of his life with the Blackfeet was his first book, presents himself from the outset as a polished writer, aware of the literary conventions of his day. Born to a well-to-do family in New York, Schultz passed up an appointment to West Point to hunt buffalo in Montana in 1877. His memoir, *My Life as an Indian*, was published in 1907, about four years after the death of his Blackfeet (Piegan or Pikuni) wife, Natahki (Fine Shield Woman), whom he married in 1879. Their son, Hart Merriam (Lone Wolf), became a painter and sculptor in Arizona, where Schultz was living when he began writing after Natahki's death. Schultz wrote nearly forty books over his long career, mostly for juvenile readers. The opening two sentences of Garcia's and Schultz's memoirs, respectively, offer a striking contrast in tone and sophistication:

> I worked for Uncle Sam mostly as a herder and sometimes as a packer since I came to Montana in 1876. I followed the Boys in Blue through all of the Yellowstone country and parts of the Musselshell country when they went chasing after some band of Indians that was out plundering or on horse-stealing raids [3].

> Wide, brown plains, distant, slender, flat-topped buttes; still more distant giant mountains, blue-sided, sharp-peaked, snow-capped; odor of

sage and smoke camp fire; thunder of ten thousand buffalo hoofs over the hard, dry ground; long-drawn, melancholy howl of wolves breaking the silence of night, how I loved you all!

I am in the sere and yellow leaf, dried and shriveled, about to fall and become one with my millions of predecessors.[11]

Garcia writes here in the expository mode with slight rhetorical seasoning, although most of his book is straight narrative, and his tone is conversational and colloquial. Schultz, writing in his mid-forties but sounding in his second sentence as if he is edging toward the grave, which in fact lay some forty years in the future, makes an effort at rapt prose, the heavily adjectival purple patch that figures in so much later nineteenth-century fiction. In fact, the anonymous reviewer for the *London Times* lashed out: "His narrative is perpetually disturbed by the emergence of an invader, an unclean spirit in the shape of a literary person, a lover of the heroic, the romantic, the Arcadian."[12]

Garcia provides nothing akin to Schultz's lyrical rhapsody. Early in the third chapter that begins, "September on the plains!" Schultz pledges his allegiance to "the illimitable plain with its distant mountains, its lone buttes, its canyons fantastically rock-walled, its lovely valleys beckoning one to the shelter of shady groves by the side of limpid streams" (44). These passages are drawn from a paragraph that runs in excess of 350 words. Self-consciously literary, too, are such moments as Schultz's lament over the passing of the "simple life" he once knew (the paragraph begins "Alas! Alas!"): "Why must the railroads, and the swarms of settlers have invaded that wonderful land, and robbed its lords of all that made life worth living? They knew not care, nor hunger, nor want of any kind" (50). Schultz blames "civilization" in his heavily romanticized portrait of Indian life, contributing to an already sizable body of writing that would suggest an Edenic, prelapsarian state that is belied later in his memoir when he recounts brutal combat among the tribes in the region. For instance, Rock Eater's account of a battle between the Blackfeet and a combined party of Crows and Gros Ventres in chapter 17 entails a merciless slaughter of some 360 of the enemy. In general, Schultz provides more stories from secondary sources than does Garcia (for example, "The Story of the Crow Woman," "The Kutenai's Story," "The Snake Woman," "The War Trip of Queer Person"), one result being that his memoir comes off with less immediacy and intimacy than Garcia's. On the other hand, Schultz performs a service by preserving Native American life narratives that might otherwise have been lost.

Both Garcia and Schultz might be regarded as adventurers, and they lace their books liberally with stories of violence and near violence, of war, murder, and suicide, of passionate and romantic courtships. Both writers were drawn into the exotic tribal culture when it was verging on its last moments of partial autonomy. Schultz refers to the passing of the buffalo in 1883, just half a dozen years after he arrived in Montana. While large supportive casts are involved in both memoirs, the writer's self remains at the center, and any other issue (mistreatment of the Indians, for example, or destruction of the buffalo) is subordinated. Neither writer comes off as deeply introspective, but both are well aware of their place in history. Of the two, Garcia, who includes an account of his wife's part in the Nez Perce War in the later pages of his memoir, asserts the greater awareness of historical context. Both writers reflect on their lives "as Indians" from the perspective of the past: they are no longer, if in fact they ever really were, "Indians." Their lives and their perceptions, however, were clearly shaped by their interaction with the native inhabitants of the region as much as they were by geography or landscape.

What were Garcia's and Schultz's intentions in writing their life narratives? Certainly they wished to revisit their own small roles in the drama that might be titled "The Passing of the Frontier" or "The Tragedy of the Northern Plains Indians." Schultz, as his subsequent books indicate, intended to explain and celebrate tribal life; his memoir is the more instructive of the two, in that he strikes some balance between information and entertainment, while Garcia does not appear to have aimed at much beyond telling of his adventures. Andrew Garcia's narrative of his life among the Indians is rough-hewn, colloquial, and often humorous. Certainly more than Schultz, Garcia writes a lament for a lost world. Schultz, however, paints the more vivid and colorful landscape of the northern Rockies; simply put, he devotes considerably more space to descriptive writing than does Garcia, most likely because he is new to the region. For neither writer, however, does the landscape function as more than setting for narratives apparently intended to entertain (particularly Garcia) and to instruct (particularly Schultz). Moreover, neither writer pays much attention to the lives of the settlers, the farmers, ranchers, and miners who were already well underway in their creation of communities.

The Female West of Anne Ellis and Annie Pike Greenwood

At about the time Schultz observed the disappearance of the last buffalo herds in 1883, Nannie T. Alderson (1860–1947) of West Virginia was newly wedded and headed for Miles City, Montana. Her life on the ranch, which ended when the cattle market plummeted in 1919, is recounted in *A Bride Goes West* (1942): "There is an old and rather brutal saying out west, to the effect that this was a great country for men and horses, but hell on women and cattle."[13] Alderson amends the former portion of the old saw by adding children to those who appreciated the greatness of the West. Also in 1883, eight-year-old Anne Ellis (1875–1938) was growing up in poverty in the gold-mining town of Bonanza, Colorado. She records her early years in the memoir, *The Life of an Ordinary Woman* (1929), which concludes with the death of her second husband. Ellis's life is not one of freedom on the plains and of exciting adventures, but of disappointments disrupted by rare moments of pleasure like political rallies and berrypicking. A passage late in the book is indicative: "One day, in my ceaseless round of work, just after putting a large washing on the line and scrubbing, I have a miscarriage. If I think at all, I am pleased over this, and never stop working day or night."[14] Both Garcia and Schultz lard their memoirs with exotic adventures. Anne Ellis lives closer to the bone: "Our chief amusements were discussing our neighbors, school entertainments, and dances" (126); "That Christmas we decide to have a community tree, followed by a dance and supper" (190). Simple amusements expressed in flat, unadorned language.

In *Plain Anne Ellis* (1931), the sequel to *The Life of an Ordinary Woman,* she briefly outlines her evolution as a writer. Encouraged by friends who heard her tell stories from her childhood, Ellis, then in her fifties, simply put pen to paper and got to work, even though she "could neither spell, punctuate, nor write a clear sentence."[15] One of her sisters offered the observation that many if not most memoirists have received: "a story of our life was just as well kept to ourselves" (212). Many *women* who write memoirs, it should be added. Particularly among earlier writers of life narratives from the northern Rockies, it is the woman who tends to write about the family. The complaint of familial uneasiness about memoir, while not universal, is certainly common, but one could hardly imagine writers like Andrew Garcia or James Willard Schultz, or least of all trappers like Ferris and Russell, being much concerned about the response of family members to their revelations, inasmuch as they reveal very little about other members of their family.

It may be well here to reflect on Paul John Eakin's concerns about the "sterile binary logic of categories," particularly as they have been applied to gender in autobiographical writing: "If female, then relational, collectivist, and, for some reason, nonnarrative; if male, then autonomous, individualistic, and narrative."[16] Eakin notes that he keeps encountering women's autobiographies that are "individualistic and narrative in character" and men's that show "important evidence of relationality." As will be evident hereafter, however, considerable effort has been devoted to identifying distinctive traits of gendered life narrative writing, particularly by feminist critics and scholars.

Among contemporary memoirists, women appear to be particularly conscious of the impact of their writing on their families. "I tried to leave out anything that might trouble my family," Annie Dillard writes of her memoir, *An American Childhood* (1987).[17] Mary Clearman Blew professes discomfort over writing even about deceased friends and relatives: "I feel an uneasy balance between writing about the dead as their lives 'really' were and writing about them as a projection of my own experiences."[18] "I couldn't have written *The Road from Coorain* [1992] while my mother was living," Jill Ker Conway observes, because "The danger is that in telling your life story you'll hurt some people's feelings."[19] She adds that she showed her manuscript to the people she was writing about "and let them say whether it was appropriate or not, or whether they minded." At issue is whether one exposes or reveals primarily oneself or primarily others. To the extent that a memoir focuses more on others than on the writer's self, it could be argued that most writers of life narrative operate fifty or more percent of the time as biographers; therefore, they may feel obligated to treat others not simply as self-projections. If that is possible, one might add.

Anne Ellis apparently did very little by way of attempting to transform the raw materials of her life. Consider, for example, this typically lean descriptive passage early in the book: "It is now the latter part of September, the loveliest time in Colorado. The quaking aspen and scrub oak are all colors of red, yellow, green, and orange" (19). By way of contrast to this denotative composition, consider the following highly affective passage from Annie Pike Greenwood's *We Sagebrush Folk* (1934) on an evening in southern Idaho: "It was so very, very quiet out there. Stars were pricking the dark sky, and there was the feel of a new-born world in the delicious cool air. I always feel night through the pores of my entire body. It intoxicates me."[20] Both styles have their appeal, but no reader is likely to welcome both with equal enthusiasm.

Like Andrew Garcia, Anne Ellis was largely "unschooled," but she was fairly well-read. Each chapter of her two memoirs is prefaced with an epigraph, sometimes by other writers, but usually the wisdom of "A.E." (Anne Ellis herself). In *The Life of an Ordinary Woman* she comments on her reading of Shakespeare and Dickens, Hugo's *Les Miserables*, Rider Haggard's *She*, and George Eliot; in *Plain Anne Ellis* she reflects on writers as diverse as Sherwood Anderson, Carl Sandburg, Mary Austin (who became a friend), and D. H. Lawrence. Nevertheless, her writing shows little evidence of literary sophistication, and it is almost totally devoid of rhetorical ornamentation. She provides sketches of local characters she encounters in the mining camps, and her ear for their colloquial speech equals that of Garcia and Schultz. Ellis rarely elaborates a scene beyond two or three pages, her untitled chapters generally taking off from some particular event: "One day we have our pictures 'took'!" (84); "We now get our first cow, paying seventy-five dollars, which is a lot of money in these days." (95); "And now a man comes to town who has been horn-swoggled into buying one of the mines" (151).

Most of her sequel, *Plain Anne Ellis*, which appeared just two years after *The Life of an Ordinary Woman*, records the slow rise of Anne Ellis from her early life of penury. Eventually she was to be elected and reelected treasurer of Saguache County, Colorado, and she was able to send her children to college. Forced by her asthma to move to Albuquerque, New Mexico, she began her writing career. She died in Denver in 1938, shortly after receiving an honorary doctorate from the University of Colorado. Hers are unpretentious memoirs of a hard-working woman's triumph over poverty and of a self-taught writer's capacity to tell her own story. Although she depicts life in the rugged mining camps with a certain vividness, focusing often on the communal aspects (dances, musical and dramatic entertainments), Ellis rarely turns her gaze on the landscape, and in this her writing is similar to that of Garcia. Carol Bly describes her as "absolutely pragmatic."[21] Both Ellis and Garcia concentrate on characters and events, often presented with fairly slight awareness of dramatic pacing.

While *Plain Anne Ellis* garnered positive reviews, they were less enthusiastic than those accorded her first memoir. E. F. Kelly, writing for the *New York Times*, praised "that utter frankness about herself, the quality that gives immortality to the great diarists and memoirists."[22] Margaret Wallace, on the other hand, while she recognizes the book's "sincerity," notes an "occasionally unlovely egotism."[23]

Annie Pike Greenwood's (1879–1956) rather bulky memoir of irrigated farming in the southern Idaho desert between 1906 and 1924 was also well received, but drew more criticism for its egotism than did Ellis's, possibly reflecting a shift in critical attitude toward the genre in the 23 years that separate the publication of their books: "The cleverness is at times too insistent and the first personal pronoun too frequent, especially in the earlier chapters."[24] E. F. Kelly suggested that the book "might with advantage have been a good deal cut down and condensed," but he praised the story for its "vivacity and cleverness and humor."[25] The most apposite review was that of F.B. writing for the *Boston Tribune*: "To attempt to give any adequate idea of the mass of data which Mrs. Greenwood marshals in the many pages of this unique story, her vivid memory running quicksilver-like through it glancing from now one now another experience as her fancy wills, rather than as chronology would dictate, seems to us about as satisfactory as describing the swiftly changing patterns of a kaleidoscope."[26]

If Anne Ellis suffered somewhat from being undereducated, it may be argued that Annie Pike Greenwood suffered from being, for a woman in the patriarchal context of the rural turn-of-the-twentieth-century West, somewhat overeducated. The daughter of a doctor who was the administrator of Utah's first mental institution, Greenwood in her girlhood memories tells of "a fringed-top phaeton" and a "twenty-room home on half a city square" in Provo (5, 7). Although she was not Mormon, Annie Pike was educated at Brigham Young Academy, then a two-year school, and she had no interest in becoming a farmer's wife: "Most men long for the soil. Adam, I am sure, regretted the lost Garden of Eden, but I suspect that Eve fed him the apple in order to get off the farm" (5). Nevertheless, she married Charles Greenwood who gave up "a perfectly good salary from the million-dollar sugar-factory in Garden City, Kansas, to go to a perfectly unknown, sight unseen, undeveloped wilderness farm in Idaho" (6).

Confronting the sagebrush desert near the Minidoka Mountains, Greenwood adapts quickly, at least up to a point, and raises four children between 1912 and 1924, although she sees herself as an "anachronism" with her Paris model hat and Best & Company of New York suit (12). The family acquires 160 acres not far from the town of Hazelton through the Carey Act of 1894 and embarks on irrigated farming (sugar beets, wheat, potatoes). Unlike Garcia, Schultz, or Ellis, Greenwood constructs her book from a series of eleven apparently essay-like chapters with one-word titles reminiscent of those from Thoreau's *Walden*: Wilderness, Education (her experiences teaching in one-room schools), Birth, Death, Recreation, Outdoors, Sex (considerably shorter than the others), War (World War I), Politics (a member of the Non-Partisan League and the Progressive Party, Greenwood turned from her support of Hoover to become an avid F.D.R. fan at the time of her writing), Faith, Economics. She appears to be considerably more aware of world events than are other regional memoirists of the time, and her progressive thinking was, and still is for the most part, out of step with that which distinguishes Idaho's deeply conservative political and social values. In none of these sections does the material cohere sufficiently to succeed as an essay in any conventional sense of the term, but her writing tends toward the expository mode, while narrative predominates in the memoirs of Garcia, Schultz, and Ellis.

Greenwood's book has no narrative arc or plot-like organization, although she arranges the chapters in loose chronological order. The chapter entitled "Faith," however, which has little to do with religion and a lot to do with faith in herself, functions as something of a climactic essay. In this piece Greenwood decides to teach at the high school level, even though she admits it is "the profession I disliked — and still do dislike, though not teaching in and of itself" (405). By this time her son Walter has run away from home, and her husband remains on the farm with the older of the remaining sons, so she must face the "hostility" of some parents and of the devious, self-designated "Professor" Larson on her own. Through clever maneuvering Greenwood wins out over those who have contrived the "contemptible plot" (412) to oust her from her teaching position, but the most important product of the episode may well be this particular essay, which possesses sound narrative structure and dramatic unity.

At several points in her sprawling book, Greenwood steps aside to inform the reader that "This is not my autobiography." Presumably, she feels she is not sufficiently attentive to her "inner life" to be writing autobiography: "I would try to be a skillful analyst of the interior of *me* if I were writing my autobiography" (65). Later, "If this were my autobiography, a book that I shall never write, I would tell you what I have suffered through a heart too filled with the passion of life and living" (220). Later still, "This book is not autobiography, yet much is in it that will offend the sensibilities of those who live more strictly personal lives than I have ever lived. This must be. I do not write here of myself, as myself, but only as a woman of a certain type, whose life was so ironically twisted" (360). Noting, after Matthew Arnold, that she has "reached that most glorious age" when she can "see life steadily and see it whole," she asserts, "I am allowed the privilege, I hope, of writing of myself as though I were some one else" (360).

Of course Annie Pike Greenwood does not succeed in writing about herself as if she were somebody else, even though her self-portrait is not always flattering and she is at times openly self-critical. In her brief prefatory note Greenwood claims to have "written only the truth." But in her afterword, editor Jo Ann Ruckman points out that Greenwood excises any account of her nervous breakdown "suffered sometime around 1920."[27] Ruckman also notes that soon after the farm went under in 1924, Greenwood left her husband, and they later divorced. Greenwood achieves what might be called a portrait of a way of life, and in that respect she surpasses the limitations of many memoirists. Her efforts to establish and to participate in the rural community near Hazleton are only partially successful, and her often lively and witty memoir relates a story of failure, the last word being the essay entitled "Economics," which tells of how they had to sell the farm that she had come to love, but was glad to leave.

The four memoirs I have surveyed above enhance or illuminate each other in various ways. Anne Ellis and Annie Pike Greenwood offer very different versions of women's lives during the settlement period in the northern Rockies. Ellis's *The Life of an Ordinary Woman* deals with poverty and a life eked out in the Colorado mining camps, but she manages to discover herself through her reading and writing. Apparently, Greenwood knew herself as a reader and writer from the outset; her struggle was to discover herself as a farmer's wife, and in that respect her success was only partial. Given her social and cultural advantages, and her sense of herself as a writer throughout her ordeal in Idaho (she submitted work to the *Atlantic* and other magazines), Greenwood resembles James Willard Schultz in some respects more than she does Anne Ellis. Their memoirs are often intentionally literary in nature. Anne Ellis might be regarded as the female counterpart of Andrew Garcia. But if Garcia's and Schultz's memoirs may be said in some ways to sustain significant aspects of the mythology of the Old West, the same cannot be said of Ellis's and Greenwood's. Theirs are, above all, studies of family and community, and in this respect they contribute to what William Kittredge and others have called for. "In the American West," Kittredge writes, "we are struggling to revise our dominant mythology, and to find a new story to inhabit."[28] The old myth, Kittredge argues, was "too simpleminded," or else the world has proven to be "too complex." In *Taking Care* Kittredge makes an appeal for giving "some time to the arts of cherishing before much of what we adore simply vanishes," and he offers "generosity" as "the prime moral and political virtue."²⁹

Five Foremothers: Mary Hallock Foote, Annie Clark Tanner, Margaret Bell, Elinore Pruitt Stewart, and Mary MacLane

Those acquainted with autobiographical writing from the Rockies prior to the recent renaissance in memoir, which I date from Ivan Doig's *This House of Sky* (1978), may object that I have cast too narrow a net. Certainly a number of other early life narratives deserve some notice; for example, Mary Hallock Foote's (1847–1938) *A Victorian Gentlewoman in the Far West*, which was the source, in manuscript, of Wallace Stegner's Pulitzer Prize–winning novel, *Angle of Repose*. In some ways Foote's memoir suggests comparison with that of Annie Pike Greenwood. Both are the work of cultured, educated women who find themselves living in the rural West under challenging circumstances. In fact, Foote provides an extensive portrait of her life in New York, where her family lived near the Havilands of china fame and entertained the likes of Henry Ward Beecher and Frederick Douglass. Educated at the Cooper Institute in New York City (later, the Cooper Union), Mary Hallock (her friends called her Molly) had a considerable reputation as a book illustrator before marrying the engineer Arthur Foote and coming to the West (first to New Almaden, California) in 1876 at the age of 29. She soon began writing and developed a considerable reputation following publication of her first novel, *The Led-Horse Claim*, in 1883. Her life in the mining camp of Leadville, Colorado, may be properly described as "rustic," but Mary Hallock Foote employed women like Anne Ellis; she did not live like Anne Ellis. Anne Ellis ate; Mary Hallock Foote dined. Whenever she wished, Foote could take the train back East, and she did so fairly often. Rodman W. Paul, who edited her manuscript (it was first published in 1972, a year after Stegner's novel) proposes that Foote never really became a "westerner."³⁰

When her husband went to the Wood River area in central Idaho in 1882 to manage a silver mine ("the darkest part of darkest Idaho"³¹), Molly stayed in Milton, New York, and she was not excited in 1884 when she landed in Kuna, about fifteen miles southwest of Boise: "No one remembers Kuna. It was a place where silence closed about you after the bustle of the train, where a soft, dry wind from great distances hummed through the telegraph wires and a stage road went out of sight in one direction and a new railroad track in another." What she saw was "pallid sagebrush" and a treeless plain: "as moonlight unto sunlight is that desert sage to other greens" (275). But she apparently adjusted well as her husband set about his ambitious irrigation project, and she began housekeeping in the Boise River canyon about ten miles from the town. Despite their uncertain finances, they assembled a domestic staff that included a Chinese cook, an English governess-tutor, and a nurse for the baby.[32] Although Annie Pike Greenwood may have experienced such conveniences while growing up, she had no such luxuries on her sagebrush farm. The Footes were to remain in Idaho for about eleven years before moving to a mine in California after the irrigation project failed.

In 1883, the year that James Willard Schultz recognizes as that of the demise of the last buffalo herds, a nineteen-year-old Mormon woman named Annie Clark became the second wife of Joseph Marion Tanner, although the Church of Jesus Christ of Latter-Day Saints, under pressure from the U.S. government, was moving toward abandoning polygamy. The church officially gave up the practice known as Celestial Marriage in 1890 and Utah became a state in 1896. Annie Clark Tanner's (1864–1941) autobiography, first published in 1941 as *A Mormon Mother*, remains a moving story of faith, poverty, abandonment, and survival. Whether or not her story is "tragic," as her son Obert, an emeritus professor of philosophy at Brigham Young University, claims in his foreword, it is certainly poignant. Laura L. Bush describes the book as "subversive" and as "an explicitly transgressive autobiographical act."[33] What most women would recognize as spousal neglect, if not outright abuse, begins shortly after the wedding ceremony, as Joseph Tanner, her teacher at Brigham Young Academy (it became a university in 1903), let two weeks elapse before consummating the marriage. Within six months he had taken a third wife.

Annie Clark Tanner taught school, but the early part of her autobiography is concerned mostly with the legal challenges to polygamy during the 1880s and with her father's trial on that charge. Haunted by her father's trial and brief term in prison, Tanner goes underground, being passed from household to household to avoid the authorities. At one point she casually mentions not having seen her husband for a year and a half. She reports the births of her children with surprising nonchalance, ticking off the births of four between 1895 and 1900, one of whom died of whooping cough when two weeks old, in less than a page. Her report of the child's death is directly followed by this one-sentence paragraph written in the flat passive voice: "Another son, Sheldon was born in this house on May 29, 1900."[34] Too frequently Tanner's life narrative reads as a simple accounting; she lacks an instinct for the story and a flair for vivid detail.

Tanner moved to Provo briefly around 1911 so that one of her sons could attend Brigham Young University. She takes some pride in observing that her children "were not reared under the old tradition, namely, that obedience is the greatest of all virtues," but rather, "They were encouraged to think things out for themselves" (227). In 1912 her husband informs Annie that he will see her no longer, nor will he provide for their children (she had two still at home, aged eight and ten). She makes ends meet by working as a nurse. Annie Clark Tanner concludes serenely: "My life has been simple, full of love, devotion, and service for my family" (335). As Bush observes, "Tanner shrewdly sandwiches her criticism of polygamy [and implicitly of male hegemony] between equally compelling accounts of continuing religious faith and devotion to God" (59).

Of the books so far examined, Tanner's best fits the designation of traditional autobiography, as it marches dutifully from the beginning to the end of the writer's life. And if one were to reflect on the themes of these memoirs, aside from something like "my adventures among the Indians" (Garcia, Schultz) or "root hog or die" (Ellis, Greenwood), Tanner's is the mostly clearly focused. Without lashing out against the Mormon doctrine of Celestial Marriage, she argues the case against polygamy and indirectly against spousal abuse or neglect. Neither of the women memoirists whose lives become at times struggles for survival (Ellis, Tanner) seems to have had the opportunity to wax poetic about the landscape or to reflect on how it might have shaped their lives. In effect, their lives were shaped more by the cultural landscape and the socioeconomic facts of their position than by the physical landscape. Both Greenwood and Foote offer numerous colorful comments on the beauty and severity of the landscape, but as with Schultz, they were professional writers with some literary aspirations, and they knew their lives were shaped significantly by the sagebrush and aridity in which they lived.

Like Greenwood and Foote, Margaret ("Peggy") Bell (1888–1982), whose memoir of her childhood on the Montana Hi-line during the 1890s (until about 1905) was published in 2002 as *When Montana and I Were Young*, aspired to be a writer. Her editor, memoirist and fiction writer Mary Clearman Blew, notes that the Montana poet and author Grace Stone Coates, whose work garnered national attention in the late 1920s, helped Bell rewrite and revise her memoir. Blew commends the book for its "documentation of frontier childhood" in northern Montana "during the twilight of the cattle frontier,"[35] but even more for its "story of survival, of growing up poor and female in a frontier world controlled by men" (xxi). Bell's father deserted his family and her mother married a vicious abuser she names Hedge Wolfe, whom Blew describes as "one of the really memorable villains of western literature" (xxii). Like Andrew Garcia, Margaret Bell has a story to tell that, at least up to a point, has what one might describe as a plot. As Norman Maclean writes in "USFS 1919: The Ranger, the Cook, and a Hole in the Sky," "Life every now and then becomes literature — not for long, of course, but long enough to be what we best remember, and often enough so that what we eventually come to mean by life are those moments when life, instead of going sideways, backwards, forward, or nowhere at all, lines out straight, tense, and inevitable, with a complication, climax, and, given some luck, a purgation, as if life had been made and not happened."[36]

Writers of life narrative may occasionally fabricate the "luck" that constitutes the "purgation" in Maclean's premise. William Zinsser simply advises, "you must give yourself a plot" (163). Blew speculates that "the romantic interest introduced toward the end [...] is fiction," but she believes we can be "reasonably certain of the general outline of Peggy's life" (xxvi). Alongside such recent memoirs as Frank McCourt's *Angela's Ashes* (1996) and Dave Eggers's *A Heartbreaking Work of Staggering Genius* (2000) the fictional liberties taken by such early memoirists as Garcia and Bell seem mere trifles. But these are just speculations. How much is fabricated in *any* memoir or autobiography can generally be ascertained only by the writer. If the writer successfully establishes her or his credibility, readers are likely to accept the verity of the text, and it is my premise that the readers' belief in the verity of the text significantly affects their response to it. In a way, it is as simple as the difference between a "claimer" and a "disclaimer":

> "The following film is based on actual incidents."
>
> "All incidents, situations, institutions, governments and people in this film are fictional, and any similarity to characters or persons living or dead is strictly coincidental."

Most memoirs are "claimers." Some early memoirists acquire credibility, I suspect, through their lack of sophistication. Writers like Garcia, Ellis, and Tanner have a certain odd advantage over those memoirists who are sufficiently well educated and well read to know and imitate the literary conventions of their day. Schultz, Greenwood, and Foote sometimes come across in their books as self-consciously literary, and their life narratives may lose some credibility as a result.

The memoirs of Annie Pike Greenwood, Anne Ellis, Mary Hallock Foote, Annie Clark Tanner, and Margaret Bell exemplify the broad social and cultural range and the varied settings from which women wrote during the settlement period between the 1880s and the end World War I in the northern Rockies: Idaho, Colorado, Utah, Montana; farms, towns, mines, ranches; from patrician Foote to proletarian Ellis and Bell. Without much doubt life narrative from the state of Wyoming during the period is best represented by the letters of Elinore Pruitt Stewart (1876–1933), first published in 1914 as *Letters of a Woman Homesteader*. The twenty-six letters to her former employer in Denver begin in April of 1909 and end in November 1913. They form the basis of the screenplay for the low-budget ($600,000) movie *Heartland*, filmed in 1979, produced by Montana writer Annick Smith, and regarded as a cult classic.

Born in Arkansas and raised in the Indian Territory (Oklahoma), Stewart was fourteen when her parents died, and she helped raise five of her siblings. She married an older man and was soon widowed, leaving her with a newborn daughter whom she supported by working as a nurse and writing articles for the *Kansas City Star*. She and her daughter later moved to Denver, where she worked as a cook, and in 1909, when her daughter Jerrine was two years old, she relocated to southwestern Wyoming, near the Utah border. Within a few weeks after going to work for the Scottish rancher Clyde Stewart, she filed on an adjoining homestead and a week or so later they married (the homestead near McKinnon is now on the National Historic Register). Three of their four children survived to adulthood.

Her former employer had some of the letters published in *The Atlantic Monthly*. The following descriptive passage from her second letter suggests Stewart's awareness that she was writing for a rather sophisticated audience attuned to (or perhaps afflicted with) the literary tastes of the day, pathetic fallacy and all:

> It seemed as if we were driving through a golden haze. The violet shadows were creeping up the hills, while away back of us the snow-capped

peaks were catching the sun's last rays. On every side of us stretched the poor, hopeless desert, the sage, grim and determined to live in spite of starvation, and the great, bare, desolate buttes. The beautiful colors turned to amber and rose, and then to the general tone, dull gray.[37]

Most of the letters are carefully focused on local characters, such as "A Charming Adventure and Zebulon Pike [Parker]" or on particular episodes, such as "The Horse-Thieves" and "The Adventure of the Christmas Tree." Throughout, Stewart appears more conscious of landscape than are any of the early memoirists mentioned previously: "The larks were trying to outdo each other and the robins were so saucy that I could almost have flicked them with the willow I was using as a whip. The rabbit-bush made golden patches everywhere, while purple asters and great pink thistles lent their charm" (231). Certainly more than such writers as Garcia, Ellis, Tanner, and Bell, Elinore Pruitt Stewart has an eye for the picturesque. Infatuation with her own quotidian (proving to her eventual husband that she can run a mower, catch a string of trout for a picnic dinner, pop a sage grouse with a shotgun) never quite overcomes her fascination with place.

Nineteen-year-old Butte, Montana, writer Mary MacLane's fascination with the copper-mining city in which she was coming of age might best be described as "dread." MacLane (1881–1929) refers to the area throughout with a refrain that acquires symbolic impact: "sand and barrenness."[38] Cathryn Halverson describes MacLane's recently reprinted *The Story of Mary MacLane* as "one of the most notorious books of 1902."[39] She documents the impact of the self-styled genius and eccentric MacLane's memoir, presented in the form of a diary purportedly covering events and offering meditations that occurred between January 13 and April 13 of 1901, the year of Queen Victoria's death. The book sold 100,000 copies in its first month. In her introduction to the 2002 reprinting, Julia Watson describes the text as "a performance, not a factual biography," and she detects MacLane's exploitation of the fashionable *fin-de-siècle* "decadence" that has been conventionally connected with the Symbolist poets.[40] MacLane portrays herself as an intense and versatile, but also lone and unhappy, "genius" who dotes on the devil. To this she adds the fashionable nihilism of the 1890s. "Tortured," as she phrases it, "with the dull, dull misery of Nothingness" (19), she concludes that "the world is made up mostly of nothing" (35), and she appears almost relieved eventually to pronounce "the pathetic burlesque-tragedy of Nothing" (225).

Certainly one source of MacLane's unhappiness is the provincial and obscure town of Butte, or as she phrases it "this uncouth, warped, Montana town" (10). MacLane likens herself to the Russian memoirist Marie Bashkirtseff and to the Lord Byron of *Don Juan*; Keats is her favorite poet, and she cites Shakespeare throughout. Like Byron, in the form of such alter-egos as Childe Harold, MacLane is too intelligent and sensitive for Butte; no one, certainly including her family and the "dry, warped friends of the dry, warped people of Butte" who are "buried in this dusty, dreary, wind-havocked waste," understands or appreciates her (15). She is, in effect, the would-be wandering heroine of her own dark mind. Watson's reference to MacLane's "anxiety of place" (vi) clearly applies at one time or another, albeit with far less vehemence, to the memoirs of Anne Ellis, Annie Pike Greenwood, and Mary Hallock Foote. Halverson refers to MacLane's portrait of a modern West as a "site of contention" rather than the mythic West, a "site of nostalgia" (61). Like Ellis, Greenwood, and Foote, MacLane was to escape her corner of the northern Rockies, and she used the success of her memoir to achieve that end, but she returned from the East in 1909 to write "lively editorials for the *Butte Evening News*" (ix) and to work on the sequel to her memoir, *I, Mary MacLane: A Diary of Human Days* (1917), which was not nearly so well received. Butte, presumably unlike New York City, was "sordid, beastly, and time-serving — but withal full of romance and poetry and the wideness of the West."[41] Apparently destitute, she died in Chicago in 1929.

Observing that MacLane "seeks to escape" the conventional, romantic "scripts of gender" (40) of her day, Halverson proposes that she "portrays provincial American arenas as a lethal version of femininity" (41). Julia Watson characterizes MacLane, with her "ambivalent relationship to her western roots" (xxii), as "the woman writer citizens of Butte have loved to hate" (xvii). She concludes that MacLane "fashioned an impudent autobiographical 'I' that spoke to an emerging Modernist sensibility" (xxi). In some ways, given her hyper self-reflexivity (the capacity to be ironically aware of herself being aware of herself), MacLane anticipates certain elements of the postmodern sensibility.

A Few Forefathers and a Few Reflections

From the foregoing one might infer that Rockies memoirs from the period of settlement came to be dominated by women and, with the significant exception of Mary MacLane, by a woman's particular interest in family and domestic matters. There is at least some degree of validity to this inference. Memoirs like those of Garcia and Schultz are less numerous than those of writers like Anne Ellis and Annie Pike Greenwood. Among the notable memoirs of the 1930s into the 1950s, for example, are Nell Portrey Davis's *Stump Ranch Pioneer* (1942), which tells of a family's migration from a failed sheep ranch in Colorado in 1936 to northern Idaho, and Grace Jordan's *Home Below Hell's Canyon* (1954), which concerns an Idaho sheep ranch in the Snake River gorge in the early 1930s. It is perhaps significant that such memoirs, like most of those mentioned previously, were published by prestigious Eastern presses (Davis's by Dodd, Mead and Jordan's by Thomas Y. Crowell; Ellis's, along with Stewart's, by Houghton Mifflin and Greenwood's by Appleton-Century). This suggests a reading public that was curious about what was perceived between the turn of the century and World War II as the last frontier. The intermountain West, with the exception of Alaska, offered the last free or cheap land, and between the railroads and irrigation, aided and abetted by developers' hype, the landscape, as Mary Clearman Blew memorably phrases it, was quickly being transformed into property.[42]

Various male writers from the region have left life narratives that are not quite as exotic as those of Garcia and Schultz. John D. Fitzgerald (1907–1988), for example, best known for his children's books, including The Great Brain series, also produced a family memoir set in the Utah Territory, *Papa Married a Mormon* (1955). Frank C. Robertson (1890–1968), who turned out some 130 genre Westerns, wrote *A Ram in the Thicket* (1950), a memoir focused on his father and the family's itinerant life in Idaho, from the panhandle to the Mormon community of Chesterfield in the southeastern corner of the state, between the 1890s and Great Depression, when he began to publish his stories and novels. Pulitzer Prize–winning Montana novelist A. B. Guthrie, Jr.'s autobiography, *The Blue Hen's Chick: A Life in Context* (1965), might be regarded as following a sort of *Künstlerroman* pattern, as it concerns his evolution from journalist to novelist. Ivan Doig considers it to have influenced his memoir, *This House of Sky* (1978).[43]

Whether the writings of Enos A. Mills (1870–1922), the man known as the founder of the Rocky Mountain National Park, qualify as memoir could be debated. Prompted by his mother's tales of the 1859 Colorado gold rush, Mills homesteaded in the Tahosa Valley facing Long's Peak, which he first climbed when he was fourteen. He helped construct the hiking trail up the 14,255-foot mountain in 1886 and guided his first party to the summit in 1889, the same year he met naturalist John Muir in San

Francisco. Largely self-educated, Mills began lecturing and writing for magazines, and in 1908 Theodore Roosevelt invited him to be a government lecturer on forestry. In 1909 appeared the first of his dozen and a half books, *Wild Life on the Rockies*. His nature writing (or ecomemoir) might be said to fall somewhere between the poles of Henry David Thoreau and Ann Zwinger; he is not as meditative and philosophical as the former and not as scientific as the latter.

Mills focuses clearly and steadily on nature, and he personifies nearly all that he encounters, from a pair of wolves to a thousand-year-old yellow pine: "Never have I seen so much individuality, so much character, in a tree."[44] While some might argue that Mills is more accurately described as a "nature writer," I suggest that he fashions himself as a character at least as carefully and intentionally as do such memoirists as Garcia and Ellis. Certainly, his writings have an agenda, as John Dotson has observed: "Mills' major themes are reverence for nature, the integrity of animals, the rightful place of human beings in nature, and the ennobling effects of both knowing and protecting nature for the common good."[45] Mills generally portrays himself alone in nature, often depicting himself at ease under difficult circumstances: "All that day I stayed by the fire, but that night, instead of trying to get a little sleep there, I crawled into a newly formed snowdrift, and in it slept soundly and quite comfortably until morning" (124). He represents himself throughout as a man who lives at ease in nature under frequently trying conditions.

Curiously, Wallace Stegner's (1909–1993) memoir, *Wolf Willow* (1963), does not concern his boyhood in Salt Lake City, where he lived between the ages of twelve and twenty-one, but the half dozen or so years before that, starting in 1914, when the family alighted briefly in Eastend, Saskatchewan, on the border with Montana. His biographer, Jackson J. Benson, indicates that Stegner did consider Salt Lake City his "hometown,"[46] but we read of his connections with the Rockies mostly in essays scattered through books like *Where the Bluebird Sings to the Lemonade Springs* (1992) and his autobiographical novel, *The Big Rock Candy Mountain* (1943). In one of his best-known essays, "Thoughts in a Dry Land," Stegner may have been thinking of himself when he defines the Westerner as "less a person than a continuing adaptation" (55). "Both fiction and autobiography," Stegner observes in an essay near the end of *Where the Bluebird Sings*, are the writer's attempts to "impose order on the only life the writer really knows," namely, his or her own (219).

Aside from Stegner, only about half of the writers cited in this chapter would likely be surprised to think that their efforts were regarded as literature at all. Only James Willard Schultz, Mary Hallock Foote, Frank C. Robertson, Mary MacLane, and to a lesser extent Anne Ellis, Annie Pike Greenwood, and Enos Mills, saw themselves as writers, or came to see themselves as such (particularly in Ellis's case). Andrew Garcia, Annie Pike Greenwood, Margaret Bell, Elinore Pruitt Stewart, and Annie Clark Tanner, among others, were one-book authors, most likely driven by what Leigh Gilmore calls "the fantasy of autobiography": "An autobiography is a monument to the idea of person-hood, to the notion that one could leave behind a memorial to oneself (just in case no one else ever gets around to it) and that the memorial would perform the work of permanence that the person never can."[47] It may be that every autobiography or memoir incorporates an ideology; it is certain that every writer of such a text is in some sense an idealist.

Part of that idealism, in some cases, has to do with the writer's enthusiasm for a landscape that others respond to only minimally or negatively. "Sagebrush," Wallace Stegner reminds us wryly, "is an acquired taste" (53). Schultz, Foote, Stewart, Greenwood, Davis, and Mills, for example, celebrate a world they see as either starkly beautiful or at best only occasionally lush:

> From the top of the hill we could see the Hubert place, a tidy gray house, with a few young trees and a beginning row of fruit-bushes. The farm lay on the edge of the desert, barbed wire marking a line between green alfalfa and gray sagebrush [Greenwood 454].

Other writers, including Garcia, Ellis, Tanner, Bell, and Jordan, apparently found little time in their active or hard-pressed lives to reflect on the landscape, which is not to say, of course, that they were unaffected by it. The fact that they were generally writing in retrospect on the places where they came of age or worked may have been less of a factor than their absorption in other matters. Bell and Jordan, for example, focus on the hard work required to maintain their ranches on marginal land in northern Montana and the Snake River Canyon of Idaho, respectively. MacLane, as has been observed, found the landscape around Butte to be as dreary as her life; obviously, she believed herself to have been powerfully shaped, albeit negatively, by that landscape.

If we read these life narratives today, however, we are not likely to be entertained or moved as much by the writer's sense of landscape as we are by his or her way of living in the particular place. This entails, to some degree, our fascination with the details of unfamiliar activities and personalities, the attraction of the exotic in both time and place. Anne Ellis ekes out an existence in the mining camps of Colorado; Elinore Pruitt Stewart scrapes out a living by farming wheat on a Wyoming homestead; Margaret Bell struggles with cattle and an abusive stepfather; Grace Jordan helps run a sheep ranch in a remote, snake-infested canyon; Nelle Portrey Davis subsists in the forests of northern Idaho; Annie Pike Greenwood attempts to bring slivers of culture to the sagebrush desert and irrigated farms of southern Idaho. Much of the interest for a reader of any of these life narratives has to do with the writers' portrayal of the sometimes eccentric personalities they encountered, and much of it has to do with their assemblage of episodes from their lives recast as small stories: Hedge's sexual assault of young Margaret Bell; Elinore Pruitt Stewart's encounter with Zebulon Pike Parker, who provides her and her daughter with refuge from a sudden blizzard; Annie Pike Greenwood's squabble with her "dislikers" at the Grange.

Saying it all comes down to the quality of writing may be an oversimplification, but clearly some of the memoirists are better story-tellers, better at creating characters, have keener insight, and show a stronger sense of style than others. One of the greatest dangers for a memoirist is the pitfall of self-indulgence. MacLane glories in it, carrying her Romantic egotism to sometimes comic and sometimes bathetic extremes. Greenwood, and to a lesser extent perhaps Foote, also might be said to err in that direction. The best of these memoirists are distinguished by (1) their ability to tell a good story, which includes the development and pacing of episodes, and most importantly the discovery or imposition of narrative structure, the shaping of their life story; (2) their ability to re-create characters (including themselves) vividly; (3) their capacity for self-reflection and self-criticism; (4) their sense of historical scope (that is, their awareness of what is going on in the world around them and of their place in the current of events); (5) their personal progress or development (their dawning self-awareness); (6) their thematic agenda or conceptual range; (7) their credibility or authenticity; (8) particularly given the present context, their sense of place, which involves both vividness and accuracy, but which does *not* necessarily involve infatuation with the landscape. In his preface to *Arctic Dreams* (1986) Barry Lopez poses two questions germane to regional autobiography and memoir: "How do people imagine the landscapes they find themselves in? How does the land shape the imaginations of the people who dwell in it?"[48]

Chapter Three

Ivan Doig and Mark Spragg: Fathers and Sons in Place

In the opening stanza of "Lake Chelan," Oregon poet William Stafford offers what might be regarded as a definition of regionalism:

> They call it regional, this relevance —
> the deepest place we have: in this pool forms
> the model of our land, a lonely one,
> responsive to the wind. Everything we own
> has brought us here: from here we speak.[1]

Whether writers elect to speak to or embrace a particular region in their work and how they choose to reflect that region are obviously of interest to readers. Surely readers throughout the United States, or throughout the world, are attracted to Ivan Doig's *This House of Sky* or Mark Spragg's *Where Rivers Change Direction* partly because they wish to connect, for some reason, with Montana or Wyoming. Whatever else readers encounter in these memoirs, they will find something about the northern Rockies, and to suggest that place is irrelevant for readers of life narrative would be as ludicrous as to argue that it makes no difference whether William Faulkner placed most of his characters in Mississippi. Novelist James Welch situates nearly all of his characters on the Montana Hi-line, the protagonist of his last novel, Charging Elk, being a rare exception; and Flannery O'Connor's characters clearly thrive in the Southeast and not in the Midwest, New England, or in California, where we expect to encounter John

Steinbeck's denizens. In his important essay, "Region, Power, Place," William W. Bevis examines the problems of regional art in a culture attracted to postmodern theory which is "itself aggressively urban": "The no-place of capitalist modernity is a kind of culture, and we will call its dominant trait 'liquidity.'"[2] Contrary to that culture, Bevis, argues, regionalism is substantial and inherently "subversive" (22).

Perhaps even more than writers of fiction, writers of life narrative might be expected either to celebrate or to assail the impact of particular places in their lives; indeed, one of the most perilous pitfalls for the memoirist is nostalgia over a former haunt. Annie Dillard's *An American Childhood* (1987), located in Pittsburgh during the 1950s, is as regional as Pete Hamill's *A Drinking Life* (1994), located in and around New York City, which is as regional as Kim Barnes's *In the Wilderness* (1996), situated in the Idaho panhandle. One may as readily wax nostalgic over an urban neighborhood as over a snow-capped mountain or a crystal clear trout stream, particularly when one's past is involved, even when, as in Barnes's case, that past was not very pleasant and occurred not so long ago (her memoir was published when she was just 38). Nostalgia implies sentiment, perhaps even sentimentality, and the age of sentiment (sometimes called "sensibility"), the period during which sentiment was fashionable, even laudable, is long past. In his positive review of *This House of Sky* for *Time* magazine, Frank Trippett warns that "personal memoir" is "notorious for snaring even gifted writers in thickets of anecdotage and sentiment," but he indicates that Doig avoids such traps and exercises "a talent at once robust and sensitive."[3] Nevertheless, no writers of life narrative can altogether avoid sentiment, nor should they. In an interview, Doig refers to the difficulty of accumulating the "emotional ingredients" for his book.[4] The emotional baggage of one's memories (to employ a less honorific metaphor) may weigh as much or even more than the conceptual freight or the literal, physical platform. There is the landscape, the father and mother, friends and acquaintances, and the congeries of events as seen and recorded; and there is the place, parents, other people, and episodes as *felt*. All these fundamental elements of the memoir are subject to change, but the landscape, particularly when rural, might be the least vulnerable. Nostalgia entails a longing, and longing implies loss. Few, if any, writers of memoir can avoid such longing, and those who read memoir are perforce drawn into that state. Linda K. Karrel finds that "Doig privileges a nostalgic and essentialistic version of the rural folk that the memoirist's persona simultaneously celebrates and rejects."[5]

Harold P. Simonson argues that "a sense of place restores one's relationship to the land and the community, and therefore to oneself."[6] Regionalism, Simonson insists, is not to be confused with local color or sentimentalism or escapism, but with "physical places that one can identify with and connect within his own soul." Writers of life narratives offer intimate and vivid portraits of the regions they know, or have known, as "home," and in the end, Simonson writes, "home is what brings wholeness and axial centeredness to people, and is therefore perhaps the only resolution any of us can know" (4).

Ivan Doig

Ivan Doig opens his memoir, *This House of Sky* (1978), subtitled *Landscapes of a Western Mind*, with the following dramatically powerful couple of sentences:

> Soon after daybreak on my sixth birthday, my mother's breathing wheezed more raggedly than ever, then quieted. And then stopped.[7]

Compare this with the opening sentences from two of the memoirs mentioned above:

> (from Mark Spragg's *Where Rivers Change Directions*)
> When I was a boy my father had horses, over a hundred of them, some of them rank, and I sat them well. He believed that horses were to use and that boys were nothing if not used.[8]

> (from Pete Hamill's *A Drinking Life: A Memoir*)
> At the beginning of my remembering, I am four years old and we are living on the top floor of a brick building on a leafy street in Brooklyn, a half block from Prospect Park. Before that place and that age, there is nothing.[9]

It is not my intention to analyze rigorously the differences in rhetorical purpose here, but to reflect briefly on the varying impact such opening passages might have on the reader. The first person singular pronoun appears in all three examples, but in Doig's opening sentence the reader's attention is addressed outward, toward the speaker's dying mother, and in the passage quoted from Spragg's memoir, the speaker shares the stage with his father. Doig's focus throughout remains fastened not on himself, but on other characters in his life, particularly his father and grandmother.

Spragg, on the other hand, rarely shifts his focus away from himself, and his opening sentences offer exposition rather than narration. But he conjures an animal that carries symbolic weight in Western writing. Spragg's horse might be said to wield power or affect comparable to Hamill's Brooklyn.

In his urban memoir Hamill opens with description of place; he directs our attention immediately to the setting. Doig moves quickly after his opening passage to set the scene in the "high spilling slopes of the Bridger Range of southwestern Montana" (3). Doig's first sentences are striking because of their immediate, dramatic impact; they are, not coincidentally, the sort of sentences one might encounter in a feature written by a skilled journalist. By the time he entered high school, Doig realized his interest in books would likely draw him away from his father's life as a sheep herder and from his own powerful love affair with rural central Montana. At Northwestern University he studied history and journalism, completing his master's degree in 1962, after which he served briefly in the U.S. Air Force. He wrote editorial and feature pieces and served as assistant editor for *The Rotarian Magazine* before leaving for Seattle with his wife, also a journalist, in 1966 and undertaking graduate work in American history at the University of Washington. He received his Ph.D. in 1969, but instead of becoming an academic, Doig embarked upon a career as a free-lance writer and editor. In *Earthlight, Wordfire: The Work of Ivan Doig* (1992) Elizabeth Simpson bibliographs dozens of freelance pieces Doig wrote for such publications as *Pacific Search* magazine and the *Seattle Times*. In these writings, as in his novels, his concerns for historical detail and strict authenticity reflect his education as a journalist and historian. *This House of Sky* had its origins in tape-recorded interviews with his father and grandmother in the summer of 1968, when he was at work on an essay about African-American singer Taylor Gordon of White Sulphur Springs for the *Montana Magazine of History*.[10] *This House of Sky* proved to be Doig's first major book, and it set the standard for subsequent memoirs from the region.

One fortunate result of these interviews is that the voices of Doig's father and grandmother, and those of other Montanans of their generation, resonate with remarkable credibility and individuality. His dialogue, the element of the memoir most vulnerable to accusations of overfictionalization, not only seems or feels realistic to the reader, but also is, at least to some degree, verifiably or certifiably realistic. We hear Charlie Doig's voice (all dialogue is italicized) throughout the book:

> The winter of 'twenty-one, I helped that scissorbill feed his cattle. He worked a team of big roans on the hay sled. Oh, they were a pair of dandies [...] Pete started working over that mare with his quirt again. 'Damn ye anyway,' I says to old mister Pete. 'Beat up on a horse like that would ye?' [13–14].

Although Charlie Doig does not speak the Queen's English, his voice is distinct from that of his friend Clifford, a rancher with whom Ivan boards while going to school:

> Well, hell, y'know, me an' Charlie was like brothers. Closer, maybe. I seen your dad was havin' a hard time gettin' over your mother's passin' away [15].

And both of these men speak in a way that sets them apart from Ivan's maternal grandmother, Bessie, whom his father invites into the household after a failed second marriage. Doig represents her as talking in "a small private language" of her own:

> I'll have a sipe more of coffee, but if I eat another bite I'll busticate.... Get that swatter and dead that fly for me, pretty please?... Hmpf, I been sittin' so long my old behinder is stiff [130].

Perhaps it would be more accurate to refer to the passages above as monologues, inasmuch as Doig does not attempt to present conversation in his memoir, and the result is that while readers have access to what might be called legitimate Western voices, they are not called upon to suspend their disbelief when confronted with pages of dialogue during which the characters are made to speak fortuitously apt lines.

Ivan Doig also sets the bar high when it comes to his description of place. Reviewers and critics have been as quick to admire his lyrical prose as they have been to praise his journalist's and historian's commitment to accuracy. Consider, for example, the mingling of fact (notably place names) and rhetoric (one is inclined to say "poetry") in the first descriptive paragraph of the book:

> It starts, early in the mountain summer, far back among the high spilling slopes of the Bridger Range of southwestern Montana. The single sound is hidden water — the south fork of Sixteenmile Creek diving down its willow-masked gulch. The stream flees north through this secret and peopleless land until, under the fir-dark flanks of Hatfield Mountain, a bow of meadows makes the riffled water curl wide to the west. At this

interruption, a low rumple of the mountain knolls itself up watchfully, and atop it, like a sentry box over the frontier between the sly creek and the prodding meadow, perches our single-room cabin [3].

The passage begins denotatively, flirts metaphorically with words like "diving," "willow-masked," and "flees," then gives way to connotative language and metaphor altogether in the last sentence. Like a poet, Doig likes to torque the language: The word "rumple" usually appears as a verb, while "knolls" generally shows up as a noun. Presumably, this is the sort of passage the reviewer for the *Christian Science Monitor* had in mind when he praised Doig's "movingly beautiful prose" that has the power to haunt the reader.[11] "Once I began *This House of Sky*," Doig observes in an interview, "I began working on what Norman Maclean has called the poetry under the prose" (O'Connell 297). In his introduction prepared for the 1992 paperback edition, Doig offers the following excerpt from his January 1975 journal: "It would be magnificent to do the entire book with this slow care, writing it all as highly charged as poetry — but will I ever find the time?"[12]

One reason the writing of *This House of Sky* proved so time consuming was the intricate and complex nature of the undertaking. Frank Trippett noted early on that memory acted as a "protagonist" in the book (92), and Elizabeth Simpson suggests that "In many ways, this is a book about memory" and that the book "is predicated on the idea that personal identity is in part a function of memory" (18, 19). As Simpson observes, however, memory comes with a "disconcerting frailty" and tends to "become patterned and troped" (18). The one-to-three-page italicized passages at the end of each of the seven sections of the book, in fact, reflect "an editorial decision that emphasizes the ephemeral nature of the material" (19). Doig comments on the nature of memory throughout the book: "Memory is a set of sagas we live by [...] why is the pattern of remembered events so uneven, so gapped and rutted and soaring? I can only believe it is because memory takes its pattern from the earliest moments in the mind, from childhood" (10). "Memory, the near neighborhood of dream, is almost as casual in its hospitality" (106). "Memory is a kind of homesickness, and like homesickness, it falls short of the actualities on almost every count" (239). These inter-chapters constitute a sort of textbook on memory. The last pages of the book present an italicized memory of his own nearly fatal accident that occurred about the time he was at work on his memoir. He calls it "A final flame-lit prism of remembering" (312).

At one extreme, then, memory and memoir inevitably connect with imagination (sagas), dream, and nostalgia. But Doig is also the consummate journalist and historian, who buttresses memory with "strict authenticity," which he acquired by returning to Montana to expand and verify "by talking to other people and seeing the places where things actually took place" (O'Connell 304). *This House of Sky* includes no photographs, but in the text Doig refers to several of them, and Elizabeth Simpson includes more than a dozen in her book-length study of his writing. Doig's close description of his father and mother as they appeared when they were young derives from "the album pages of those campsites," a pair of "almost-strangers" grinning up at him "off the stiff black pages" (5). The Fourth of July 1928, for example, is recorded in his mother's photo album: "*Ready for the Big Day:* Dad and his brother Angus have doffed their black ten-gallon hats for the camera, grins in place under their slicked hair, and bandannas fluttering at their necks like flags of a new country" (50–51). Moreover, as may be inferred from the foregoing, Doig maintains what might be described as a historian's attention to dates: "The start of memory's gather: June 27, 1945. I have become six years old, my mother's life has drained out at 31 years" (9). In the second section of the book he traces the Doig family's migration to Montana from 1890 through his parents' marriage in 1934 and his own birth in 1939, reflecting briefly on such historical events as World War I and the influenza epidemic of 1918–1919. The African-American Gordon family in White Sulphur Springs is commemorated and dated with Rose Gordon's valedictory address of 1904, and when Charlie Doig and his second wife, whom Ivan calls Ruth, decide to give up on operating a café and return to herding sheep, we are told it is the autumn of 1948. When Ivan's grandmother, Bessie Ringer, enters the narrative to help raise him after the breakup of his father's second marriage, Doig introduces her at age twenty heading to Montana by train in the spring of 1914.

Anticipating his eventual emergence as a novelist, Doig demonstrates skill in the portrayal of both male and female characters in *This House of Sky*. William Bevis observes that "Ivan's young life took place in a matriarchal world, while his myths and obsessions were patriarchal."[13] In personal correspondence with me, Doig indicates that he mentioned to his potential publishers two memoirs that had influenced him, Mari Sandoz's *Old Jules* and Wallace Stegner's *Wolf Willow*. He did not mention two "more traditionally shaped memoirs," both of which he admires, A. B. Guthrie, Jr.'s *The Blue Hen's Chick* (1965) and Nannie Alderson's *A Bride Goes West* (1942, reprinted in 2003).[14] The memoirs written by men are balanced with those written by women, and as Bevis notes, a sort of tension between the genders runs throughout Doig's memoir. The dominant character, Charlie Doig, decides to raise his son in his own image: "My boyhood would be the miniature of how he himself lived" (54). Presumably, Charlie Doig intended for his son to be, as he was, a fine horseman and an excellent foreman, a man devoted to life in the sort of "unsparing landscape" critics like to label "hardscrabble" (22), and perhaps, like himself, a man of "muscle and feistiness" (46). Early on Doig presents a physical portrait of his father, "just five and a half feet tall," "slim down the waist and hips," and "cocking the dry half-grin which sneaks onto my own face as I look at him" (5).

But, as Bevis has observed in *Ten Tough Trips*, it was "the women" who offered Ivan Doig "what he really needed" (167). Certainly his maternal grandmother, Bessie Ringer, acts as a worthy counterbalance to Ivan's father. As she aged, Doig discovers from his study of photographs, she "broadened and squared." By 1950, when she became a part of eleven-year-old Ivan's family, she was 57 (his father was then 47), her face strong, "almost mighty," built around "the careful clasp of a mouth which always seemed ready to purse with no relenting." She was just over five feet tall, and "where my mother was a wand of a woman, this grandmother was an oak stump" (114, 115). Bessie Ringer never quite dominates the book, never quite replaces Ivan's father, but she exerts a powerful presence. Karell argues that "Bessie's character is fused with sentimentalized portraits of rural western women when she is cast as the enduring, nearly ageless caretaker," and she finds that Doig's father, too, "is represented stereotypically. He is the quintessential western loner, a tough but fair boss with an enviable work ethic" (125). Implicitly, then, at least for some readers, Doig creates characters who embody features of the Old West mythology. Certainly that premise merits some speculation.

Charlie Doig rarely behaves like a "loner." He actively seeks the support of a woman, particularly to help him raise his motherless son, and he also recognizes the need for his young son to be part of a family and of a community. Toward that end, he boards out his son with a number of families, each of which Ivan brings to life with apparent affection and gratitude. Moreover, nearly every important male in the memoir is balanced by an influential woman. Taylor Gordon, the black singer from White Sulphur Springs who goes on to write his memoir, *Born to Be* (1929), is no more magnetic than his sister Rose. Mrs. Frances Carson Tidyman, Ivan's English teacher when he enters high school in Valier, discovers his talent with language and proves to be even more influential than McCarthy, his football coach, who advises him to go into journalism. Psychologically, in effect, Ivan seeks out his departed mother's approval by foregoing the macho Western myth. Bevis finds that the book "writes itself into the crack between nostalgia for our rural roots, and the success story of the mobile individual who got out" (169).

Although I have presented *This House of Sky* as an exemplar of the new memoir from the Rockies, it was named a finalist for the National Book Award, not in the category of "Biography and Autobiography," as Doig rather proudly notes, but "Contemporary Thought." Not that the two categories are mutually exclusive, of course, but if the book is commendable for its credibility in the genre of memoir, as well as for its admirable style, portrayal of character, and narrative shape, perhaps it deserves the most acclaim as what might be called a "memoir of ideas." Harcourt Brace Jovanovich marketed the book as a memoir, but the subtitle, "Landscapes of a Western Mind," suggests a conceptual layer not necessarily expected of life narrative. (Doig credits acquisitions editor Carol Hill for the subtitle.) In his review James P. Degnan commends the book for its celebration of "the traditional middle class values," which he lists as "fidelity, self-sacrifice, hard work, deferred gratification, common sense, dependability, concern for the rights of others, and desire for the good opinion of others."[15] Elizabeth Simpson suggests that the book "goes well beyond the conventions of biography and autobiography" and lists half a dozen "profound and elusive issues": "the relationship of past to present; the nature and function of memory; the creation of personal identity; the political and ecological impact of the westering impulse; the cultural and personal qualities that permit one group to prosper on land where others starve out; the apparent arbitrariness of death" (11).

As A. Carl Bredahl has perceived, *This House of Sky* relies heavily on narrative, but Doig rejects "traditional plotting" and structures the book in seven sections that "develop a continuity from the narrator's remembering, remembering the past in order to understand the present and facilitate the future."[16] The book follows the author's progress from age six through his high school years, but other characters, not Ivan Doig himself, occupy the foreground. To that extent, until the sixth part, some 240 pages into the text, when Ivan leaves Montana for college at Northwestern University, the book conforms more nearly to definitions of memoir than to those applied to autobiography. The focus tends away from the self, and the organization does not appear to follow "a dutiful line from birth to fame."[17] In the sixth section, however, the close focus and the narrative rhythm of the book are disrupted, as if leaving Montana might somehow, as Yeats put it, "trouble the living stream." Each of the first five sections covers about three years of Ivan's life, but the sixth, "Ivory" (which is how Ivan's name appears in Ebonics), only about one-third the length of *each* of the three central parts of the narrative, follows Doig from age eighteen to 27. He takes his bachelor's degree, serves briefly in the U.S. Air Force, takes his first jobs in journalism, gets married, and receives his Ph.D. at the University of Washington in 1966, having left Montana in 1956. The final section, "Endings," shifts the focus back to Doig's father, who dies slowly of emphysema in 1971, and grandmother, who dies quickly of a heart attack in 1974.

Bredahl describes the sixth section as "the choppiest in the book" (22), and it is surely the least coherent. Karell finds the section "stylistically abrupt" and "lacking the lyricism, detail, or eloquence that comprise Doig's consciously honed writing style in other sections" (127). What Doig does in that section, however, appears to be fairly common among some memoirists who evolve their life narratives somewhat on the model of the novel. Not quite satisfied with a memoir-as-novel paradigm; they yield to what might be called the model of memoir-as-autobiography. The writer of life narrative is often seduced by an impulse to tell the entire story, to bring everything up to date, and perhaps for a writer like Ivan Doig, a trained historian, it was impossible not to yield to that impulse. As a model for the new surge of life narrative writing from the northern Rockies, some might argue that *This House of Sky* qualifies more as predecessor than paradigm. But the techniques of creative nonfiction are much in evidence in Doig's book, and most subsequent memoirists from the region have acknowledged some debt to it.

Although he was to return to the memoir in *Heart Earth* (1993), his short, poignant book on his mother's last year, Doig has made a name for himself as a novelist, starting with *English Creek* in 1984, which was to become the centerpiece of a trilogy that also includes *Dancing at the Rascal Fair* (1987) and *Ride with Me, Maraiah, Montana* (1990). In these novels of the McCaskill family, and in other novels set in Montana, Doig fashions a fictional world for the inland Northwest that is reminiscent of Faulkner's Mississippi. As Elizabeth Simpson notes, however, "many critics believe it [*This House of Sky*] to be Doig's best work" (22).

Mark Spragg

Like Ivan Doig, Wyoming native Mark Spragg (1952–) gained initial attention as a writer through a memoir, *Where Rivers Change Direction*, which won the 1999 Mountains and Plains Booksellers Award. And although Spragg's book is constructed as a collection of fourteen personal narrative essays, and therefore suggests the structure one might associate with a book of short stories, it coheres so tightly through the first ten pieces, which follow his maturation from age twelve through sixteen (1964–1968), that initially we might suspect his paradigm is the novel, a sort of Bildungsroman. Spragg subsequently demonstrated his talent for the novel with *The Fruit of Stone* (2002). A second novel, *Unfinished Life*, appeared in 2005, and a movie based on it was released in the fall of 2005. Hailing the publication of Spragg's second novel as a "sparkling hat trick," Bill Ott, in a starred review for *Booklist*, places his memoir in a category with those of William Kittredge and Ivan Doig.[18]

Although he now lives in south central Montana, Mark Spragg has not roamed far from "the anachronism that we considered our normal lives" in the Shoshone National Forest, just six miles from the east gate to Yellowstone Park,[19] and he maintains his Wyoming residency. Doig devotes a section of his memoir to his college days at Northwestern, but Spragg is largely silent about his college experiences at the University of Wyoming in Laramie, where he complains about how the sidewalks and paved roads caused his feet to ache: "Four years of college on concrete has nearly crippled me. [...] I did not attend graduation. I packed the car and did not look back" (198). (A lesser man, perhaps, would have given up on wearing cowboy boots.) Unlike Doig, whose memoir summarizes his work as a journalist before he earned a doctorate in history, Spragg unveils few of the external details of his life after age sixteen. When I contacted Spragg he indicated that his second wife, Virginia, collaborated with him on the screenplay for *Unfinished Life*. The movie features Jennifer Lopez, Robert Redford, and Morgan Freeman and is directed by Lasse Hallström, whose achievements include *My Life as a Dog* (1985) and *Shipping News* (2001). Spragg's work as a screenwriter has involved him in two prior films, *Gross Anatomy* (1989), which is set in a medical school, and *Everything That Rises* (1998), a made-for-television movie that does not derive from Flannery O'Connor's story, but is set in the contemporary West. He professes no particular pride in either of those endeavors, but is optimistic about the prospects for *Unfinished Life*.[20] Spragg also edited a small book of photographs and essays for the Sierra Club, *Thunder of Mustangs* (1997). In the final essay from *Where Rivers Change Direction* he is 36 years old (the year is 1988 or so), and he has remarried.

Both Ivan Doig and Mark Spragg proved most generous in responding to my queries and supplying information not available in such sources as *Contemporary Authors*. The major gap in Spragg's case concerned the period between his graduation from the University of Wyoming, where he majored in comparative literature, and his memoir. He filled in the gaps over the phone. For example, Spragg credits Robert Roripaugh, Wyoming's poet laureate from 1995 till 2002, with having urged him to abandon his study for a master's degree and devote himself to writing.[21] He reports that he managed the family ranch for a while and tried his hand at teaching high school, but found that it left him insufficient time for his writing. Spragg then worked manual labor — oil rigs, building fences, shoeing horses — while writing short stories and essays. Several essays in *Where Rivers Change Direction* first appeared in short versions (just four or five pages — he regards them as "lyric exercises") in the Sierra Club magazine. Then a friend, Ron Bishop, who had been a successful script writer (he wrote for the *Gunsmoke* television series, and his credits include *How the West Was Won* and *The Red Pony*), encouraged Spragg to turn to script writing in order to make a more reliable income. Spragg met his wife Virginia about twelve years ago when she was a counselor at Northwest College in Powell, Wyoming. He describes her as his first and most important reader and editor.

Spragg considers his decision to write his memoir an effort to honor his dying mother, but he indicates that it was otherwise "absolutely unpremeditated."[22] He recalls having read no other memoirs before writing *Where Rivers Change Direction*, but he now particularly admires the work of Ivan Doig, Kim Barnes, Annie Dillard, and Tobias Wolff. As a boy, from ages ten through sixteen, he kept journals (Spragg says he has about forty of them), and in these he recorded scraps of conversation that helped him with his reconstructions of dialogue. He tends to be sparing with dialogue in most of the essays, as in the following subtly humorous exchange between himself at age thirteen and John, the ranch hand who is in his forties and who serves as a sort of father figure. The passage occurs as they prepare to break camp after John has cut his hand:

> "Make sure you don't feel sorry for me today," he says and lowers his cup. "It won't help either one of us."

"No sir, I won't."
"We'll butcher that elk after breakfast and let the stove cool. It won't take as long as you think to tear down camp."
"I didn't think it would take long."
"Well, it won't."
"Should I look at your hand?"
"I already did. It wasn't hard to find" [61].

If anything, young Mark's exchanges with his somehow distant father require even shorter sentences. Although in his study of closure in the book Brian Dillon praises Spragg's "use of dialogue to reveal character and push the plot forward,"[23] only in the essay on the alcoholic cook, "The Circusmaster," does dialogue appear as a predominant feature.

As in Doig's *This House of Sky*, Spragg gives us the lay of the land starting on the first page. "It is easiest for me to remember the land," he begins (1). Presumably this is because that landscape, "the high Yellowstone Plateau, straddling the Continental Divide," has not changed that much over the years, and Spragg has never strayed far from home.

> I see tar-black butterflies at work in the meadows along the Shoshone River, the grasses come thick in seedheads. I smell white-cupped blossoms, bursts of lavender, the weedy scent of the bloodred Indian paintbrush, the overpowering tang of the banks of low-growing sage. I can hear my boots scuff against the black and rust and corn-yellow lichens that covered them [2]

Spragg's descriptive passages are distinguished by exact observation (sight, sound, smell) and a keen awareness of color, but he rarely dabbles in metaphor. "Everything that means home to me," he writes in the first page of "A Ditch Burning," is "a by-product of the North Fork of the Shoshone":

> The floor of the Wapiti valley is a descending fall of water-smoothed rock. Its random and volcanic ridges crumble down to the river, down with the flow of water, brought every year imperceptibly lower and more jagged by the runoff of thunderstorms and snowmelt. The river and its tributaries support the grasses and wildflowers that by midsummer grow belly-deep to a grazing horse. There is Douglas fir. Spruce. Varieties of pine, some juniper, aspen, and at the river's banks the water-drunk cottonwood. The trees shed their needles, cones, leaves, layering the forest floor, each season adding to the mulch of acidic duff [254].

Such descriptions, nearly barren of rhetorical ornament (the "water drunk cottonwoods" are as close to figurative speech as he gets in either of these passages), may promote the reader's credibility. There is a trade-off, of course. Such passages are not particularly moving or emotionally powerful, but they have the advantage of almost scientific accuracy, and they possess a certain musical quality, the lyricism of things as they are.

Like Ivan Doig, Spragg mentions photographs from time to time, but the salient feature of his memoir is the dream, or in some cases the dreamlike moment. While reader credibility is heightened by reference to photographs, it may well be threatened by dreams, particularly when those dreams appear to be too fortuitous, too coincidentally right for the context. Near the end of his first essay, "In Praise of Horses," Spragg dreams that "I stood on the horse's rump and pissed a yellow arc into the air," then "screamed into the vault of the black night sky, and turned and walked to his withers and sat" (22). This is only the beginning of a remarkably well-defined dream. The pinto is described in detail, and Spragg tells us that he held his arms "high like the armatures of long, slim wings" as the horse broke into a run. He concludes, "I saw God looking at me in the dream and knew it was a horse I had to thank" (23). "A Boy's Work" ends with a dream of himself running wild in a forest: "I lie down upon the soil to feel its care for me, and imagine I am recognized, that I am held dear. I think that I will fall in love with a girl who is raised on this same wilderness" (119). Perhaps it is sufficient to observe that this dream, which follows fifteen-year-old Mark's discovery of a note from his mother that she has left food for him in the fridge and that she loves him, is not quite as "common" (118) as he suggests. Spragg scatters several other dreams in his memoir, each of them revealing something of his subconscious. The dreams are clearly reconstructions of the adult writer's consciousness, or perhaps even of what might be called his extended consciousness. As is often the case in dealing with memoir, we are suspended between the "exact truth" and the "emotional truth" of the story. Memoirists who insert dreams into their books risk losing some of their credibility with the reader, but dreams also lend the life narrative special innerness and intimacy.

Spragg's organization of his memoir as a set of essays also offers both advantages and disadvantages. An obvious disadvantage is that each essay will call individual attention to itself (as is the case with particular stories that make up a collection), and some will inevitably be less effective than others. "Wapiti School," for example, while it offers some comic relief in his reminiscence of puppy love, does not fit comfortably among such essays as "In Praise of Horses," "Bones," and "Adopting Bear." Nearly every essay offers evidence of Spragg's flair for what I would call lyrical aphorism, a clever and memorable sort of phrasing that comes off looking not so much pithy or wise as it looks or feels beautiful: "The gift of horses liberated me. It was horses that allowed me early on to step away from the love affair I maintained with myself" (9). "I like to believe that horses were fashioned moments before us. I like to believe that they sprang from the earth snorting, lifting man loose from the imagination of God" (59). "When I am older I will believe that following in their wake has filled me with the inconsolable joy of animals" (172). Spragg echoes his phrasing later when he writes of his mother's "inconsolable joy for life" (266). "The winds wail a hymn of transience" (221). "Wyoming has taught me to be thankful for pain. There is pain that saves the body; there is pain that saves the soul" (229). "I cling to the sound of water to be brave in the world. I go to the sound of water to remember that God is not mute" (229). And of his mother dying, like Doig's father, from emphysema: "[M]y mother said simply that we live on a water planet. That all streams flow into one" (256).

The relationship of father to son in Spragg's memoir is reminiscent in some ways of the difficult connection described in Edmund Gosse's classic Victorian memoir, *Father and Son* (1907). Although the adolescent Mark Spragg's life is by no means as restricted as that of Edmund Gosse, whose father wished to direct him into the clergy of the fundamentalist Plymouth Brethren, it is clear that Spragg's father, like Gosse's, operates on the paradigm of son-as-clay-to-be-shaped, presumably so that he will one day take over the "family business," the "oldest dude ranch in Wyoming" (1). Gosse's father saw his son as a future minister; Spragg's father casts Mark in the mold of ranch hand. As his father himself suggests later, "'When we work together I guess I'm your boss'" (122). Like Gosse's father, Spragg's father appears only rarely in what might be called intimate contexts with his son, and like Edmund Gosse, Mark Spragg eventually, quietly, takes "a human being's privilege to fashion his inner life for himself."[24]

Doig's father dominates *This House of Sky*. The mind that the West landscapes is primarily Charlie Doig's and only indirectly (albeit importantly) that of the author. But while Spragg's father is a powerful figure in several essays that comprise this memoir, it is the author himself whose mind is landscaped in *Where Rivers Change Direction*. "I went to work for him when I was eleven," Spragg writes (1). Paid thirty dollars a month, he is given a bed in the bunkhouse and takes his meals with the rest of the crew; by the time he's fifteen, Mark is considered competent to lead four- to five-day pack trips. Initially, we get only a spare portrait of Spragg's father. He smokes cigarettes almost incessantly, it seems, and he is a man of few words and curt syntax. At age twelve, Mark sees his father as a man of "medium height": "If he were to turn to me, hold out his arms to me, and I were to walk into him my head would not brush his collarbones. I am only as tall as the top of his heart" (26). Significantly, however, his father does not hold out his arms to his son, and several of the essays depict young Mark in what readers might perceive to be a search for a surrogate father. The most promising candidate is John, who is in his forties when Mark is thirteen. In "Bones" Mark tends to John when he accidentally slashes himself with a knife while hunting elk. Spragg's description of his dilemma back then (whether or not to run for help) is suggestive: "But I know if I abandon him it will change the family that this man and I have made" (52).

In "Greybull," the essay that comes nearest to revealing some affection between father and son, we acquire more physical details of the father: "I know that our faces appear alike: same jaw, same forehead, same eyes." Spragg adds little else to this description other than the fact that his father has "tightened his face" by "squinting into the day's work" and his cheeks are "smooth shaven and browned." "Our similarities," he adds, "have always surprised and unsettled us both" (123). But why would that be, the reader might ask: surely we should expect such similarities, nor would most of us find those similarities "unsettling." At the end of the day, his father arranges for Mark to purchase the horse he has admired at an auction, gives him a raise from a dollar to five dollars a day, and informs him that he will deduct what his son owes him from the raise. The father tells his son he's "worth it." His son responds, "I'll work harder." The father responds (playfully, but with double edge), "If I wasn't satisfied I'd have fired you back down to just being my kid." Then the father adds, "I'll take what you owe me out of the raise. Lunch is my treat" (137). Presumably, there are at least two ways of regarding this scene. Perhaps the father is attempting to teach his son such conventionally "American" values as self-reliance and personal economy.

Other readers might object to the father's lessons as relics of the myths of the Old West currently under interrogation. Or perhaps the father is simply a man who cannot bring himself to give. Any way one regards the transaction, it is clear that the father-son connection has been somehow "commodified." The father does not *ask* his son about paying him back, nor does he offer that option, at least as Mark Spragg writes the dialogue.

Some Westerners might be proud to think of the father's fiscal toughness as regional — old-fashioned, rural values — but in fact that particular brand of parsimony is quite common everywhere.

"The Well Rising," one of William Stafford's earlier poems, ends, "I place my feet / with care in such a world" (52). The world in which Mark Spragg comes of age is filled with perils that a boy might not be aware of. Horses, for example, while Spragg regards them as kindred spirits, throw him on more than one occasion. And although he reflects that "At eleven it was my ambition to be a bear" (182), he imagines that a grizzly awaits him in the darkness, and he fears he might be a coward. The experienced hand, John, cuts his finger to the bone. Mark's favorite cats become dinner for the coyotes. A neighbor informs him, when he is attempting to find some solitude after his college days, that years ago she chopped off her abusive father's hand. On several occasions, as a boy, Spragg witnesses the harsh and ugly reality of death: "The horse was a big-boned paint we called Samson. He looks now to be just a large, sodden, and unfinished puzzle. Part of his neck and shoulder are eaten away. The hide hangs in scallops over the wounds. [...] The eye socket on the upturned side of his head has been pecked hollow. My father puts his toe to a length of gut and turns it. Maggots writhe, glistening in the bright air" (188). Two observations about this lurid passage: first, the horse has a name (rather an ironic one, in fact), so it is not simply a generic dead horse; second, it is Mark's father who reveals to his son the most lurid feature of the corpse. The world is a dangerous place, Spragg's father seems to be warning — step carefully.

After "Greybull," which is placed almost exactly in the middle of the book (it comes seventh of the fourteen essays), Spragg's father is not mentioned again until the last essay, "A Ditch Burning," which is devoted to Mark's dying mother. Prior to that essay Spragg's mother has been only a shadow figure, as she is in "A Boy's Work," when Mark observes her at night through the window of his parents' cabin. She is seated at the table with Spragg's father, and he cannot hear their conversation: "She sips coffee from a mug my brother made her as a school project and nods as my father speaks. She grimaces" (110). We also see her briefly when she reflects on the death of her infant daughter when she was just a few months old, following a premature birth. She tells Mark that his soul is "smiling at God," that his pair of cowlicks reveals that he has "a happy soul" (31). For the most part, however, the mother has no voice. That is, until the final essay, in which Spragg informs us that his mother, at age 64, has divorced his father, who has moved to Las Vegas (they had sold the lodge some years earlier). In this essay Mark Spragg comes to the realization that it is his mother, not his father, who has made him into "a man stronger than she imagines" (283). As Melody Graulich has observed, we find that "his mother has flowed like an underground river beneath the landscape of manhood, changing the course of his life" (272). Brian Dillon argues, however, that Spragg withholds from the reader the easy scene of closure one often gets from memoir, concluding that Spragg's consciousness of the damage he has done to animals serves as "the primary origin of his shame" (171) and that he leaves the reader with the image of a man "all too aware of the inadequacies in his development" (169).

At the end of the last essay we are made aware of Mark Spragg's coming to manhood, the manifest theme of the book from the outset, when, ironically, inasmuch as he has struggled against the impulse throughout as childish, he is able to weep. In the opening essay, "In Praise of Horses," fourteen-year-old Mark cries because he has ridden a sick horse too hard, but he also sees that he is "crying for myself, and because I was afraid that careless boys grow into careless men" (21). In "A Boy's Work," when he is compelled to shoot and cut open a gangrenous horse for bear bait, fifteen-year-old Mark takes pride in not crying: "I think a boy would cry. I think maybe I have begun to be a man" (115). Presumably, he is in error here, but typically boys from the United States are taught to regard tears as unmanly. In "Adopting Bear," after a frightening experience with a grizzly, sixteen-year-old Mark does not "sob," but he does "start to cry" when he realizes he is safe (194). In the essay "Wind," which might be proposed as the Wyoming state symbol, the deaths of two friends move Mark to "weep a little" as he contemplates "the many ways men die" (229). (As Gretel Ehrlich observes in her memoir, *The Solace of Open Spaces*, "If anything is endemic to Wyoming, it is wind."[25]) In some ways the weeping motif in Spragg's memoir is reminiscent of the Plains Indians "Crying for Pity" stage of initiation rituals. Fearful of pain and death, the individual cries not only because he feels sorry for himself, but also as a lament for suffering in the world and in hopes of bringing on a vision. At the end of his memoir, Spragg believes he has acquired self-knowledge and that he has "glimpsed the dark cloud at the base of my soul" (281). He remains fearful at times that he has led "a careless life," but his weeping this time, as his mother is dying in the next room, "will not be crying because I am afraid. I will be crying because she willingly suffers for my ease" (283).

Reviewers of *Where Rivers Change Direction* have been so extravagant in their praise that those who contributed blurbs (the word appears to have been coined around 1910) for the book jacket were hard pressed to keep up with them. Martin Padget, in the *Times Literary Supplement*, commended the writing as "fresh and innovative" and found the "storytelling" to be "robust, elegiac and ethically motivated."[26] Paul Gediman, in a starred review for *Publishers Weekly*, praised the "clean, crisp prose" and "piercing voice from the heartland" and commended "this resonant autobiography" that "weds the venerable Western tradition of frontier exploration of self and nature with the masculine school of writing stretching from Hemingway to Mailer."[27] Calling it a "soulful book" in her back-cover blurb, Terry Tempest Williams added, "Here is a book for women to read to learn the hearts of men. Here is a book for men to read to curse what they have lost." Not surprisingly, the editors of the paperback edition (the book was first published in hardcover by the University of Utah Press) set Williams's pronouncement in bold type. Although commentaries on the Internet may not presently have much clout when it comes to conventional critical appraisals, they may one day come to have nearly equal status with print reviews, and at times these amateur reviewers can be downright eloquent: "The words are sculpted into exquisite granite sentences like the mountains that surrounded him as he grew up on a dude ranch in Wyoming in the 1960s."[28]

A Comparison of Ivan Doig and Mark Spragg

About 22 years separate the publication of *This House of Sky* from *Where Rivers Change Direction*, and in that time the parameters of nonfiction have broadened considerably. Doig writes in what might be called the "autobiographical tradition." Although he employs some techniques of the emerging neo-genre of creative nonfiction, he appears reluctant to portray himself as a character. Rather, young Ivan is one of the subjects of the author Ivan Doig's scrutiny. He rarely investigates his own inner regions. Mark Spragg, however, writing from more fully evolved limits of creative nonfiction, actively promotes himself as the main character, the protagonist, of his memoir. It may not be quite accurate to say that at the end of *This House of Sky* we know more about Charlie Doig and Bessie Ringer than we know about Ivan Doig, but surely we have a more vivid sense of them as characters than we do of the narrator. At the end of *Where Rivers Change Direction*, however, it is obvious that other characters in the memoir perform as a supporting cast. The book centers on Mark Spragg, his fear and anxiety over pain and death, and his struggle to find his place in the world and to embrace his own compassionate nature. As Linda K. Karell observes, "The memoirist's challenge is to make language bridge the fissures of forgetting without promising false healing" (132).

Both writers explore parental roles in some detail. Ivan Doig begins with his mother's death, and Mark Spragg's ends with his mother's death. Karell suggests that "nostalgia is itself an attempt at forgetting" and that the "deepest yearning" in *This House of Sky* is for a "further collaboration" with his "absent mother," which Doig pursues in the subsequent memoir, *Heart Earth* (130). Spragg fulfills that yearning in the final essay of his book. While the father asserts a powerful influence in both life narratives, Spragg's is taciturn, while Doig's is generally quite voluble. Gretel Ehrlich may be deferring too far to the stereotype when she writes of the "profound" silence of Westerners brought on by their "solitude," a "laconic style" that affects even syntax: "Sentence structure is shortened to the skin and bones of a thought" (6). But Spragg records his father's speech as if he were verifying Ehrlich's observations. Doig's mother appears only at a distance and early in the book, but her surrogates play important roles in his memoir. In the section entitled "Flip" (Doig's grandmother's dismissive term for her), we follow Charlie Doig's effort to provide a "second mother" for his young son (he is nearly nine when they marry). By the time Ivan is eleven, Ruth, as he calls her, is gone and his maternal grandmother takes over, though she never quite edges out his father. In Spragg's memoir, however, the father vanishes from the picture to be replaced by the mother.

Melody Graulich has observed how "The threat of violence — from humans, from weather, from animals, from chance accidents — looms over Spragg's boyhood," and how, "Like the violence, the threat of his father's disappointed expectations shapes his growing up." The father, Graulich concludes, "casts a dominating shadow over the text. He is simultaneously a presence and an absence."[29] While Doig's father apparently honors his son with his decision to make his boyhood "the miniature of how he himself lived" (54), even to the point of introducing young Ivan to the nine bars of White Sulphur Springs, Spragg's father appears to have diminished his son in what might be regarded as a similar intention. The difference derives, in part, from Spragg's father's methods. The "deep ingredient" of Doig's father's "adventuring" as a young man was horses (39), but by the time Ivan is on the scene, horses play only a small role. Not so for Mark

Spragg, whose father, to repeat, "believed that horses were to use and that boys were nothing if not used" (1). The son, presumably, must prove his practical worth. "It was his hope," Spragg writes, "that we [horses and boys] would redeem one another." His choice of a theological term here is suggestive, the implication being that the brothers are in need of redemption, although the memoir does not pursue that lead.

Both memoirs focus on life out-of-doors in a northern Rockies landscape that has distinctive features and that the writers set before us in quite different ways. Doig herds sheep on the Blackfeet reservation with his father and grandmother near the Two Medicine River in 1954:

> Open and overawing as it was, this summer land somehow seemed tense, pulled taut and inward, with its contradictions. All this flatness and yet some purposeful tilts to it, our own ridge dropping after any few paces southward, slanting off to a sharp coulee which pitched deeper and darker, like a flume through the base of the cliffs above the Two Medicine [204–205].

Spragg begins his essay, "Recoil," with four paragraphs devoted to a definition of place, from which these are the opening sentences:

> The sage is blanched olive, aqua, and gray. The soil pale and rutted: as an abraded layer of bentonite and alkalis, swirled like some volcanic patisserie with comma-shaped hyperbolas of silica, lime, and ash. Last year's prairie grasses are scattered sparsely, brittle as dried quills, broken over by the winds, surviving perennially on the few smears of inconsiderable nutrient. This is top land, not bottom. Moisture is rare, and there is nothing to hold it [235].

The lay of this land is not spectacular, and neither writer attempts to make it look more vivid than it is, but both Doig and Spragg bring a writer's interpretive vision to bear. Doig tends to personify the landscape, finding it somehow "tense" and "purposeful." Spragg creates the impression that he sees with a geologist's empirical objectivity (bentonite and alkalis, silica, lime, and ash), but no technical report would permit such similes as the soils "swirled like some volcanic patisserie."

"This place is violent, and it is raw," Spragg writes of Wyoming (220). Doig's portrait of Montana is not quite so dramatic, but it, too, emerges as a land of blizzards and barren mountains. They also embody the region in its animals. Both life narratives, for example, include what one might consider an almost obligatory bear story. Although horses do not play as important a part in Doig's memoir as they do in Spragg's, Doig offers a menagerie of sheep and sheep dogs, and he describes the lambing process in detail. But Doig and Spragg also define the region by peopling it with memorable individuals. Doig re-creates dialect in his narrative, so his characters speak with highly distinctive voices: "Mother him like hell now, don't ye? See what a helluva dandy lamb I got for ye old sister?" (163). But Spragg's characters acquire their own understated inflections: "'My friend's had a rat piss in his eye.' Jack makes the statement flatly. [...] 'I can kick your ass.' 'That hasn't happened yet,' says Jack, but quietly, slowly" (151). Whatever else these writers accomplish, they provide physical identity and voice for those distinctive aspects of a particular place that set it apart from what William Bevis describes as "liquidity," or anonymity.

Charlie Doig and Spragg's father, Ivan Doig and Mark Spragg are shaped by what they do for a living and by the place they do it. Had these characters worked for a software firm in Cheyenne or a university in Missoula, they would not likely attract our attention, or if they did, it would be in a very different way. This having been said, one might pose a difficult question: If these two memoirists were to have children who wished to write their own life narratives, what would they be like?

Chapter Four

Mary Clearman Blew's and Teresa Jordan's Western Family Albums

Do all memoirists, whether intentionally or not, proceed from, or eventually discover in the process of their writing, some didactic, that is, instructive, purpose? Are all life narratives, by nature, inevitably "exemplary"? "Where I Lived" is important to Henry David Thoreau, but "What I Lived For" is even more important, both to him and presumably to most of his readers. In the first chapter of *Hole in the Sky: A Memoir* (1992), Oregon/Montana writer William Kittredge says he hopes his is not a "cautionary tale," but "a book that is useful."[1] Colorado memoirist Craig S. Barnes subtitles his book, *Growing Up True* (2001), "Lessons from Boyhood." Idaho memoirist John Rember offers a serious pun when he asserts that the stories we tell amount to *"a way of saving our lives"* (his italics).[2] The form is "useful in getting at the truth," Thomas Larson writes in his introduction to *The Memoir and the Memoirist* (2007): "I have found the memoir's pragmatism to be its genius."[3] As Paul John Eakin observes in the last chapter of *How Our Lives Become Stories* (1999), where he confronts the "ethical dilemmas of life writing,"[4] ethical problems become more complex "if we conceptualize identity as relational rather than autonomous" (16). Eakin contends that nearly all life writing (particularly memoir) is in fact "relational," involving others as much as or more than the writer's self. Presumably writing one's life story would be advantageous, perhaps even therapeutic, for the writer, but aside from engaging characters and a good story, what is in it for the readers?

From the memoirs of Ivan Doig and Mark Spragg readers may take something about the relationship between fathers and sons; something about the value of physical labor out of doors and involving animals; and something about the landscapes of the northern Rockies, both their beauty and their hardness. Presumably, any memoir will tell us something about time, memory, change, loss, and death. In Spragg's case, and perhaps to a less obvious extent in Doig's, the reader acquires lessons in manhood. Frequently, in the early portion of his memoir, Spragg reiterates "I am just a boy,"[5] and one of his happier moments occurs in the essay "Wintering," when an owl appears to be telling him that "for a man I am bending toward a rightness" (217). Elevated by his father to the status of partner in the sheep herding business rather than employee, Doig is rarely dealt with as if he were a boy at all. After a harrowing experience driving sheep through a blizzard in northern Montana, he writes, "As much as at any one instant in my life, I can say: *here I was turned.*"[6] Subsequently he is discovered as a potential writer by high school teachers and he leaves Montana. Most life narratives, whether by intent or coincidentally, are also accounts of how the writer became a writer.

Mary Clearman Blew (1939–), who grew up in central Montana, and Teresa Jordan (1955–), who grew up in southeastern Wyoming, offer lessons from a woman's perspective (my preference over such terms as "female" or "feminist") in their memoirs. Ivan Doig and Mary Blew were born in 1939, while Spragg (1952) and Jordan (1955) grew up in a quite different era; therefore, both gender and time are important factors to reflect upon. Part of what makes Blew's memoir an appropriate partner with Jordan's is that both writers have compiled books of essays that pertain mostly to their families and only indirectly to themselves. As narrators they remain peripheral characters, considerably more so than Spragg, but more than Doig as well. In any event, life narrative writing would appear always to have some didactic or instructive element. In the introduction to her biography of her Aunt Imogene, Blew explains that she was trying to understand her aunt's life, "and through her life to understand my own" and that she wanted to believe she was "following the same road."[7] Presumably, Blew's readers also will be instructed by Imogene's capacity for "independence and acceptance." None of the three models (life stories) the women in her family provide seems right for Teresa Jordan, but understanding them frees her to find her own narrative. Her readers may learn that they, too, have the power to "perceive a relationship fundamentally different from any" that has existed in their families and to act on that perception.[8]

Mary Clearman Blew

Like Ivan Doig, whose *This House of Sky* she knew well before she undertook her own memoir, which differs from it considerably, Mary Clearman Blew grew up in a ranching family in rural central Montana. Doig's White Sulphur Springs is located about eighty miles southeast of Blew's Lewistown, as the crow flies. Reviewers occasionally have noted connections between Doig's and Blew's memoirs; Barbara Howard Meldrum, for example, finds Blew's narrative "much more than simply a woman's version of *This House of Sky*," and she regards it as "less linear, more associational and thematic than Doig's."[9] Ivan Doig himself, in a review written for the *Washington Post*, claimed that he had been "looking over [his] shoulder" ever since he was old enough "to realize that my boyhood Montana had girls in it as well."[10] He describes *All But the Waltz* as "a now-necessary chronicle of what might be called uncolonizing, coming to terms with century-old illusions about wringing prosperity form the high dry plains" (X6). In *Landscapes of the New West* (1999) Krista Comer goes so far as to propose that the "new regionalism" did not start with Doig or Norman Maclean, but with the "murkier cultural waters [...] linked to the changing social tides created by the civil rights movements and contemporary feminism,"[11] and she finds Blew's memoir an apt culmination of her study.

Blew, like Doig, took a doctorate, but in English literature rather than history. After completing her bachelor's and master's degrees at the University of Montana, she went on to complete her Ph.D. at the University of Missouri in 1969, writing her dissertation on Juvenal and Ben Jonson's satires. Unlike Doig, Blew has pursued an academic career, which includes ten years teaching at Northern Montana College in Havre and seven years at Lewis-Clark State College in Lewiston, Idaho. It was her move from Montana to Idaho that triggered her memoir. At the time, she reports, she had been reading William Kittredge's *Owning It All* (1987) and Kim Stafford's *Having Everything Right* (1986).[12] She has taught at the University of Idaho since 1994. In "Reading Abraham," from *All But the Waltz*, Blew speculates that if she kept transcribing her great-grandfather's letters, perhaps she would "learn something about the magnet pull of place, perhaps even how to break it" (21). Place is attractive (in both senses of the word), but it can also be constrictive. Blew's lingering fascination with her Aunt Imogene may have to do with the fact that Imogene did eventually discover a new place for herself away from the ranch.

Among Blew's books are three collections of short fiction, starting with *Lambing Out and Other Stories* (1977) and most recently *Sister Coyote: Montana Stories* (2000), and several anthologies, including *Circle of Women: An Anthology of Contemporary Western Women Writers* (1994), edited with Kim Barnes, *Written on Water: Essays on Idaho Rivers* (2001), and *Forged by Fire: Essays by Idaho Writers* (2005), edited with Phil Druker. *Writing Her Own Life: Imogene Welch, Western Rural Schoolteacher* (2004) is a biography of her aunt, who appears in *All But the Waltz* and is featured in the memoir, *Balsamroot* (1993). Her first novel, *Jackalope Dreams*, appeared in 2008. So far as genres of fiction might suggest a paradigm to some writers of memoir, Doig's *This House of Sky* is novel-like while *All But the Waltz* resembles a collection of short stories in structure. In fact, in her review Victoria Amador describes *All But the Waltz* as "in its way, a series of short stories chronicling the history of Blew's family in Montana."[13]

Mary Clearman Blew's *All But the Waltz: A Memoir of Five Generations in the Life of a Montana Family* (1991) opens with a short essay, "The Sow in the River," in which she offers a memory from the summer of her third year, only to confess that her memories "seem to me as treacherous as the river."[14] To prove her point, Blew offers a dialogue in which her father informs her that her memory of a sow and her piglets seeking refuge from the flooded Judith River is altogether false. "Every ripple is suspect," when it comes to memory, Blew writes (10). It occurs to her that she may have dreamed about the sow, and she concludes that memory "lights upon a dream as readily as an extended event" or "a set of rusty irrigation pipes." On the one hand, memory is all we have, but on the other hand, "What I remember is far less trustworthy than the story I tell about it" (11). Well aware of the tension between what actually happened and what is remembered, Blew also perceives the tension between what is remembered and the story in which that memory eventually finds itself immersed. As Linda K. Karell observes, "for Blew memory is as treacherous and punishing as it is vital to the meaning of the stories we tell about our lives."[15] "What we learn in memoir writing," Thomas Larson notes in *The Memoir and the Memoirist* (2007), "is that memory has far more of its own agency than we thought, that the very act of remembering may alter what did occur" (34).

Not coincidentally then, the first substantial essay in Blew's memoir relies only rarely on her memory, and mostly on research and what a historian like Ivan Doig would refer to as "primary sources," photographs and letters of her great-grandparents. Clearly, Mary Blew accepts the notion of collaboration in writing that shapes the thesis of Karell's book, with which she is familiar:

> All writing is collaborative, however — collaboration between the writer and her tradition of story; collaboration between the writer and her reader; collaboration between the writer and the thin edge where her daily lines press into the future. And drawing as it does upon letters, memories, and family stories, this book [*Writing Her Own Life*] is, at the very least, multi-authored [11].

Neither Blew nor Karell, however, mentions the collaborative aspect of photography in writing (the text of *All But the Waltz* includes a dozen photographs). In fact, none of the life narratives I have mentioned are as significantly connected with the reality or truth of photography as Mary Blew's. If memories are so unreliable, Blew appears to imply, perhaps photographs can supply some verification.

But then one ought to inquire into the reality and truth of photography. Of course the family photo album does not reflect the conscious art of an Ansel Adams, but similar issues pertain when it comes to interpretation. The University of Oklahoma reprinting (2001) of the Viking Penguin text features a cover photo of Mary at age 2½ (it is dated May 1942), about her age when she saw the sow on the island in the flooded river. Dressed in striped overalls and wearing a man-sized cowboy hat and boots, the child casts an impish blue-eyed, close-mouthed grin at the camera. Both hands are plunged into her pockets. Behind her stands a log cabin. Below her feet the editors have imposed a snapshot of a man (presumably Mary's father) working a pair of collared horses in a corral; a line of bare mountains, perhaps the South Moccasins, in the background. The cherubic child seems to rise straight out of the mountains. Her father and the horses are at the bedrock of her being. At this point, of course, I am interpreting the photography, and Mary Blew undertakes a similar kind of interpretation periodically throughout the book. Once one introduces (or imposes) one's words, the photograph acquires a meaning different from what it might have for another viewer. But what truth or reality did the photograph itself express anyway? Unmediated, that is to say, what did the photographer attempt to signify? "Here is my beautiful daughter." "Look how independent this cute little rascal is!" "She may look sweet, but that smile conceals all sorts of deviltry." Or, as to Mary's father, the snapshot having been taken, presumably, by her mother: "Here is my husband doing what he loves." "These two darned horses gave Jack fits." "My husband likes me well enough, but he *loves* his horses."

In his study of photography and autobiography Timothy Dow Adams asserts, "The forms of photography that most clearly turn life into literature are the portraits and the self-portrait, those forms of light writing that in many ways parallel life writing."[16] Both Mary Blew and Teresa Jordan distribute portraits throughout their memoirs, but significantly, perhaps, neither offers a self-portrait *except* from childhood: we see Mary at the ages of about three and eight and Teresa at what I judge to be about four. She rather teasingly also offers us a glimpse at the back of her head in her wedding photo that accompanies the concluding essay. This use of photography might be said to confirm Sidonie Smith and Julia Watson's observation that memoir tends to reflect more on the lives of others than on that of the writer.

In "Reading Abraham" Mary Blew begins with a framed, formal photograph of her paternal great-grandparents taken in 1890. As Karell indicates, Blew's memoir offers a "critique of rural nostalgia and rural life's limited and limiting opportunities for women" (133). That critique begins promptly with Blew's assertion that she has come to disapprove of her great-grandfather Abraham Hogeland and believes he would have disapproved of her. She regards him as "a paterfamilias, an oppressor, a traditionalist like my father, who had tried to keep me home on the ranch" (16). Handed a bundle of his letters, her first impulse was to stash them in a chest and consign them to oblivion. She provides a thorough description and an interpretation of the photograph (her italics):

> *He has crossed one knee over the other. His left hand lies casually on his thigh; his right hand rests in the pocket of his dark worsted suit trousers. Though his accoutrements are those of the paterfamilias—the mustache, the formal clothes, the watch chain across the vest—his posture exudes an easy energy, a humor that contradicts the formality. Those are laugh lines under his eyes. Under the mustache, Abraham is enjoying himself* [18].

Blew employs the word "casually," as opposed to such possibilities as "firmly" or "diffidently." Clearly, she sees her great-grandfather as a complex person, part stern "paterfamilias" and part a man of good "humor." Blew finds the likeness, particularly to her father, to be "disturbing," and she feels angry because Abraham is the avatar of all she detests about the stereotypical Western male. Her father was one of those stereotypes, and she defines his "unwanted legacy" in these "censorious, deluded" words that were directed at her: "Somewhere you got the idea in your head that you know something, but you don't know a goddamned thing" (17).

When she finally begins to struggle with Abraham's blurred pencil scrawl, Blew discovers that this surveyor who came to the Montana Territory from Pennsylvania in 1882 in order to "convert landscape into property" (22) was a would-be poet, and she begins to feel a sort of grudging "intimacy" with him as a fellow writer, similar to that which a scholar might feel for the subject of her literary research. In particular, she identifies with Abraham's accounts of the landscape: "I knew where to find his road, and these things I knew not so much spatially, geographically, as internally, as I might slowly recognize a map of my own arteries" (21). But in the end she finds his statements about the Jocko Indians to be condescending and concludes that her great-grandfather's vision, like her father's, was "linear," and she connects her own lot as an "uppity woman" to that of the Indians (36). Nevertheless, like Abraham, Blew feels herself a long way from home, and through him she is reminded of the lonely act of writing generally and of the terrifying "endlessness" that all writers attempt to counter through their words.

In the next of the remaining nine essays, "Dirt Roads," Blew attempts to come to terms with her father's death in 1983. At the age of seventy her father, Jack Hogeland, simply jumped into his red pickup, drove off to eastern Montana, and died, thus fulfilling the "romantic and despairing mythology" of the rugged Western loner (45). Her initial reaction Blew describes as "a mixture of awe and rage." The essay is prefaced by a snapshot taken in 1947 showing Mary, her younger sister Betty, her mother and father, all on horseback. Blew also refers to a couple of absent photographs in the text: a "formal wedding photograph" of her paternal grandparents (her grandfather Albert, a legendary cowboy, a "top hand" and "breaker of bronc to saddle," died when her father was just three years old [46]); a snapshot of her father posing by his team of colts near a water tank. In her interpretive comments on the family photo, Blew notes that her father's hat "characteristically, shades his face" and that he "faces the camera, self-aware. He knows he is a cowboy" (48). As she interprets her father, he felt betrayed when Mary went on to graduate school instead of being satisfied with the life of a rural schoolteacher who would remain connected with the ranch. But although she indicates her desire to be "free of the cowboy," Blew confesses in the terse final sentence of the essay, "The myth has its grip on us all" (54, 55). In fact, while Mary Blew has left Montana, the ranch, and the cowboys, it could be argued that she has never quite freed herself from its myths. She is an award-winning quilter, like her foremothers, and she still rides horses, sometimes with her daughter Elizabeth, a veterinarian, to whom the memoir is dedicated.

The third essay, "Leaving Montana," focuses on the relationship between Mary Blew's widowed grandmother Edna Hogeland and hired hand Bill Hafer, who stayed with her for forty years, although they never married. The rather odd couple recalls the mutual need for companionship of Ivan Doig's father Charlie and his mother-in-law Bessie. In his review of *All But the Waltz* Doig suggests that Blew's "ultimate theme" resembles his own: "how bumpily a family is seamed together" (X6). Although they do not marry (or remarry a second time in Charlie's case), the men depend on what might be described as surrogate wives, and Blew's grandmother, like Doig's, relies on her surrogate husband, at least up to a point. Blew directs our attention to a "bleached color snapshot from the 1950s" (67) showing Grammy in the branding corral about to rope a calf, but Blew introduces no photographs of Bill. Instead, she points out that in a family photo of her parents' wedding, Bill "is not present" (74). Charlie's mother-in-law is family, but Bill Hafer is not.

The essay "Little Jake and the Old Ways" concerns Blew's father Jack and his relations with a young Hutterite cowboy named Jake in the late 1940s. Doig describes it as "a fine, morally complicated tale" (X6). Young Jake obviously idolizes Jack Hogeland, who eventually sells his ranch to the Hutterites, despite the fact that they were often the objects of prejudice in Montana. The essay is accompanied by a photo of Jack with his horse Pet in 1937, but the only photograph dealt with in the text is drawn from an old issue of *National Geographic* in which the photographer captured Jake branding cattle. Subtly, Mary Blew suggests that the prejudice she observed in her great-grandfather's treatment of the Jocko Indians has diminished over the generations.

The sixth essay, which occurs near the midpoint of the book, marks a significant transition in the text between what might be called the man's or cowboy's world and that of the women, "the unrelenting female life" (113). Entitled "Auntie," this essay is illustrated with a snapshot of Mary's father in 1937 watering a pair of horses, but the text begins with the summer of 1942 (Mary was not yet three), when her favorite aunt, Imogene, suffered a mowing accident that nearly cost her foot, quite possibly her life. Aunt Imogene was already teaching in Port Angeles, Washington, by then, but her break with ranch life did not end, as she returned to Montana for the ritual of haying, still done at that time by horses. Blew moves easily back and forth among glimpses of the 1942 mowing accident, more recent events, and much earlier memories, including those of her maternal grandmother Welch, who taught in rural one-room schools in Montana, as Imogene did before moving to the Olympic Peninsula. Curiously, we do not really "see" much of Imogene Welch, and she is not represented either in an actual photo or in a summary of a snapshot (a dozen photos of Imogene appear in *Writing Her Own Life*). By moving about freely in her chronology here and elsewhere, Blew creates a non-linear consciousness in her memoir.

The seventh essay, "Getting Married," concerns Mary Blew's mother, Doris, her courtship and early years of marriage. Several significant details of Doris's life are not provided until the ninth essay, "Unwanted Child," but Blew hints at what is to come when she writes, "my mother was never a child" (127). Blew mentions poring over several snapshots in an effort to better understand her mother, but they seem to illustrate only what she already knows, that "my mother always seemed so unhappy" (129). She focuses on the picture that accompanies the essay and shows her mother in 1940 sitting in a rocking chair, with month-old Mary on her lap. I think most viewers will see in the photo a pretty young mother gazing lovingly down at her child. Blew, however, interprets the photograph differently: "I can almost see the years settling in, the web of lines contracting her face. She has gained perhaps fifty pounds since her wedding day" (130). With the birth of her first child, as Blew perceives it, her mother "never thought she came first again" (132). The essay might have ended on that cold note, but Blew proceeds with a Depression-era story about the family's purchase of a house by paying delinquent taxes. In this story, as retold by her mother, young Doris backs off the angry former tenant with a piece of firewood, and so the essay ends, with Mary concluding, "I will never know her. I only hope I may be half as brave as she" (136). In effect, this story retrieves Doris for the reader; it counters the image of her as a bitter, perhaps even self-pitying woman.

The next essay picks up from the Depression-era story at the end of "Getting Married" and occurs in 1934, when Doris's sister Sylva married Ervin Noel and moved with him to Fort Peck to work on the dam, a WPA project. Written in the dramatic present tense, this essay is the most story-like of the lot, clearly relying a great deal on imaginative reconstruction.

"Going to Fort Peck" is followed by "Unwanted Child," in which Blew suddenly leaps a couple of decades to December of 1958 and her own pregnancy at age eighteen. With Mary's college plans disrupted, it appears that her son will be the "unwanted" child. Her mother-in-law crows triumphantly that Mary will have to drop out of college, while her mother exclaims only, "'Oh Mary, no!'" (166). Then we discover that her mother was also an "unwanted child": "She was only two years old when the fifth and last child, the cherished boy, was born" (166). The bulk of the essay becomes an inquiry into her mother's anger and unhappiness. In addition to constant financial problems and the demands of the ranch, the salient feature of her mother's unhappiness is her feeling of being unloved, her resentment over her mother's (Mary Blew's namesake, Mary Welch) preferential treatment of her siblings. At the end of the essay Blew returns to the present of December 1958, shifting from the first person (I) at the doctor's office when the essay began to the narrative third person (she) who "lies propped up in bed with the sleeping scrap in her arms" (178). The startling metaphor of the infant as a "sleeping scrap" is repeated for effect. Both Blew and her young husband (he is only twenty) are bullied and cajoled by his parents, other relatives, and neighbors. All of this concern "over whether or not one Montana girl will finish college": "What kind of genius," the fifty-year-old Mary Blew asks, "would she have to be to justify it all?" (178).

Maintaining her free-play with history and chronology in the book, Blew does not directly respond to the rhetorical questions with which she completes her ninth essay, but drops back more than thirty years in "January 1922" to tell the story of her grandmother Mary Elizabeth Welch, who taught for dozens of years at several rural schools throughout Montana. Blew selects the time her grandfather A.P. suffered a nervous breakdown, and she *imagines* a black-and-white photograph of them as they drive to the teacherage: "his face, once handsome," is shrinking over his skull, "his nose and chin drawing together and releasing his eyes into a jerky life of their own"; Mary Welch's face is "drawn with twelve years of privation and silent grief" (182). Where appropriate photographs are lacking, the memoirist may resort to the imagination without falsifying the record. As Blew asserts in her essay, "The Art of Memoir," "When I speculate, I say so."[17]

Reading the memoirs of writers like Ivan Doig and Mary Blew, one wonders why success eluded their immediate forebears. Presumably, the land itself has always been too marginal to support the small rancher or farmer. Only the large-scale operations have thrived, and the scions of those fortunes appear not to have written down their life narratives. Do most effective memoirs proceed from lives that have not been easy, or that have been downright difficult, even (or perhaps preferably?) wretched? Consider, for example, Frank McCourt's *Angela's Ashes* or Reinaldo Arenas's *Before Night Falls*. Perhaps this tradition in memoir flows from the fictional source of such novels as Charles Dickens's *David Copperfield*. Celebrity memoirs, of course, run counter to the hard-life narratives, but those penned by writers with literary aspirations only rarely celebrate the achievements of the self or of kinfolk who have lived comfortably and prospered. It may be argued that writers like Doig and Blew have prospered, at least in relative terms: their lives appear considerably more comfortable than those of their parents. But then the focus of their memoirs is not on their own present lives. "What is the best early training for a writer?" Ernest Hemingway asked himself in 1935, answering famously, "An unhappy childhood."[18]

Blew refers to a snapshot of her grandmother taken in 1915 as she shells peas: "Her face and body already are set in familiar taut lines, carved deeper by the unrelenting light and shadows of the sun. Her hair is beginning to gray around her face." With the hard drought years of 1919 through 1921 still ahead of them, Mary Elizabeth Welch "will not look up," as Blew interprets the photograph, "and yet her contained rage makes it hard to look away from her" (191). The essay concludes with Blew's grandmother's funeral. It was she who taught Mary Blew how to read, and she sees in her own hands the same "quick movements" of her grandmother's. Even more significantly, Blew sees her own face as "seared with the indelible lines of hers," which she describes as "permanent lines of sadness" (198).

The sadness of that life, which Victoria Amador refers to as "melancholy grace" (8), might be regarded as the understory of this memoir, and it is the subject of the title essay, "All But the Waltz," which completes the volume. While Mary Blew enters the text of her memoir several times, she seems for the most part to tease her readers when it comes to self-revelation. In the first three essays ("The Sow in the River," "Reading Abraham," and "Dirt Roads") we learn what she thinks about memory, patriarchy, and the Western (male) myth, but she nearly disappears from the text except as a peripheral "character" until "The Unwanted Child." Here, too, she tantalizes her readers (perhaps the cowboy's term "dallies" is appropriate), offering half a dozen pages on her dilemma as a young woman facing motherhood and shifting to her own mother for more than half of the essay (about ten pages) before returning to herself in the last two pages. Then she adroitly shifts gears again, diverting our attention in "January 1922" to her grandmother before she confronts herself head-on in "All But the Waltz."

It is the summer of 1982 and Blew, dean of the College of Letters and Science at Northern Montana College (now Montana State University-Northern), is pregnant with her third child. Her husband, Robert Blew, the jesting "Marlboro man," has become ill. The essay purports to reflect upon Bob's "hidden sadness" (212), but more than a little of her own melancholy comes through these pages. Dying of pulmonary fibrosis, her husband, an oil wildcatter, is susceptible to mood swings, and his financial problems are complicated by his cavalier attitude toward filing his income taxes. He opposes divorce with a dogged refusal to believe she wants it, and Mary must resort to restraining orders. If she could believe they have no problems, if she could "accept the invitation to waltz with this rattling skeleton" (220–221), it would be another matter, but she cannot, or perhaps, will not. Typically, the woman who can have all of the dances *except* the waltz is being marginalized from the most important, most intimate dance. In this essay, however, the woman herself refuses the waltz in an assertion of independence that acquires for her the sort of freedom mythical Western males have too often demanded for themselves, or perhaps taken for granted. But not, one might add, without cost. Their daughter, Rachel, is seven when her father dies. The essay and book end at the cemetery, where Mary Blew pictures herself as "dry-eyed," like her grandmother Mary Welch years before when A. P. died. Blew depicts herself as haunted by her grandmother and husband in a struggle that seems never to end. Krista Comer draws attention to the connection between Blew's father and her husband: "Like her father, her husband has been fatally proud, a masculine man to the end, and it has cost him and his family his life" (229).

Teresa Jordan

The ten essays that comprise Wyoming-bred Teresa Jordan's memoir, *Riding the White Horse Home: A Western Family Album* (1993), resemble in their perspective the eleven that comprise Mary Clearman Blew's *All But the Waltz*, published two years earlier. Both are ranch memoirs written from a woman's point of view, and both writers deal more with members of their family than they do with themselves. In both books the essays are accompanied by photographs. Blew would very likely disagree, however, with Jordan's premise that "it's easier to be a rancher's daughter than a rancher's son." (36). Moreover, the generation that separates the writers and their parents (Jordan is Blew's junior by about sixteen years) is significant. The penury of the Depression does not haunt Jordan's mother; in fact, she goes away to college at the University of Arizona, and Jordan describes her mother's "proving grounds" as "primarily within the walls of a comfortable home" (46). As one reviewer noted, "Jordan makes it clear that despite the hardships of cattle ranching, it is in some ways a privileged and even elitist way of life."[19] Jordan acknowledges that she knew of Blew's memoir, but says her own book was "pretty far along by the time I read Mary's," and although she is "very impressed" with it, she does not think it "had a great deal of affect on mine."[20] Both Blew and Jordan worked with the same editor at Random House, Dan Franks, and Jordan notes that Franks also worked with Gretel Ehrlich on *The Solace of Open Spaces* (1985), the "memoir that probably influenced me most in terms of understanding the literary potential of personal experience." She also mentions such "women's ranch memoirs" as Agnes Morely Cleaveland's *No Life for a Lady* (1941; reprinted in 1977) and Nannie Alderson's *A Bride Goes West* (1942; reprinted in 1969 and 2007). While Blew's memoir ends with divorce and a windy October funeral, however, Jordan's concludes with an essay celebrating her marriage, at age 36, in the summer of 1991, for which she returns from Salt Lake City to Wyoming.

Born in Cheyenne, Wyoming, in 1955, Teresa Jordan attended Colorado State University before transferring after her sophomore year to Yale, where she received her bachelor's degree in history summa cum laude in 1977. While she was at Yale her mother died, and shortly after her graduation her father sold the ranch. As she indicates in her memoir, Jordan moved frequently (and restlessly) about the West in her years after college, from Casper, to Denver, to Portland (three times), to Missoula, where she spent a year in graduate school at the University of Montana, to Butte. While living in Salt Lake City Jordan edited three books: *Cowgirls: Women of the American West* (1982), *Graining the Mare: The Poetry of Ranch Women* (1994), and *The Stories That Shape Us: Contemporary Women Write about the West* (1995). More recently, with the success of *Field Notes from the Grand Canyon: Raging River, Quiet Mind* (1999), illustrated with her own water colors, Jordan has turned to painting and photography. She received her B.F.A. degree in drawing and painting from the University of Utah in 2002 and presently lives with her husband, folklorist Hal Cannon; they divide their time between Salt Lake City and a ranch near Elko, Nevada. She wrote her latest book, an illustrated journal, *Field Notes for Yosemite: Apprentice to Place* (2003), in collaboration with Gretel Ehrlich, a part-time Wyoming resident. Jordan and her husband co-host the regional radio show, *The Savvy Traveler*. She reports, "I've never been entirely comfortable with the self (even through the lens of community) as subject matter," and she adds that by the time she finished the book she was "removing the letter 'i' from my keyboard."

While Jordan has moved in the direction of the visual arts, her memoir reveals more of her training as a historian than as a painter. The opening essay, the prologue "Walking the Hogbacks," features some descriptive passages, but we encounter geology rather than poetry as the writer tells of finding fossils with her great-grandmother Nana, who died when Teresa Jordan was eight. The ranch, in the family for four generations, from 1887 until her father sold it in 1978, is located "fifty miles northwest of Cheyenne, fifty miles northeast of Laramie, and twenty-six miles southwest of Chugwater" (6). The Iron Mountain area, where the ranch is located, Jordan describes in terms reminiscent of Mark Spragg and Gretel Ehrlich as "great country for wind" (8).

Her memoir, Jordan writes, is "a book about loss" (16). It is something of a commonplace that all memoirs inevitably concern the theme of loss, and in fact the same might be said of history. In the second essay, "Legends," we most clearly encounter Jordan's flair for history. A photo of her great-grandfather J. L. Jordan on horseback prefaces the essay, and it opens with a memorable sentence, not about her great-grandfather, but about her grandfather Sunny: "My grandfather disliked children and cats" (21). One can almost hear the ghost of Mark Twain or W. C. Fields muttering, "He can't be all bad." Jordan's affection for Sunny mingles with fear of his anger, a "gruffness" he used to disguise any embarrassing "tenderness" (22). But the main story of "Legends" concerns J. L., who came out West in 1886 from Maryland at the age of 25. The collaboration in this essay derives from Jordan's use of brief passages from J. L.'s letters and her splicing in of information about Owen Wister's visits to Wyoming and his early Western stories, including "How Lin McLean Went East" (1892). Like Lin McLean, Jordan suggests, her grandfather Sunny split from his father J. L. and embraced the role of "the disappointed prodigal, orphan" and loner (28).

Unlike Blew in "Reading Abraham," and, as will be seen hereafter, William Kittredge in *Hole in the Sky*, Jordan has no issues with her grandsires: "He could *do* things. These simple words capture much of what I respect most about my great-grandfather, my grandfather, my father, and the other men who surrounded my upbringing. They could *do* things" (31). Jordan admires the Western men's capacity to work with their hands. This sentiment is reminiscent of Norman Maclean's observations on his writing of *A River Runs through It and Other Stories*, that they proceeded from a perspective similar to his "basic belief that what seems most beautiful in all I see about me is what men and women can create with their hands, issuing from their hearts and heads."[21] Surely an important part of the nostalgia recorded in recent memoirs from the Rockies emanates from writers who generally do not do manual labor, or have not done any since their youth. Writers like Doig, Blew, and Jordan reflect upon a way of life that required a great deal of hard physical work. Such nostalgia might invite the critics to sneer, "we see that *they* aren't out there mending fences or laying irrigation pipes." But the nostalgia over manual labor, most notably over that which the writer has done in his or her past is often an earned sentiment. Consider the poems of writers like Philip Levine that look back to his work in the factories of Detroit, or Gary Soto's on laboring in the fields of California, or B. H. Fairchild's on the machine shop in southern Kansas.[22] One more step might take us to "transferred nostalgia," the writer's pride over the manual labor of his or her parents, as in the poems of Washington's Tess Gallagher, whose father worked as a logger and stevedore, or David Wagoner, whose father worked as a smelter in the steel mills around Gary, Indiana.

Like Mary Blew, Teresa Jordan sets about correcting certain aspects of traditional Western mythology. "The history of the West," she points out, echoing William Kittredge's call for community, "is the story of cooperation, not isolation" (32). This cooperation, however, does not necessarily work within the family, and in "Legends" Jordan comments on the conflict between her grandfather Sunny and her older brother Blade. How her father weighed in on the matter is not clear, but she cites a rancher friend to the effect that "the West can be understood as the history of fathers fighting sons" (34). Based mostly in western Washington, Tobias Wolff's memoir, *This Boy's Life* (1990), although it concerns strife mostly between stepfather and stepson, comes to mind, as do various portraits Wallace Stegner draws in his fiction and nonfiction of his footloose father. Readers from other areas may not agree that such struggles are in any sense regional. One might premise, however, that father-son tension is likely to be the greatest when property is involved, whether that property is a thousand acres of Wyoming cattle land, or an insurance agency in Ohio, or a plumber's supply in Florida.

The next essay, "Mothers," balances "Legends," which is gendered male. It opens with Teresa Jordan baking bread, the sort of domestic image that Mary Blew appears to be reluctant to offer in *All But the Waltz* (although in fact she is a superb cook). Jordan soon establishes that she is writing from the perspective of about a dozen years since her mother died in 1976 (Jordan provides a family tree with dates at the front of the book). In the essay Jordan attempts to come to grips with this mother, who was "a typical ranch wife," but of the 1950s through the 1970s, not of the harsh 1930s or 1940s: "She hadn't been a pioneer; she hadn't overcome poverty or extraordinary physical hardships; she didn't work outside; she was afraid of horses" (46). In short, Teresa Jordan's mother's life could hardly have been more different from that of Mary Blew's mother. Despite her normal school education, for example, Doris Hogeland would not likely have spent her time reading Ayn Rand or, later in life, *The Sensuous Woman*. Jordan discovers that her mother was a "menopause baby" (50), and therefore was, like Blew's mother, in some ways an "unwanted child," but Jordan appears to be unable to make much of her mother's early hardship. Instead, she employs intertextuality, summarizing the film *Now Voyager* (1942), a favorite of her mother that concerns the mother of an unwanted daughter. Jordan also uses a collage technique featuring gaps in the text and abrupt transitions so that we move quickly from the movie, to her visit with her mother's closest friend, to her own birth and infancy, back to the movie, then to Jordan's cousin Donna, then quite suddenly to a line of dialogue that prefaced her mother's trip to Mexico with her older sister, then on to Jordan at age eight with her first horse.

Throughout the text of the essay, Jordan scatters references to baking as she tries to decipher the code that is her mother: she poses the question whether all mothers are so "indistinct" (49). She believes her mother differs from other mothers, that, presumably unlike those others, she has lived "a life that fulfilled her" (65). It appears that Jordan, driven by the agenda of contemporary feminism (Betty Friedan, Germaine Greer), feels some need to find a dramatic center to her mother's life that she simply cannot locate. To her daughter's argument that the ranch is her father's "career," Jordan's mother responds that it is "*our* career. This is something we've done together. And you can't imagine how satisfying this work has been" (65). We will encounter similar views hereafter in Judy Blunt's *Breaking Clean*. Finally, Jordan is compelled to accept that her mother "had chosen to be a wife and a mother," but she finds some satisfaction in the realization that her mother "had also chosen to be a full-fledged business partner in the family corporation" (65), and she comes to appreciate the "full measure of respect my parents afforded each other" (66).

When Jordan attempts to draw her mother's attention to her father's occasional anger, she fails to arouse a spirit of rebellion. This apparent effort of the memoirist to problematize the life of a relative or friend may create problems for some readers. Are we to suspect there was more conflict, and therefore more drama, in the relationship than was manifestly evident? Are we to suppose that the writer's mother was herself unaware of, or that she meekly acquiesced to, a subordinate position? Jordan insists, "She had created her life as a matter of choice and a triumph of will" (68–69). Although the will to conform oneself to convention may not sound to many readers like a "triumph," Jordan makes the assertion with no tincture of irony. In any event, her efforts at interpretation end when her mother dies of an aneurysm before her fiftieth year. On the other hand, Jordan has not followed in her mother's footsteps, nor did she appear headed in that direction before the family ranch was sold.

In "How Coyote Sent the White Girl Home," Jordan tells of leaving the family ranch, although it might be more apt to say that the ranch left the family. The national trend with farming and ranching has gone that way for several decades. Echoing Robert Frost, Jordan points out in "The Death of the Hired Man," that millions of ranch jobs have disappeared since 1950, and while some of those jobs were held by hard-working men with little education, more ranch owners than hired hands went down. The future appears to favor the very large corporate farm or ranching operation, on the one hand, or the gentleman amateur, the dilettante rancher, on the other, those, in effect, who can afford to dabble at ranching. Lest this latter portrait sound overly disparaging, suffice it to say that the latter species of rancher or farmer *may* prove to be the better steward. Perhaps the dabbler will be more likely than the corporate agribusiness person to leave his or her land to the Nature Conservancy. Jordan offers a personal perspective on the nature of ranch work in the essay, "Newtime: A Calving Diary," which pays tribute to the ranchers' ironic "reverence" for the animals they are nurturing for the slaughter (108).

The most poignant essay in the book, "Bones," begins as a commentary on the dangers of ranching, exemplified in her account of her father's broken leg, which he suffered when she was eight. The essay concerns "accommodation," the way ranch families adjust to calamities, but about two-thirds of the way through, Jordan turns to her latent theme throughout the book — the loss of her mother. She introduces the theme by pointing to a pile of bones to which she would take a colt in order to help it overcome its fear. If one takes time, Jordan says, "the horse will eventually approach what scares him. He will see that bones are just bones. He will move in the world more freely." The bones obviously represent death, and most ranchers are able to confront most of the "bones" they encounter, but "For my family, the pile we shied away from was grief" (124). Jordan describes her struggle with grief, her efforts at evasion and isolation, and her attempt to cope with the emotional loss through therapy. In the concluding paragraph, admiring their "stark beauty," she observes that "all bones are ancestral. Our homage is sincere and yet irreverent, a wry celebration of the fact that we still wrap our own bones with skin" (129).

Parallel to Mary Clearman Blew's essay "Auntie," about her favorite aunt Imogene, Teresa Jordan pays homage in "Marie" to the great-aunt whose diaries she has inherited. Like Blew in her subsequent memoir *Balsamroot*, Jordan quotes frequently from the diaries, in the process creating a sort of intertextuality that makes the essay a product of collaboration albeit, as with her use of photographs, at one remove. This kind of textual collaboration differs considerably, of course, from such intentional projects as Horace Axtell and Margot Aragon's *A Little Bit of Wisdom: Conversations with a Nez Perce Elder* (1997) in which, as the title indicates, the collaboration is live. Like Blew's aunt Imogene, Jordan's great-aunt Marie is the person whose life she might wish to emulate, though apparently for quite different reasons. Even though Blew regards her aunt as a happy person and only later, through her diaries, discovers her disappointments and lack of fulfillment, she does not go so far as Jordan in depicting a woman whose most memorable trait was "contentment." Jordan writes, "I believe I have never met another person so entirely at ease with her life" (134). In fact, Marie's diaries, stretching from 1938 to 1963 (she died in 1984 at the age of 85), reveal "a woman who was just like the Marie I thought I knew" (135). Happily married, apparently, to John, who proved more successful as an entrepreneur than as a rancher, Marie records a life of hard work and what one might call civic benevolence to their hired help. The longest entries, we are told, are obituaries for various animals and pets, and Jordan presents a picture of almost unnerving complacency: "The two of them had a sense of both appetite and generosity, and when you were around them you couldn't help feeling that the world was a splendid place" (147). As it turns out, however, the congenial domesticity of great-aunt

Marie proves to be no more attractive to Teresa Jordan than that of her mother.

The essay structure offers the writer an opportunity to create various narrative rhythms or sequences in the book. Mary Blew, for example, carefully creates a thematic sequence of marriage essays that pivot on "Auntie," which concerns her old maid aunt, and includes the last five essays in the book. The rhythm, however, may amount to no more than the juxtaposition of a pair of essays so that one may enhance or counterpoint the other, as in the case of "Mothers" and "Legends" above. Similarly, to balance what some readers might find the almost cloying sense of well-being that pervades "Marie," Jordan introduces in "The Death of the Hired Man" a tribute to and lament for the hard lives of the foremen and workers who made their ranch function. Jobs for skilled manual laborers, particularly professional cowboys and handymen like Leonard Cheser, have virtually vanished in rural America. At the end of the essay she pays tribute to a man named Kelley who "retired to Chugwater and raised a garden until age and drink caught up with him." Kelley, Jordan observes, "could never flip burgers at Wendy's." He was "flawed," but "he had dignity, he had skills and artistry, he paid his own way. There was a place for him in the country; there is no place for him now" (176).

For "The Death of the Hired Man" Jordan provides a photograph of Leonard Cheser, as she does of her great-aunt Marie and her great-uncle John, but she does not offer commentary thereon in her essays. In "Writing My Grandmother's Life," however, Jordan constructs an essay on her paternal grandmother, Effie Lannen Jordan, largely on the basis of photographs. If every family has a difficult relative among the leaves on the family tree, "Gran" is Jordan's case in point: "I have never heard an affectionate story about her," Jordan observes (180). In her "Grandmother," Jordan draws a portrait in sadness and disappointment, the antitype of great-aunt Marie, of Jordan's mother, and of most of the hired men and their families. She is the wife of "Sunny," Jordan's not-particularly-likable paternal grandfather, who figures prominently in "Legends," early in the book. "Legends" is the second essay and "Writing My Grandmother's Life" is the penultimate, so they function as near bookends to the collection. Effie's life from the outset appears to be a testament to the premise that "a woman can ask for too much" (179).

The point of departure for this essay, however, is not the snapshot of Effie as a college girl, but an elaborate dream that features silent twin girls, six or seven years old, who live in a Victorian house and whose job it is to control the passage of trains that run through the house. The girls seem to be "excited" by the passengers' "fascinating and unimaginable lives" (181). When a second train approaches and the girls do not get to the controls in time, it comes to a screeching halt, and the girls sense they have done "something terribly wrong." In the final image from the dream, all is quiet and the girls, who cannot see each other, have an opportunity to board the cars. We do not learn whether they seize that opportunity. Subsequently, Teresa Jordan finds among the pictures of her grandmother one taken at age three, and she discovers that her own photo at age three resembles it. This recognition provides her no comfort, for she describes Gran as a woman full of "bitterness and lethargy," inclined to fix the world with a "cynical sneer" and a "perpetual pout" (182). As she digs through the photographs, however, Jordan comes to realize her grandmother was not witchlike, but, as a younger woman, "beautiful, endearing, charismatic" (183). This positive demeanor soon disappears from the photographic record, however, to be replaced by "a sense of wariness" (183) and eventually, following her wedding, "a look of defeat" (185). Jordan points out that "No wedding photographs have survived. Probably, she burnt them in one of her periodic fits against the man she would neither live with nor divorce for forty years of a fifty-year marriage" (185). This portrait of her grandmother, in which Teresa appears to be the twin, sets the stage for the final essay in the book.

After reviewing various photographs of her grandmother, one form of collaboration, Jordan introduces a second form with her citations from Carolyn G. Heilbrun's *Writing a Woman's Life* (1988), which Heilbrun describes as "a feminist undertaking."[23] Teresa Jordan appears unable to decipher or interpret her mother's life, or perhaps she simply cannot bring herself, for obvious reasons, to pass judgment on it. The same does not apply when it comes to her willingness to pronounce a verdict on her grandmother who, despite her intelligence and "incisive wit" (191), hadn't "the slightest idea what she wanted" (190). Unaware, or perhaps unwilling, to part from conventional paradigms of what her life might be, Effie Lannen Jordan remained passive and invisible, as instructed by patriarchal tradition, and her life was miserably unhappy; moreover, she made those around her unhappy as well.

From her story of her grandmother's life Jordan concocts her own story: "I could imagine a peer relationship in which I had my work, my partner had his, and we built a home and family together" (195). The final essay in the book, "My Life as a Bride," amounts to a brief epilogue that tells of Teresa Jordan's marriage in 1991 to Hal Cannon at the Community House overlooking Chugwater Creek. Jordan describes the photograph of Effie from her days at the University of Kansas that prefaces "Writing My Grandmother's Life" as "all style and attitude"; she stands, "hand cocked on hip" wearing an "outrageous, corded 'cap'" and looking like a "flapper" (184). The photograph resists interpretation. Effie perhaps intends to appear sensual or fashionably bored, but she also looks sad. The photo Jordan places before "My Life as a Bride" denies us any opportunity to read the bride, as the camera catches her back while her husband, facing the camera, embraces her. She wears a white dress, flowers are wreathed in her hair, and she holds a bridal bouquet, the ribbons of which blow, as does her husband's hair, in the inevitable Wyoming wind. The essay counterpoints the one on her unhappy grandmother and provides a hopeful, celebratory conclusion, a healing story combined with a promise to fight for the Iron Mountain region of Wyoming and for "hundreds of other places like it throughout the rural West" (206). In a poem entitled "Looking Back" appended to her memoir, Jordan writes, "I want to belong to the ground / again" (209).

Comparison of Mary Clearman Blew and Teresa Jordan

Mary Clearman Blew prefaces *All But the Waltz* with a family map of Fergus County in central Montana. Readers can locate great-grandfather Abraham's homestead, the Welch homestead, the Ballydome and Duck Creek schools, the Judith River, the Judith, Snowy, and Moccasin Mountains, and the county seat, Lewistown. Teresa Jordan's *Riding the White Horse Home* opens with her family tree, beginning with her great-grandparents, all of whom are mentioned at least in passing and all of whom died before she was born. She carefully identifies her relatives (that is, "my grandmother," "my great-aunt") and provides their dates of birth and death. This variance in context anticipates Blew's somewhat greater attention to place. Certainly, Blew's memoir features a greater variety of specific sites than does Jordan's, but neither writer lavishes as much attention on descriptive detail as does Ivan Doig or Mark Spragg.

The greater points of divergence in these two memoirs concern time and narrative perspective. While both writers explore their family's westward migration beginning in the 1880s, Blew's essays dwell mostly on the decades between 1916 and 1942, while Jordan's concern mostly the 1960s and 1970s. Among other things, this means that the hard times of the Great Depression provide a darker historical backdrop for Blew's essays. In Jordan's essays, as in those of Mark Spragg, the first-person pronoun figures far more prominently than in Blew's. Although Teresa Jordan offers us a "family album," we see considerably more of her in *Riding the White Horse Home* than we do of Mary Clearman Blew in *All But the Waltz*. In short, Jordan's is the more self-revelatory of the two life narratives.

Unlike Mark Spragg, neither Blew nor Jordan (with the single notable exception mentioned above) makes much use of dreams in their essays. Both writers proceed from documented family history, and they make extensive use of photographs. Neither writer is much inclined to sentiment or nostalgia. As Jordan notes, "I was raised to be Western, which is to say stoic" (13). Perhaps the point of greatest divergence in these memoirs, aside from the historical contexts noted above and implicit in the fact that Jordan is sixteen years younger than Blew, is that Jordan appears far less troubled over her father and consequently, in some ways, over men in general. The supposed "conflict with her father" that prompts reviewer Roland Wulbert to consider Jordan's memoir "a contribution to the literature of feminism"[24] is pretty much imperceptible, I think, except for her disappointment over his sale of the ranch. At the end of "Legends," she portrays her six-foot-three father sitting "a fine figure on a horse" (38), and she thinks of him somewhat paradoxically as "a kindly man with lily-white arms, driving a station wagon, offering Coca-Cola and apologies" (39). The sudden death of her mother haunts Jordan's memoir, along with the loss of the family ranch, in which she detects a vanishing way of life in the West. The woman in Jordan's memoir who is most injured by conventional male myths of the West is not the writer, but her paternal grandmother.

One point of irony on which these two memoirs diverge is the fact that Blew's family, particularly her father, resent her decision to leave the ranch, while Jordan's family urge her to do so and eventually make it impossible for her to return. In both cases "going off to college" draws the writers away from their former lives. "In my twenties, while I was in graduate school," Blew writes, I knew my father felt angry and betrayed. For years after I left Montana he would not even speak to me" (80). "From as far back as I can remember," Jordan writes, "when family discussion ran to what I would be when I grew up, ranching was never considered. [...] They [her parents] were preparing me for success. And they were preparing me, though they didn't realize it, to abandon them" (76, 77). While

Blew and Jordan have left their family homesteads and their home states, however, they have not left the West. Blew has established a career as a writer and academic; Jordan has returned to the land, although not as an active rancher. Like Blew, she does some teaching, along with her writing and painting.

These memoirs leave us in very different places: in a cemetery and at a wedding. Mary Blew wrote her title essay last, along with the introductory piece, so only a few years separate the funeral in Kansas from her writing. Her daughter Rachel, born in the fall of 1982, is seven, the year is 1989, and Blew is in her second year of teaching at Lewis-Clark State College in Idaho. "[I]t will never end," she laments: "Perhaps my grandmother [her namesake Mary Welch] could have told me that. Her shade follows, as does his [her former husband's], through the windswept grass as Rachel and I walk hand in hand down the gravel track from the knoll" (223). Teresa Jordan wrote her final essay in 1993, just a few years after her wedding in Wyoming on the Point at the "top of the breaks where I could see forever" (10). "But perhaps," Jordan writes, "that was just the image my mother and I, so many years before, had wanted to avoid — the wedding, and even the marriage, as something separate from a larger sense of life" (207).

Chapter Five

Coming to Womanhood with Kim Barnes and Judy Blunt

Sidonie Smith concludes in *A Poetics of Women's Autobiography* (1987), "ultimately, every woman who writes autobiographically ends up interrogating the prevailing ideology of gender, if only unconsciously and clumsily."[1] In a subsequent study of women's autobiography, Smith provocatively asserts, "If the topography of the universal subject locates man's selfhood somewhere between the ears, it locates woman's selfhood between her thighs."[2] The foremost theoretician on the subject of gender in autobiography, Smith insists there is "no isolable core of selfhood" for women because the "act of heterosexual intercourse" and "the experience of pregnancy" necessarily involve an invasion and occupation of the female body by the male "other" (12). Implicitly, her role as daughter, and potentially her additional roles as sister, wife, and mother as well, always in some ways constrains a woman's identity. More so, that is, than a man's identity is constrained by his role as son, and potentially as brother, husband, and father. Moreover, Smith asserts, if the woman "claims her own equal powers of self-conscious reasoning" in the face of male paradigms that conventionally restrict the woman to emotional focus, domesticity, and maternity, she risks placing herself in "posture of carnivalesque monstrosity" (14).

Such statements contribute to what might be considered an extreme portrait of the dilemma confronting women as writers and particularly as autobiographers. The male's "official account of the community," presented as "universal," valorizes "individuality and separateness while erasing personal and communal interdependencies," and in that process he reenacts "the erasure of the feminine that facilitates male entrance into the public realm of words, power, and meaning" (19). In her comments on letters written by women during the eighteenth century, Patricia Meyer Spacks observes how the correspondents found "ways to avoid the troubling threat of [presumably male] egotism."[3] Is egotism, one wonders, a gendered trait?

Susan Stanford Friedman draws on Nancy Chodorow's *Psychoanalysis and the Sociology of Gender* (1978) and Sheila Rowbotham's *Woman's Consciousness, Man's World* (1973) in her essay on women's "autobiographical selves," arguing that a woman's identity is neither "purely collective" nor "purely individualistic," but a "new identity" that "merges the shared and the unique."[4] The woman as an autobiographical self, Friedman suggests, "does not feel herself to exist outside of others," but "very much *with* others in an interdependent existence that asserts its rhythms everywhere in the community" (56). Regardless of whether one agrees with Smith and Friedman, some tension, some conflict is expressed in women's life narratives between their sense of familial, communal, and social responsibility and their desire for independent, individual, and personal identity. But is that tension or conflict significantly greater for women than it is for men? As Paul John Eakin observes in the passage cited in chapter 2, "relationality" is detectable in many male autobiographies. "All selfhood," Eakin asserts, "is relational despite differences that fall out along gender lines."[5] If the convention of the autonomous self has been at least somewhat compromised by the premise of the socially constructed or relational self, then the new and evolving models of women's identities (no longer subservient to the patriarchy, or at least increasingly less so) may cause additional anxiety over the complex self that would derive from the merging or blending that Friedman admires. Teresa Jordan's memoir, as I read it, moves in the direction of a communal self that Friedman commends; Mary Clearman Blew's memoir strains against that impulse. Blew's next memoir, *Balsamroot* (1994), written about three years after *All But the Waltz*, testifies to the tension indicated above: "The problem Auntie [about to be committed to a nursing home] and I have got here is me. I have never been worth a good goddamn at self-sacrifice."[6]

In *Writing a Woman's Life* (1988) Carolyn G. Heilbrun identifies the publication of poet May Sarton's *Journal of a Solitude* in1973 as "the watershed in women's autobiography."[7] Heilbrun asserts that she calls it a "watershed" because in that memoir Sarton "retold the record of her anger," for "above all other prohibitions," women have been forbidden to express their anger in print (13). Moreover, she writes, women have been dissuaded from acknowledging their desire for power and for control over their own lives. Criticizing Mississippi author Eudora Welty's memoir, *One Writer's Beginnings* (1983), for its "bittersweet" nostalgia, Heilbrun argues that "Nostalgia, particularly for childhood, is likely to be a mask for unrecognized anger" (15). The "exercise of power and control" (17) in both private and public life, she observes, at times requires the expression of anger.

Kim Barnes's *In the Wilderness: Coming of Age in Unknown Country* (1996) and Judy Blunt's *Breaking Clean* (2002) derive from conflict with the traditional, patriarchal paradigm, and they repudiate that model, occasionally expressing anger in the process and coming to power and control. But to what extent do Barnes and Blunt attempt to alter what Sidonie Smith calls the "topography" of "woman's selfhood"? Do their memoirs promote a communal perspective, as opposed to the individualistic or egotistical values conventionally ascribed to the patriarchy, or do these writers (inevitably, some might argue, in the self-indulgent act of choosing to write memoir) repudiate communally prescribed roles? Clearly, to the extent that the patriarchy traditionally commanded silence, Barnes and Blunt have joined the ranks of those who speak out, and in doing so they demonstrate both voice and agency.

Kim Barnes

Born in 1958 in Lewiston, Idaho, Kim Barnes spent her preadolescent years in logging camps near the North Fork of the Clearwater River in the Idaho panhandle. She was twelve when her father, having converted to Pentecostalism, moved the family from its rural Eden to the small city of Lewiston. Her two memoirs, *In the Wilderness: Coming of Age in Unknown Country* (1996) and *Hungry for the World: A Memoir* (2000), follow her childhood and adolescence in Lewiston, a city of around 26,000 when she graduated from high school in 1975. Barnes's publications began with a poem in the *Seattle Review* a year after her graduation from Lewis-Clark State College in Lewiston in 1983. In July of that year she married poet Robert Wrigley, who had been her instructor in a poetry writing class. After receiving her M.A. in English from Washington State University in 1985, Barnes taught as a lecturer at the University of Idaho for four years before taking a similar job at Lewis-Clark State in 1991. She taught at LCSC for nine years, including a leave of absence to earn her M.F.A. in 1995 at the University of Montana, where she studied with William Kittredge. She and Wrigley have two children, a daughter, Jordan, born in 1987, and a son, Jace, born in 1989. Both Wrigley and Barnes presently teach at the University of Idaho. Barnes's first novel, *Finding Caruso* (2003), is set in 1957 on the Clearwater River in northern Idaho; her second novel will be released soon. In 2006 she coedited with fellow author Claire Davis an anthology of essays entitled *Kiss Tomorrow Hello: Notes from the Midlife Underground by Twenty-Five Women over Forty*.

Although Barnes was successfully placing her poems in magazines like *Shenandoah* and the *Georgia Review*, Mary Clearman Blew, who taught at Lewis-Clark State from 1987 to 1994, convinced her to expand into prose and encouraged her, as Barnes phrases it, to "allow the truth of my emotional convictions."[8] Barnes and Blew coedited *Circle of Women: An Anthology of Contemporary Western Women Writers*, published by Viking Penguin in 1994. Coincidentally, both Kim Barnes and Judy Blunt are not represented by prose entries in the anthology, but by poems. Reviewers largely overlooked Barnes's first memoir, even though it was short-listed for a Pulitzer Prize. But the sometimes rather naïve and occasionally ungrammatical commendations of *In the Wilderness* offered by the general reader (from Amazon.com) possess special appeal: "A book that changes readers' lives. It's filled with the kind of grace we should all be envious of" (Los Angeles, CA, 18 May 2001). "It soars above the current crop of mangy memoirs that fill books with words, but fail to get to the soul of the matter" (Oakland, CA, 10 March 2001). "Barnes's honesty makes her story effective," wrote Roberta Bernstein of *Hungry for the World*, which garnered somewhat more critical attention than *In the Wilderness*, "but one gets the sense that even after two books she is not yet ready to reveal everything."[9] Presently, in fact, Kim Barnes is working on a third memoir, tentatively entitled "Out of the Fire," which will complete the trilogy.

In the Wilderness behaves very much like a novel, and the chapters are not titled, as is the case when writers construct the book as a collection of essays. Barnes's narrative divides near the midpoint, at the end of the sixth chapter, when twelve-year-old Kim and her family move from the Edenic forests, where her father has worked as a logger, to what seems to her the big city of Lewiston on the Clearwater River, where her father will drive a truck. Barnes describes the wilderness setting with a lyrical grace to which readers have responded enthusiastically.

> When not in school, we filled our days exploring the near woods, digging after ground squirrels, amassing piles of found treasure: feathers blue as river water, bones of deer, old buckets and chains, nests stitched through with colorful bits of moss.[10]

In addition to the imagery, the subtle patterns of sound attract us — the rhyming of "ground" and "found," for example, and the nonintrusive use of alliterative b-sounds that unites the latter portion of the sentence: blue, bones, buckets, bits. Although she describes Lewiston's spring and summer as "idyllic" and the valley as "rich in color," it is a place that "seemed never to stop": "Even at night the traffic continued, the stores stayed open and people went on about their business as though they had no home to go to" (123).

The paradise Barnes grew up in is a littered version that the locals called "Dogpatch." If the found objects of the passage cited above are admirable because of their natural appeal ("feathers blue as river water," "bones of deer"), they also appeal in a different way, perhaps only to a child, because they include recent artifacts of human manufacture, that is, trash: "old buckets and chains." The "dump with its brown corked bottle" and "bits of metal and porcelain" attract the children as readily as the deer bed, "fragrant grass crushed beneath an overhanging branch of yellow pine," where they would lie amid the aroma of musk and "pick tufts of hair from the needles, imagining the warmth of a fawn nestled tight in the curve of its mother's flank" (5). The children play, and hunt grouse, and fish whenever they wish. One aspect of this prelapsarian world is the father, whose eyes are "so blue they seemed clairvoyant" (7). When Kim's younger brother Greg gets lost one autumn evening, she describes her family's confidence in her father finding the boy in terms of religious faith, repeating the phrase "we believed" in a sort of refrain that concludes with a passage reminiscent of a Christian hymn: "If only he'd come, *now, now*." The fact that the boy turns up of his own accord in certain ways prefigures what ensues. The father is not all-seeing, omniscient, or omnipotent. When financial hard times hit the timber industry during the mid 1960s, he holds out longer than others in the family, but as Barnes observes, "The circle was broken" (49), a statement that recalls the familiar hymn, "Will the Circle Be Unbroken?"

Although Kim remembers her mother using cosmetics and wearing her swimsuit, it is she that first turns to Pentecostal fundamentalism. But her father soon follows, and he becomes more radically involved. Barnes appears remarkably kind in her efforts to understand her father's conversion. Given the "haphazard set of circumstances and catastrophes that had beset his family" (she describes his father's death in an automobile accident in Oklahoma in the second chapter), she speculates he was "intrigued by the unequivocal dictates of the religion" (50). Like the Old Testament children of Israel, or so Barnes suggests, her family left the demons of destruction for salvation in the wilderness, but now the wilderness had proven insufficient. "What he believes," Kim Barnes writes, "is that it was the Spirit that spoke to him" (51). Here and elsewhere in the memoir she carefully avoids lashing out against the way of belief she eventually found inimical, nor does she criticize her father and his motives. The reader, however, will likely conclude that her father was motivated mostly by fear. Promptly, he asserts his role as the patriarch: "My father's authoritative presence became absolute" (52). And her mother all but disappears: "The woman is to be chaste and modest, subservient to her husband's guidance, lest the mar of her sex tempt her to stray into the ways of the world." Her mother's beauty becomes a hindrance, so she yields to drabness, and to powerlessness as well: "Because her husband was the hammer and she the nail, she built a house of acquiescence" (52). Young Kim predictably embraces the strict dictates of the church.

Soon the Barnes family falls under the influence of the preacher, Brother Lang, and Kim finds herself sinfully attracted to Luke Lang, although nothing comes of her fascination except feelings of guilt. Briefly, Kim finds herself hailed as a healer, but ironically, she discovers that Brother Lang, who proclaims his own powers, is little more than a charlatan when he takes away her glasses and declares her eyesight healed. After three days of blurred vision Kim resumes her glasses. When Brother Lang later feels himself threatened by an attractive woman in the congregation who has opposed his ministry, he cleverly arranges to have her shunned, following an effort to "take the burden upon himself" and rid them all of the devil's presence after a forty-day fast (88). Barnes offers a cutting image of the preacher: "Brother Lang sat weak and smug, shriveled to a hard, leathery knot" (89). But the lesson she learned at the time was "be still, be invisible"; she learns that as a woman, a source of "temptation" and "evil" (90), she threatens everyone around her. Not long after that event, at least as Barnes develops the narrative in her memoir, one of the Lang boys gets lost while hunting, and when they find his body, his neck is "wedged in the fork of a downed tree" (103). The bizarre accident recalls the death of David's rebellious son Absalom in 2 Samuel 18:9. Barnes's father appears to feel the consequences of the death himself, as she describes him taking on the burden of pain the Lang family cannot bear.

The following spring, at least as the episode transpires in the novel-like format, Barnes's father, apparently hounded by a visionary demon from a dream the year before, determines to undertake a quest "like Jesus in the wilderness" and to stay fasting and praying in an underground bunker for forty days and nights (108). In a scene that has more than a few comical elements, Kim's Uncle Barry and family drive up for a surprise visit, but promptly depart when they realize what's going on. The next day her father leaves his lair, and nothing else is said. Only recently, Barnes notes, did she learn that her uncle threatened to have his brother committed if the vigil continued. But one result of the failed quest appears to have been her father's decision to leave the wilderness for the city. Fittingly, Barnes observes, the "symbolic end" to her life in the woods and to her childhood is her baptism by immersion at age twelve (117). Yet even as she seems to feel "the pure joy of absolute faith" (118) and begins to be aware of the gift of speaking in tongues (glossolalia), Kim finds herself still dreaming of carnal matters, herself wrapped up in a blanket and held in Luke's arms. In the summer of 1970, as they leave the woods, Barnes looks at the huge Dworshak Dam that contains the North Fork of the Clearwater and thinks of it as a wall of sorts separating her former from her future life.

In what might be regarded as Part Two of her memoir, Kim Barnes, age twelve, moves with her family to Lewiston and lives briefly with her maternal grandmother Nan, whose world is considerably more secular and tolerant than that of her parents. But this proves only a temporary respite from the narrow, restrictive world of her father, who rejects the sinful pleasures of *American Bandstand* for the glories of The Rapture. If Part One of Kim Barnes's "novel" might aptly be entitled something like "Compliance" or "Conformity," surely Part Two merits a title like "Rebellion." The lyrics of The Beatles, Cher, and Rod Stewart listened to surreptitiously over the radio fuel her rebellion, as does her evolving sense of the unfairness of her constricted life. From the perspective of 26 years the adult Kim Barnes, a successful writer and college teacher, happily married and the mother of two, can be compassionate and understanding when it comes to her parents' behavior: "How can I describe the sense of fear my parents must have felt? [...] Having left the woods, my parents found they had entered into a whole other kind of wilderness" (137). Nevertheless, she stresses the injustice. While her brother is "encouraged to participate in sports," for Kim it is "*No* to the after-school dance, the movies, the swimming pool" (139). No even to Tampons. Her "only haven" is familiar to anyone who has inquired into feminist discourse: silence (142).

Aided and abetted by her cousin Lezlie (Les) and a neighbor, Kim joins in the sinful pleasures of cigarettes, boys, and increasing lies. She does not yield to the boys' sexual advances, but develops an "emotional veneer" (157). Soon beer and wine, "bad marijuana highs," and Jimi Hendrix enter the mix, and whippings and groundings have no impact on her behavior: "I think we craved destruction" (162). She becomes numb both to her father's punishments and to her mother's pathetic appeals: "By the time I was fourteen, I felt only anger, loathing, a need to escape from the restrictions imposed by my parents and the church" (170). Suspecting her of using hard drugs, Kim's parents confront her on the eve of her planned runaway to California with a girlfriend, and they offer her a choice: a juvenile detention center or a summer with the Lang family, who live outside Spokane in the town of Post Falls, Idaho. As she reflects upon her condition years later, Barnes regards her parents' love for her as conditional, "dependent upon my obedience." What she yearns for is "unequivocable [sic] acceptance" (181), and initially she seems to find that with the Langs. She feels her bitterness dissipate, and one morning at breakfast she announces her conversion. As she indicated earlier, the two selves Barnes describes in her memoir remain with her, "both vulnerable and bitter, believing and hardened against belief" (171). In the summer of 1972 she yields to the vulnerable and believing, and she senses the possibility of a "new life" (187).

Barnes returns to the metaphor of the wilderness by way of accounting for her apparent salvation: "Some are born to the wilderness. Some come to the wilderness to be reborn" (182). But what might be called the Lang Family Wilderness comes with temptation for the still virginal Kim in the person of Luke, who is being home-schooled and whom Kim tutors. The most likely anagogical wilderness is that celebrated in Milton's *Paradise Regained*, based on Satan's temptation of Christ in Matthew 4:1–11. In Barnes's version of the story, however, the innocent Kim is undermined by the paranoid and obviously twisted suspicions of Brother and Sister Lang. This, of course, is the same Brother Lang who contrived the shunning of an attractive woman from the congregation at the Cardiff Spur Mission near "Dogpatch" several years earlier. The "presence of Satan" in the Lang home turns out this time to be Kim, and ironically, she is not suspected of harboring a demonic lust for their son Luke, which is more or less the case (she is at least infatuated with the boy), but for their son-in-law, Terry. She is seen as having "seduced" him: "I was fourteen years old and had been cast in the role of Jezebel" (197). The Langs promptly shun Kim and send for her parents. These episodes, perhaps coincidentally, constitute dramatizations of what might be called the *ur*-legend of the patriarchy as presented by various feminist theoreticians over the past several decades: Fearful, perhaps absolutely terrified, at least in primitive cultures or in earlier centuries, by the threat of the passionate and lustful, and therefore weak, female (secretive, monstrous, demonic), the rational and self-controlled, and therefore strong, male (open, intellectual, heroic) represses or directly suppresses the female, creating a myth of her inferiority and hence of her proper subordination in the scheme of things. She is best kept powerless, submissive, and, most of all, silent.

Kim does not respond to this injustice in the mode of the New Woman. Not at age fourteen a budding Virginia Woolf or Simone de Beauvoir, she distances herself from "that *other girl*" (202), the shameful and sinful seductress, and allows church to fill "every nook" of her life as she proceeds to graduate from high school with honors in 1976. In fact, she goes so far as to proselytize, getting involved with "Pastor Dave" in a Christian call-in radio show and drawing on her troubled past in an effort to reach out to her "unsaved peers" (207). The Kim Barnes of 1996, although she confesses to some "regret," does not repudiate "those years in the church, filled with guilt and perhaps even abuse" (208). "Even considering the summer with the Langs," she writes, "I feel lucky to have escaped the chasm that so many of my junior high school friends fell into." In fact, as she looks back on her high school days, Barnes sees herself as wanting a "story" from her mother, and not a story that would undermine her father's authority or counteract the patriarchy, but "a narrative to give meaning to her life and mine. I needed my mother to tell me how to find happiness in submission, how to content myself with giving and serving and silence" (210). Obviously, inasmuch as her memoir does subvert the myths and theology of the patriarchy, she did not acquire such a story.

In an essay she has released for open publication and that appears on the Internet, Barnes asks:

> What happens when, in an individual's quest for meaning through story, she finds herself building a narrative in direct opposition to the narrative that is her inheritance? What happens when the stories we tell ourselves are ones that we believe our family and community cannot accept, when we break the codes of conduct, the codes of silence and

submission, when we risk being cast out and stripped of membership in the tribe?"[11]

"Only recently," Barnes writes, did she realize the destruction of her former self was "a necessary precursor to the creation of a 'new,'" and that in embracing the spirituality inherent in her passion for writing she could find a way "to honor my family *and* stay true to my art" ("Prayer, Piety, Passion, and Prose" n.p.). She does not undervalue the role of tradition, but prefers to such terms as "deconstructing" or "demythologizing" the term "redefining."

By her senior year of high school Kim has bought herself a '67 Chevy Impala with money she has saved from her after-school job, and she finds that the "shiny newness" of her conversion has "faded" (218). In a bizarre episode Barnes tells of coming home one evening in a fog of pot-induced paranoia and, finding no one there, concluding that her family has been taken up in The Rapture. When she comes to her senses, she finds herself doubting her faith and seeking a sort of "contract" with God over what fragments of her faith she has left (226). The remaining pages of Barnes's memoir concern not so much her "compromised" faith, as her anguished break with her father. But the fact that she feels she has "forged" the new beliefs herself and that she feels herself, as when she was baptized, to be "touched by grace" enables her finally to confront her father over his arbitrary rule. The crisis comes to a point with a graduation party in Coeur d'Alene, about 120 miles to the north. Her father's refusal to discuss his grounds for denying her permission to go prompts Kim to turn to her mother, who predictably demurs. Kim interprets her mother's lack of support as fear: "To be a grown woman and live in a house with fear as the ruling principle, to be afraid of waking your husband's wrath [...]" (228). She decides to go to the party (she is eighteen), even though her father insists she will not be welcome back at home.

The last three chapters of Barnes's memoir are very short, creating the impression of time speeding up. At the end of chapter 10 Barnes writes of wanting to be "part of a community" or of a family that believed in a future, that "held the promise of something other than inherent imperfection and destruction" (232). In the next chapter she reflects briefly on her boyfriend and visits the wilderness near the North Fork of the Clearwater, but she finds it much changed. In particular, she discovers loss, not only of pristine nature, but also of herself when she was a girl and of her family.

Chapter 12 opens with a brief memory of her father teaching Kim how to shoot when she was six years old. Then she moves to 1978, two years after her graduation from high school. Like her father, who has scarcely spoken to her, Kim cannot bring herself to apologize, but in need of a family that will not shun her, she invites him to go hunting. As a peace offering, she returns his 30.06 Winchester rifle, of which she observed in the previous chapter, "It symbolized for me the metaphorical death of my father" (235). In effect, she returns to her father his control over his own life. Her brother accompanies them. But this is not to be the healing or redemptive hunt of the traditional male initiation ritual whereby the boy becomes a man by shooting the bear or dropping the six-point buck. In this event, twenty-year-old Kim is supposed to kill the deer (significantly not a buck, but a doe), but she realizes that instead of feeling "grateful" that her father has saved the first shot for her, she feels "patronized," on the verge of being judged: "This will be his test of me, his way of making me prove up" (247). The legal term "prove up" recalls property provisions of the Homestead Act. They are not out for meat, but have gone hunting only "because a daughter and her father can speak to each other only in a code made up of action and reaction." What she perceives to be a "ritual of blood" involves their "roles" as "powerful father" and "willful daughter" (248). Not surprisingly, she misses. As she writes the account, Barnes indicates that *because* he wanted her to shoot the deer, she wouldn't. When her father offers her an opportunity to make up for the missed shot by leading them out of the woods as night falls, Kim realizes she is lost. Of the silent drive back home, Barnes reflects that had her father simply "reached across and patted my knee or squeezed my arm, the wall between us might have fallen. [...] I might have believed my father's instruction a map I could follow" (251).

No such contact occurs, however, and the final, short chapter functions as a sort of coda as Barnes reflects on the last log drive down the Clearwater in 1971, then shifts to the present moment of her writing in 1994. She was then living with her husband, poet Robert Wrigley, in Lenore, Idaho, overlooking the Clearwater. In a highly rhetorical conclusion (some would say "poetic") Barnes carefully exculpates her father, rejecting the temptation to intellectualize her parents' Pentecostal fervor or to "cast my father as the villainous male, an extension of the patriarchy that doomed my mother to victimization" (256):

> I could say my father only imagined the demon roaming our house; I could say that the words I spoke in tongues were the unintelligible mut-

terings of exhaustion. I could say that no memory is more or less sound, no story more true than the one before: my father loved the land and his wife, his family and his god; my father feared the chaos of his own nature and delivered us from the wilderness into a life I am still aswirl in [257].

In the penultimate paragraph Barnes likens herself to the river that flows below her house, carrying all of the remembered events "in the quiet pools and strong currents of my being." In the last passage of the book she seems to echo Dylan Thomas's "Fern Hill" in her yearning to go "back to that place where I sang with the soul of a child" (258).

A patriarch of the old school would surely assert that it is not for the daughter to forgive the father; or to write condescendingly of him, even implicitly; or to speculate that her father might be in some ways "villainous"; or that, at least temporarily, he might have been crazy, a man plagued by the "chaos of his nature" who would victimize his wife. On the other hand, some feminists might have problems with Barnes's reluctance to excoriate the patriarchal system (if not her father personally) for its excesses. After all, the joys of her childhood and girlhood were at best diminished. Some might object, too, that the anger Carolyn Heilbrun seems to commend in women's autobiography post 1970 is all but absent from this memoir. Perhaps Barnes appears too complacent at the end of *In the Wilderness*, too much at ease with her conventional "home in the world" (255). Nevertheless, Barnes cites nearly all of the standard scriptural passages that find their way into feminist interrogations of the marginalization of women in western culture. And if her critique of the patriarchy, and of the religious fundamentalism that continues to promote it, does not appear overt, it remains both clear and subtly potent.

In *Hungry for the World* (2000) Kim Barnes produced a sequel to *In the Wilderness* that has shocked some of her readers. In this book Barnes tells the story she withholds in her earlier memoir. The first third of the book revisits scenes from *In the Wilderness*, bringing us to 1978 when, at age twenty, she becomes the object of attention (little affection is involved) of a Vietnam veteran and long-haul trucker she calls David. A frightening and sometimes sordid account of seduction and sexual exploitation ensues that will surprise readers of the earlier memoir, from which Barnes emerges in apparent control of her life. Although she makes frequent references to her dawning of sexual awareness, Kim at age eighteen has escaped the authoritarian rule of her father, and at the end of the memoir she jumps over the years to offer us an idyllic portrait of her present life as wife and mother. As she presents herself in *Hungry for the World*, she is clearly aware of what she does not want in life: not to have her mother's life, "bound by fear of a man's displeasure, his anger and strength," and not to need a man to make her feel safe.[12] What she wants seems on the one hand to be simple enough: "someone with whom I might share all the sides of myself." And on the other hand what she wants might be perceived as a fabrication couched in imagery drawn from harlequin romance novels: "I wanted to lie beneath stars in a meadow ringed by cedar, have my lover whisper to me the names of distant constellations" (103).

What she gets is a sociopath who convinces her to "lie with other men, men he would designate and direct" (151). Her overly protective father, her silent mother, and the restrictions of Pentecostal fundamentalism have not prepared her to deal with the fallen world. "This is not about sex," Barnes asserts: "It is about confusion bred into fear; it is about tyranny built on that fear — controlling the body, the mind, the soul of another. It is about being raised to believe that women want to be, must be, dominated" (153). While she has rejected those beliefs, Kim finds herself unable to escape them. Following several lurid encounters that involve visits to sex shops in Seattle she asks, "Did I believe that I deserved this final subservience, dues owed for the years I had fought to control my own existence?" and she sees herself locked in a cycle of "rebellion, punishment, submission" (194). In effect, the wilderness of sexual depravity from which Kim emerges in *Hungry for the World* is far deeper and darker than those of her childhood and early adolescence.

Kim Barnes's life narratives end in paradox. She rejects the fundamentalist community of her childhood, but implicitly embraces a community of academics and writers. Nor does she repudiate religion per se in the process. She rebels against family as defined and constricted by the patriarchy, but she establishes her own family. Nor does she turn her back on her difficult father. Near the end of her second memoir, *Hungry for the World*, Barnes asserts that her father (ironically, if not paradoxically) "gave me both reason to rebel and the means to do it" (239). She insists that she does not reject her past, but carries it with her "in the quiet pools and strong currents" of her being (257). In writing and publishing her memoirs, Barnes, like other women who write and publish their words, moves beyond the restrictions of domesticity and establishes her public voice. But at the same time, she performs in the roles of wife and mother.

By the time she wrote *Hungry for the World* Barnes had read extensively in the genre of memoir, and in a personal interview she mentioned reading such books as Harry Crews's *A Childhood: The Biography of a Place* (1978) and Chris Offutt's *The Same River Twice* (1993). She was also influenced by several poignant memoirs of gay men, including books by Paul Monette and Mark Doty's *Heaven's Coast* (1996). For writers attempting to claim authorship of their own stories she advises, "Remember to honor your family with the gift of good writing. By this I mean treat them in your writing as you would your most cherished fictional characters. Allow them complexity; understand that they are flawed and sometimes blind. Make them sympathetic. Describe their actions objectively; let the audience be their judge" ("Prayer, Piety, Passion, and Prose").

Judy Blunt

Born in 1954 in Malta, Montana, a town of some 2,000 on the Hi-Line located about fifty crow-flight miles from the Canadian border and more than thirty miles from the family ranch, Judy Blunt probably represents the last generation of rural Americans to spend several years of her childhood without the benefits of electricity, indoor plumbing, or running water. Phillips County, of which Malta is the seat, covers about 5,131 square miles and numbers around 5,000 residents, less than one person per square mile. Blunt grew up on a ranch, married a rancher, and after some thirty years of that life she left. By the spring of 2002, when her memoir appeared in print, Judy Blunt's parents were selling off their 15,000-acre ranch and most of the cattle and moving to town. If 15,000 acres (even dry ones) seems a large spread, one might consider the fact that her former husband's ranch numbers around 50,000 acres. What constitutes a profitable, or even a livable, piece of land varies considerably in the northern Rockies. For example, 2,000 acres of dry farm land in the Palouse region of northern Idaho may well include substantial parcels that can produce 80 or more bushels of wheat per acre. Dry peas, lentils, and canola (rapeseed) are also common crops in this non irrigated country that abuts the timberland of the Selway-Bitterroot chain. Two thousand acres of that sort of farmland can support a family; two thousand acres of ranch land in north central Montana could mean a ticket to the welfare office.

Although Blunt organizes her memoir, *Breaking Clean* (2002), as a collection of fourteen individually titled essays, the arrangement is largely chronological, and readers are likely to consider it novel-like in nature. Not surprisingly, given the way even avid readers tend to blur genres, one of the 27 five-star reviewers on Amazon.com concludes, "I recommend this novel to anyone who appreciates a very good story." In general Blunt's memoir, her first book, received strong reviews. Writing for the *New York Times Book Review* Elizabeth Gilbert praised the "delicate eloquence with which she captures the cost of these hard lives on people's souls."[13] Mary Zeiss Stange commended the "considerable power" of Blunt's "intimate descriptions" of the landscape.[14] Stange's comments, along with those of several nonprofessional reviewers on Amazon.com, who refer to her lyrical powers, remind us that like Kim Barnes, Judy Blunt was first published as a poet.

The memoir chronicles Blunt's girlhood on the ranch with considerable attention to the child's play she enjoyed with her siblings, particularly her younger brother and sister, who are twins. In general, memoirists from the Rockies have not devoted much of their attention to childhood activities, except as those activities had to do with the adult world of work. Consequently, we gain access in this book to an element largely missing in other regional memoirs. Readers will doubtless reflect mostly on the hard work and hard conditions on the family ranch, the rattlesnakes, the sub-zero winters, the wind, but Blunt's accounts of herself as a child at play deserve particular notice. Kim Barnes's memoir pertains mostly to her adolescence; she is twelve as the book opens, and her family is preparing to leave the wilderness. Blunt devotes at least a quarter of her memoir to such childhood activities as play, pets, and school activities.

Nearly halfway through the book, when she is fourteen, Judy Blunt leaves the ranch to attend high school in Malta, and at that point her life changes shape drastically. The novel-like structure of the book loosely resembles that of Kim Barnes's *In the Wilderness* except that Blunt carries her memoir through her thirteen-year marriage to the man she calls John, and she recounts her experiences as a ranch wife. They raised three children before she rebelled against the narrow restrictions of ranch life and at the age of 32 entered the University of Montana in Missoula. She worked at various jobs, including a stint sanding hardwood floors, while raising her children as a single parent, and she received her B.A. in 1994. Her first published book was a collection of poems, *Not Quite Stone* (1992), which won the University of Montana's Merriam Frontier Award. *Breaking Clean* won a PEN/Jerard Fund Award in 1997 and the Whiting Writers' Award in 2001. Blunt currently lives in Missoula, long renowned for its community of writers, and she teaches at the university as an associate professor of English.

The opening chapter of the book, the title essay, acts as a prologue and has occasioned some controversy. In his review for the *New York Times*, Blaine Harden cites Blunt's editor at Knopf, Robin Desser, to the effect that she urged Blunt to open with that essay because "It compresses the essence of the book in the same way that an overture contains an entire piece of music."[15] Certainly the chapter is dramatically loaded. Blunt recalls herself as a child of eight proving herself as "tough" and as a "hell of a little worker" in the family's two-acre potato field.[16] She then returns to herself as a single parent in Missoula worrying over her children before focusing on the evening her father brokered her marriage, when she was just fifteen, to a neighboring rancher twelve years her senior: "On the porch, John had presented my father with a bottle of whiskey and was asking Dad's permission to marry me" (5). The marriage did not take place immediately, but the reader will not become aware until much later in the memoir that a two-year engagement ensued, or that the two had indulged in flirtation before that moment on the porch. As Blunt records it, the drama concludes as follows, her father speaking: "'And you, you cocky sonofabitch! Don't you try planting anything too early, understand?' They were still laughing when they entered the kitchen" (7). Among the unanswerable questions is whether the off-color metaphor actually occurred or whether the "planting" is simply Blunt's interpretation of the tenor of that conversation.

Not surprisingly, as Harden reports their reactions, Blunt's former husband and his family were angry about the memoir, although their fury at the time was based on reviews and hearsay rather than actual reading. It is not likely, however, that reading the book would have altered their attitude. Blunt's dry sense of humor, for example, would probably not have won them over:

> I stuck with the bargain sealed on my parents' porch for more than twelve years, although my faith in martyrdom as a way of life dwindled. I collected children and nervous tics the way some of the women collected dress patterns and ceramic owls [8].

That she "kept up with the cycles of crops and seasons" and did it well, even "excelled" at it, might also be open to dispute from a perspective other than that of the author. But such is the nature of memoir and autobiography. The writer does not simply present her life: she interprets her life, and inevitably she interprets the behavior and motives of people whose lives have impinged on hers. Unlike Mary Blew, who distrusts memory, Blunt claims confidence in her memories, but questions her own treatment of them: "Although my memories are real, my interpretation of them is less trustworthy" (33).

More serious, perhaps, is the charge made by Blunt's former father-in-law about one of the most dramatically powerful incidents in the opening chapter:

> One day John's father, furious because lunch for the hay crew was late, took my warm, green typewriter to the shop and killed it with a sledgehammer [9].

Well, no, or at least not exactly. In response to her father-in-law's denial in the Phillips County newspaper, Blunt confessed that he had not taken her typewriter to the shop and smashed it, but had merely gotten angry and jerked the plug from the outlet. As Blaine Harden phrases it, she had a "different standard of factuality in the first chapter of her memoir" (E3). Mary Clearman Blew observes that the memoirist is confronted with "the conflicting claims of the exact truth of the story and its emotional truth" as he or she perceives it.[17] Andrew Hudgins says of the eighth of the "loving lies" autobiographers tell that some "subjective" or "emotional truth" is essential in the "lie of impressionism," which he considers the biggest and least defensible of the lies, but "inescapable for a writer attempting to create an *artistically coherent work*"[18] (italics mine). Sins, or perhaps what one might call errors in judgment, abound in memoir; they go with the territory. There are sins of omission, as in what Blunt does not tell the reader in her first chapter about her relationship with her husband-to-be. Had she stayed with her original ordering of the chapters, this "sin of omission" most likely would not have occurred. Hudgins lists such "sins" fourth in his essay, under the "lie of emotional evasion" (545). And there are sins or errors of commission like that concerning the typewriter: not furiously smashed, then, but furiously unplugged.

I have lavished so much attention on this issue not because I believe Blunt's decisions undermine the memoir, but because they pertain directly to a significant topos in the theory of life narrative writing. There may never be a definitive statement on this topos, but Sidonie Smith and Julia Watson's disclaimer surely applies: "While autobiographical narratives may contain 'facts,' they are not factual history about a particular time, person, or event. [...] [T]hey offer subjective 'truth' rather than 'fact.'"[19]

What might be called Blunt's "memoir proper" begins with "A Place of One's Own," a title that echoes Virginia Woolf's "A Room of One's Own"

(1929). The essay opens with a pre-natal "memory" from the spring of 1954, when Judy's pregnant mother confronted a rattlesnake in the chicken house. Her father, who married at twenty, Blunt describes as a "rowdy young cowboy" (12), and later, in more detail, she refers to him as a "thick, rugged man" with "hands like the paws on a grizzly bear" (23). Her mother, age 28 at the time and already the mother of a four-year-old daughter, she portrays as a "no-nonsense divorcée" (12) who, even in her seventies, "remains independent, opinionated and fiercely practical" (14). She also has a two-year college degree. Blunt presents observations and episodes that illustrate what reviewers like to refer to as the "hardscrabble" life on the remote ranch, which was late to acquire electricity.

In "Salvage," the third chapter, Blunt recounts the great blizzard of 1964, which hit when she was ten years old. With a wind chill of some seventy degrees below zero powered by winds of sixty or more miles per hour, even her six-foot, two hundred pound father finds himself helpless. In one vivid passage Blunt describes her father breaking ice that has formed over the cows' eyes and noses with a pair of pliers. In the spring the range cows give birth "in the stench of decay, their tails gone, ear tips dried crisp, ready to fall" (59). He loses more than forty head. In an interview published on the Powells Books website Blunt indicates that her depiction of the December 1964 blizzard was a "composite picture"; that is, in composing it she drew from her memories of several harsh winters. She also mentions that she tape-recorded an interview with her father in order to verify some of the details.[20] The two essays, "Church and State" and "Lessons in Silence," offer some relief from the perils of ranching with stories of Blunt's elementary education in one-room country schools. These chapters are reminiscent in some ways of Mark Spragg's essay, "Wapiti School," in *Where Rivers Change Direction.*

The next three chapters constitute a set of childhood memories built around episodes that represent (perhaps "symbolize") a child's life on the ranch. The latent subtheme concerns Judy's struggle with puberty, her resistance to the female identity that seems to impose itself on her body when she menstruates. When her grandfather tells young Judy they "don't need any more girl cats" (89), she wonders why they can't just get rid of the boy cats. The more mature Judy Blunt, however, sees the big picture:

> I knew this injustice wasn't limited to cats. Our ranching community applauded the birth of stud colts, bull calves and boy babies. We celebrated the manly man for doing the work of two men and the little woman for whipping up man-sized meals. [...] I got from television

names for what I already knew, an adult world divided neatly into Marshal Dillons and Miss Kittys. I reached for the role of the gunslinging marshal [90].

All life narratives obviously concern the identity of the writer, and nearly all women who write memoirs deal with various problems of gender, including the struggle to come to terms with their sexuality.

Blunt confronts the physicality of that struggle directly in the essay entitled "Fighting Fire," which begins with a story about Judy and the twins playing with matches and starting a fire that gets out of control. Almost lost in the fire game is the fact that the children are also experimenting with cigarettes and whiskey, including some potentially dangerous efforts at concocting home brew. The central episode of the chapter, however, concerns a large fire caused by lightning in 1966, when Judy was twelve and struggling with her maturing female body, biting off her fingernails and having her hair cut close: "A big, raw-boned girl, my mother said. Tall for twelve. A square, horsy face, I thought, eyes hidden by owlish glasses, chin jutting like a shoehorn" (97). Physically, at least, young Judy sees herself as most like her father, and at one point she lashes out against her feminine self in dramatic fashion: "After dabbing my bare chest with alcohol, I attempted to lance my budding breasts with a darning needle" (98). Her realization that her role during the fire fighting is to help the women in the kitchen as they prepare food for the men who battle the flames particularly rankles. It is "a community of men and women pulled together by the work they had done for each other, and their pride in doing it well," but Judy has not participated in that community effort, as she explains in the closing sentences of the essay: "I had not set myself aside and pitched in. In the end, I had done the one thing worse than doing nothing. I had rooted for the fire" (109). In effect, by setting herself apart from her conventionally prescribed role as a young woman, Blunt risks assuming the "posture," as Sidonie Smith describes it above, of "carnivalesque monstrosity."

In "The Year of the Horse," the final chapter of the first part of the memoir, Blunt blends several strands of narrative and exposition in a manner that has become fairly common practice in the postmodern essay. The first seven pages retell the type of cute story that becomes part of a family's mythology: how three-year-old Gail bumped heads with an Angus bull and explained, "Me and Bully Wooly were just *betending* to bump heads" (132). (Judy was four at the time.) The next four pages, expository in nature, provide commentary on the ranch's remoteness and the necessity of "community" for survival: "No one worked a homestead alone" (134). "We talked in facts" about weather and business, Blunt explains, "but stories were how we spoke" (136). In effect, she offers a brief sort of *ars poetica* here: "Listening to stories, I learned what was worth saying and what need not be spoken aloud; I learned how we remember and whom we remembered and why; how facts are shaped or colored or forgotten" (136).

The most important story of the chapter, however, Blunt reserves for the last ten pages, and even it is not so much concerned with the fact of her first horse as it is with the fact that she sees herself as no match for her giggling baby sister Gail: "I could not be dainty and perky. My voice never had that high range needed to giggle" (137). Judy's dilemma involves both the loss of her identity as a child and the imposition of her identity not simply as an adolescent or youngster, but as a young *woman*. In the summer, despite the heat, Judy dons a fake fur coat and tries to conceal the fact that she is menstruating. When she and Gail kill a porcupine, notorious for destroying trees and injuring livestock and pets with their quills, its blood on her coat and a look in her sister's eyes combine with the image of the dead animal to drive her to shame, at which she sheds her coat and accepts her menstrual blood: "It was the moment childhood became no longer possible" (146). It is also the moment at which she begins to accept herself as female. She can no longer play at being Matt Dillon.

If Kim Barnes's memoirs are tacitly feminist in nature, Judy Blunt's *Breaking Clean* becomes openly and avowedly so in the essay, "Learning Curves," which begins with Judy at age fourteen, boarding and going to high school in Malta. During the spring of 1969 she is ridiculed when she addresses her class about the inequalities women face in the United States. As Blunt points out, for small towns in Montana, as for small towns throughout the country, the fervent Sixties came into focus tardily. Stories of strong women were a part of her upbringing: "I grew up in a community of women whose strength and capacity for work I have yet to see equaled, true partners in the labor of farming and ranching" (153). But she also notes that her "brand of feminism celebrated strength through silence," and she submits that this silence could look "passive" when seen from the "outside": "The issue is power. And it's the silence that kills us" (154). Predictably, Judy has difficulty learning how to conform, but she struggles to alter her skirts and apply makeup so she will look "right," and she soon finds herself with an appropriate boyfriend. But she also finds herself completely unprepared for his advances: "I felt no physical desire for him and I did not enjoy having him touch me" (174). Reflecting on her incapacity to be "cute or giggly" and on her "legacy of wide shoulders, strong arms and broad, square hands," Blunt affirms that she "allowed the movement toward feminism" to adopt her.

"The Reckoning" focuses largely on Judy's sophomore year in high school and her involvement with an older, more experienced man ("Guy" is twenty-two and she is fifteen). In scenes reminiscent of those from Barnes's *In the Wilderness*, Judy rebels against her parents, partly because she believes they suspect her of being a "slut." When her father follows them on a date, confronts Guy, and threatens him with a statutory rape charge, Judy vows revenge, which comes in the person of "John," twelve years older and destined to become her husband. Discounting her dramatic depiction of the event in the opening chapter of the memoir, Blunt tells us that on the day of her graduation from high school in 1972 she accepted an engagement ring: "Pressed to set a wedding date, I had picked one more than a year distant" (198). The summer after graduation, she writes, "opened before me like a gift. John was comfortable and familiar, and I loved him dearly" (199). In effect, Blunt does not support the earlier *tableau vivant* of the forced marriage contract sealed by suitor and father over a bottle of whiskey. But she does portray herself as severely limited in her options. There is no place for her on the ranch now that her older brother has become a partner: "We girls would be left something of value, but we should know at the outset that we would never inherit the land" (211). One of the most dramatic events in the book occurs as a consequence of her sense of futility and powerlessness. She smashes a window with her hand and resolutely sprays the house with her blood (we learn almost coincidentally that she has been drinking). She concocts a lame explanation of what has happened, and the "transparent lies" (215) are readily accepted. The chapter concludes with her marriage, which she phrases in businesslike terms as "the vows of silent partnership" (215).

In "Learning the Ropes" Blunt details her first hard months as a ranch wife lived under the penurious tyranny of her father- and mother-in-law. She denominates the spread, ironically, the "Loving U Ranch." Despite the fact that his parents exit the ranch house and name their son the manager, father-in-law "Frank" still runs the show, and mother-in-law "Rose" (Frank's third wife) attempts to assert her authority. Blunt accepts head-on the risk of portraying Rose's latent alcoholism, but the major point of the chapter is that Judy's husband refuses to back her up in her conflict with his stepmother. Readers know from the first chapter that the marriage is doomed, but even if they had started with this chapter, they would likely have suspected something from the way Blunt avoids any comment on their honeymoon, except to note that they did have one.

In "Winter Kill" Blunt leaps ahead several years into the marriage, by which time they have three preschool-age children. The focal episode concerns their daughter's fever (it spikes at 106.1) and convulsions in the spring of 1977. She and John drive at night over gumbo roads, guided by the sporadic headlights of neighboring farmers and ranchers who drive out to light the way. The essay becomes a celebration of "the quiet strength of community" (275), but readers get other messages as well: "the cautious shutting down of self to any needs beyond those provided" (261); "the solitude I treasured took the shape of isolation" (262). The last essay in what might be considered the body of the memoir is "Night Shift," the manifest subjects of which, one might say, are smoking and calving. John, urged by his father, forbids his wife to smoke, but she refuses to back down. Although the care of livestock was reserved for the men, Judy single-handedly delivers a difficult ninety-pound calf from a nine-hundred-pound heifer. This act is as clearly a gesture of rebellion as her refusal to quit smoking: "I could run to the bunkhouse and kick the hired man out of bed. I could get John up and tell him to calve his own goddamned cows. I could drive seventy miles into town and sit down in a bar and smoke like a whore" (289). After delivering the calf, she lights a defiant cigarette and reflects that she can "do it all": "I could play their game until I dropped — but I would never own a square foot of land, a bushel of oats or a bum calf in my own name" (291).

Several readers who responded to the memoir on the Amazon.com website complained that Blunt "did not reveal the details that led to the breakdown of her marriage" (Boston, MA, 2 May 2002) and that she seemed to "hurry through the years as a ranch wife," so that the book appears "unbalanced" (Delaware, 9 May 2002). The last chapter is entitled "Afterword: Leaving Home" and constitutes a sort of epilogue that balances the first chapter, which serves as a prologue. It has taken her thirty years, Blunt says, to recognize "how a way of life can consume people from the inside out" (292). In 1986, at the age of 32, Judy Blunt left Phillips County, as she phrases it, "with a new divorce and an old car, with three scared kids and some clothes piled in back" (295). Most likely there were memorable arguments and confrontations, but the grounds for the divorce, those notoriously "irreconcilable differences," are laid out clearly enough. In effect, she was required to play a role she could no longer tolerate. Unwilling to accept the romance and mythology of the Old West, Judy Blunt insists that "farming and ranching is a business" (292), and the deep, "soul-sustaining" benefits like "freedom and autonomy" (293) that make up for the diminished profits have dwindled. Moreover, as she makes abundantly evident, ranching is not a business in which the woman very often becomes an equal partner. Obviously, Blunt's experiences as a ranch wife bear little resemblance to those of Teresa Jordan's mother.

Visiting the vacant site of her first school, Judy and her sisters discover the rock houses she and her girl classmates built in the 1950s and 1960s, and she claims she recognizes her own house at once by its layout. The rock houses are metaphoric constructs as much as anything. They are icons of domesticity: "Inside these rooms, we had enacted the social rituals of our grandmothers and mothers" (301–302). In most ways Blunt has repudiated those rituals, rejected the ranch for the town, the husband for the single life. At the end of her memoir Blunt celebrates her grateful awareness of "the enormous power of this prairie" and "a sense of peace" (303). In an interview published on the Internet, Blunt's comments are reminiscent of Mary Clearman Blew's phrase, "bone deep in landscape," from the opening pages of *All But the Waltz*: "My relationship to the landscape of Montana is visceral. My land defined my life for thirty years, and I find that it still defines my voice. It's hard to shake the dark humor, the inside jokes that are part of growing up at the mercy of harsh weather and hard soil."[21]

Comparison of Kim Barnes and Judy Blunt

Kim Barnes finds it difficult to perform in her role as dutiful daughter; Judy Blunt finds it difficult to perform in her role as dutiful wife. The comparison is not that simple, of course, but the rhetoric here conveys some truth. Both memoirists revisit their troubled adolescent years, complicated by difficulties with acceptance of conventional gender roles and of their sexuality. The sources of those difficulties, however, differ considerably. Barnes struggles with her impulse to concede the fundamentalist Christian and patriarchal premise that women are inherently sinful and dangerous: they are by nature temptresses, seductresses. Blunt feels no such impulse. Rather, she contends with women's apparent lack of power in the world, their lack of genuine autonomy and of an identity other than being nonmale. The ranch wife, Blunt suggests, is expected to act as a silent partner; a silent partner who, in most circumstances, will not inherit the one thing farmers and ranchers value most of all, the very land that has defined her character and voice. The system, or whatever one wishes to call it (the tradition, perhaps, or the culture) is unequal, and hence unfair.

Obviously the "constraints" on a woman's identity to which Sidonie Smith refers do remain, and to some extent those constraints may be magnified in rural areas and small towns. Both Barnes and Blunt struggle with their desire for independence and autonomy partly because they admire their fathers, even while they recognize from the perspective of their writing that their fathers, or at least the models of the world that their fathers embraced, have been wrong. Kim Barnes in particular is conflicted because of her own lingering feelings of guilt over her behavior and the high cost of her rebellion to her family and to herself. Repudiating its "structured hierarchy," Barnes sees herself as responsible for having torn "the carefully woven fabric of family" (231). At the time of her writing, Barnes had not reconciled completely with her father, and that adds to the conflict. Unlike Barnes, Judy Blunt struggled with life as a single parent, although she does not make that a significant element of her memoir, and that presumably has added to her sense of a conflicted self.

Both writers are also torn by their attraction to certain aspects of conventional women's roles, particularly insofar as they concern family and community. They admire their mothers, and Blunt finds several opportunities to assert and to dramatize the vital importance of communal efforts on the ranch. For example, she recognizes her parents' partnership as "an arrangement that often rewarded a woman's strength and independence" (231), but she discovers no such partnership in her own marriage. Blunt pictures herself at her wedding as "bristling with independence yet eager to please" (35). The paradox does not prove viable for her. Barnes portrays her mother as less capable, or perhaps less willing, to sustain her autonomy. She watches her mother reject "her own beauty" and her voice (because "a silent woman was a treasure") until, "It was as though my mother had disappeared" (52). We have no indication of how Judy Blunt's mother may have acted as her daughter's marriage disintegrated, but Kim Barnes's mother at crucial points proves unable, or perhaps unwilling, to challenge her husband's authority. In fact, the last we hear from her in *In the Wilderness* comes in the context of her citation of Paul the Apostle (1Timothy 2:11–12): "Let the woman learn in silence with all subjection. But I suffer not a woman to teach, nor to usurp authority over the man, but to be in silence" (231). Of course, once she chooses to write and to pursue publication, the woman's silence ends.

Chapter Six

The Indian Lives of Sidner J. Larson and Janet Campbell Hale

Although a good deal has been written about Native-American autobiography, most of it takes as a point of departure a disclaimer similar to this: "That form of writing generally known to the West as *autobiography* had no equivalent among the oral cultures of the indigenous inhabitants of the Americas. [...] [T]he notion of telling the whole of any one individual's life or taking merely personal experience as of particular significance was, in the most literal way, foreign to them, if not also repugnant."[1] "Strictly speaking," writes Arnold Krupat of the "preliterate" era, "Indian autobiography is a contradiction in terms."[2] Of course one might point out that "the whole" of a life is hardly ever the subject of memoir, either oral or written, so perhaps a simple semantic option would suffice: "Native-American *memoir*." If it all simply came down to semantics, however, we would not encounter such books as Krupat's own *Native American Autobiography: An Anthology* (1997), H. David Brumble III's *American Indian Autobiography* (1988), or Gretchen Bataille and Kathleen Sands's *American Indian Women, Telling Their Lives* (1984).[3]

Contemporary Indians like Sidner Larson and Janet Campbell Hale, who have written their own life narratives, have available to them not only such models as N. Scott Momaday's *The Way to Rainy Mountain* (1969), but also such earlier autobiographies as *Yellow Wolf: His Own Story* (1940), coauthored by Lucullus Virgil McWhorter, and Sarah Winnemucca Hopkins's *Life among the Piutes: Their Wrongs and Claims* (1883), edited by

Mary Peabody Mann (Horace Mann's widow). One of the earliest of the Indian autobiographies is that of the Sauk chief Black Hawk, narrated in 1833 to Antoine LeClaire. Like Black Hawk's, the life narratives connected with such Indians as Yellow Wolf, Geronimo, and the renowned Black Elk are "as-told-to" autobiographies. Purists could argue that only those works actually written by the subject are genuine. Paul John Eakin argues that "the potential for exploitation" is "inevitable," and finds "an unresolved tension between relational and autonomous modes of identity" in such collaborations.[4] Although Sarah Winnemucca was literate, scholars conjecture as to just how much of her own writing is to be found in her autobiography. Even the more recent effort of Christine Quintasket (Mourning Dove) of the Colville tribe from northeastern Washington, who achieved some fame as the first Native-American woman to have a novel published with *Cogewea* in 1927, involved considerable editing. Jay Miller, describes the "assortment of pages" of her "Salishan Autobiography" that came to him in 1981, some forty years after her death, as "drafts" of an autobiography.[5]

Today the as-told-to format has become a staple in the subgenre of the celebrity autobiography. As I have noted elsewhere, collaboration has played a long and ongoing role in autobiography, and some theoreticians have argued that all life narrative writing is in certain ways "collaborative." The classic as-told-to Indian autobiography is *Black Elk Speaks* (1932), which resulted from the collaboration of the Oglala Sioux medicine man Black Elk and writer John G. Neihardt. G. Thomas Couser, however, among others, has suggested that the story lacks authenticity and "remains confined within the invisible reservations of its unconscious ethnocentrism."[6] One recent example of a collaborative or co-written Indian autobiography involving a literate subject is Horace Axtell and Margo Aragon's *A Little Bit of Wisdom: Conversations with a Nez Perce Elder* (1997). This form of life narrative (both the as-told-to and the collaborative autobiography) has its origins in the work of ethnographers who recorded the memories and stories of native informants around 1900 and who usually had to rely on translators. David Brumble surveys a number of problems that beset such narrations, including the inclination of the interviewer (usually an anthropologist) to ask "the kinds of questions that his literate, Western audience will expect autobiography to answer. [...] Then there are the hours of transcription and the editing: the ordering, cutting, and sometimes the rephrasing and the additions" (10). Typically, Brumble and others have noted, the editors attempt to impose chronology and narrative (plot-like) form on the often circular (rather than linear) sequences and the episodic structure, if such terms as "sequences" and "structure" may be said to apply here. Krupat elaborates the process in greater detail, emphasizing that what he prefers to call "*original bicultural composite composition*" (31) must not be read naïvely: "Indian autobiographies are collaborative efforts, jointly produced by some white who translates, transcribes, compiles, edits, interprets, polishes, and ultimately determines the form of the text in writing, and by an Indian who is the subject and whose life becomes the content of the 'autobiography' whose title may bear his name" (30).

The motives of the Indians who participated in these "autobiographical projects," as Brumble calls them (Eakin refers to them as "ethnographic autobiographies" [172]), varied: desire to "set the record straight" or to vindicate themselves, intent to "preserve their knowledge of the old ways for future generations," need for money (72). Brumble observes, "these books *must* distort the selves they portray" (11, italics mine). Submitting that there is "a sense, of course, in which every autobiography is a fiction of the self," he contends that "self-written autobiography is at least the subject's *own* fiction" (11). These "autobiographical projects," then, were not efforts at self-discovery or self-definition, but at self-declaration.

Scholars have debated certain premises about the nature of Indian autobiography for at least twenty years, particularly the issue of the individual self. In suggesting a term like "*communo-bio-oratory* (community-life-speaking)" as more appropriate to pre–Columbian native writing than "*autobiography* (self-life-writing)," Hertha D. Wong reminds us that "emphasis on the autonomous individual and writing" is not particularly relevant.[7] The thousands of oral history projects that have been conducted worldwide, often at retirement centers, might at least suggest some validity for another hybrid: *auto-bio-oratory*. Arnold Krupat goes to considerable lengths in support of the premise that in Native-American culture "the individual could not in any positive way be imagined to stand outside or against his society" (11); that is, the individual defined himself in terms of the community (tribe, clan, family). Consequently, Krupat points out, the individual, when he does speak out, does so without reference to his tribe, but strictly to himself.

Commenting on "coup tales" told by the Plains Indians to commemorate or celebrate their own achievements in combat, Brumble observes that "Christian notions of modesty and humility simply did not apply; the warrior had to publicize his deeds as soon and as often as possible"

(27). One is reminded of the boasts of various Homeric heroes, or of the Anglo-Saxon Beowulf's *bēot*. Brumble concludes the autobiographical narrative that various ethnographers attempted to extract from them was not "an endeavor entirely foreign" to the Indians (46). There is, then, some tradition or convention of personal or individual exploit in Native-American self-life stories; indeed, James Willard Schultz includes several of these in *My Life as an Indian*, as noted in chapter 2. Wong finds that "Contrary to some romanticized notions of communal identity, even within a specific tribe, individuality abounded" (13). Perhaps we ought to distinguish between "individuality" and "individualism," the latter being applicable to the injurious solipsism that some would argue has become a sort of Western cult. Wong notes that the "Native American concept of self differs from a Western (or Euro-American) idea of self in that it is more inclusive. Generally, native people tend to see themselves first as family, clan, and tribal *members*, and second as discrete individuals" (13). She proposes that "a Westerner *writes* an autobiography to set himself or herself *apart from* (better than, different from, richer than, more successful than) other members of his or her society, whereas a pre-contact Native American *speaks* a personal narrative to become more fully *accepted into* (a fuller participant in) his or her community" (16).

Two other traits of traditional native culture often reflected in their autobiographies are particularly worth emphasizing: first, their intimate relationship with nature, which they regard as spiritually infused and inevitably connected with supernatural phenomena; and second, their cyclical (circular) or nonlinear sense of time. Reading Indian autobiography Brumble on occasion experienced a sort of "culture shock" that he refers to as "epistemological vertigo" (3). One might think of this as a psychological response to a surreal, dreamlike sort of anti-logic or a sudden disappearance of cause-and-effect in the narration. We frequently encounter apparent incursions of the spirit world on the quotidian in novels like Leslie Silko's *Ceremony* (1977), Gerald Vizenor's *Darkness in Saint Louis: Bearheart* (1978), and James Welch's *Fools Crow* (1986). A raven, for example, converses familiarly with White Man's Dog (later to be named Fools Crow), and in *Ceremony* conventional medicine fails Tayo, while the native healing of Ku'oosh and Old Betonie saves his life. *Black Elk Speaks* introduces the reader to a world in which visions impose on historical events and in which the *spiritus mundi* frequently asserts its preeminence.

The foregoing constitutes a context, of sorts, for the study and appreciation of Native-American autobiography, and it suggests that there *is* a long tradition of personal storytelling, or the telling of stories that feature the self, in Indian communities. Autobiographers like Momaday and Chickasaw poet and novelist Linda Hogan, however, do not appear to have been influenced by Indian autobiographies or memoirs that preceded theirs. David Brumble assumed that N. Scott Momaday had read "a wide range of the Indian autobiographies" (16) in the process of writing *The Way to Rainy Mountain* and *The Names*, but Brumble discovered he was in error. While his reading helped him better understand Momaday's memoir, Brumble found that Momaday himself relied on the oral tradition. Sidner Larson, however, who is Gros Ventre on his mother's side, wrote his doctoral dissertation at the University of Arizona under the direction of N. Scott Momaday, so he was familiar with *The Way to Rainy Mountain* and through that memoir he was acquainted with traditional oral storytelling. His favorite Momaday writing is "The Man Made of Words," and he also admires Leslie Silko's "Language and Literature from the Pueblo Perspective." Through these essays, Larson confides, "one gets a glimmer of what it is we talk about when we talk about oral tradition."[8]

Sidner J. Larson

About two-thirds of the way through his first book, *Catch Colt* (1995), Sidner Larson writes: "There is no way to feel more alive than being trapped behind a bar waiting for some pathological asshole to see if he can kick the shit out of you."[9] This passage ripped out of context reveals quite a bit about the nature of Larson's memoir. It is not "lyrical" or "poetic." It is more accurately "physical," perhaps even "visceral," and profane in its effect. Larson's prose style, mostly unadorned with rhetoric, imagery, or metaphor, concentrates on physical action rather than meditation or contemplation. One is more likely to encounter a coarse epithet or profanity than a passage of purple prose in this book. Larson's approach is almost unnervingly straightforward. Consider another example, from the opening paragraph of the sixth chapter, or essay, "Crazy Lodge":

> I knew it was time me for me to leave Montana, but not because I sensed things would go so badly with the economy there during the 1980s. My reasons had more to do with some bad habits. I drank too much, chased women, worked too hard, and I was arrogant [97].

With this minimalist rhetoric Larson wastes no time in fatuous apologies. Generally, his prose features a vocabulary stripped of nuance and richness;

uncomplicated syntax; and short, almost sparse paragraphs (often five or six expository or narrative paragraphs to a single page). His discourse could be described as willfully unrefined, and he rarely presents himself as an admirable or even sympathetic narrator/protagonist.

The impetus to write his life story, Larson told me, came not from his dissertation director at the University of Arizona, but from a conference he attended at the University of North Dakota about a year before he left for Tucson. There he met Tobias Wolff whose memoir, *This Boy's Life* (1989), had just been published, and from Wolff he learned something about the "illegitimacy" upon which his own memoir was to be founded. The title of Larson's book, which evolved from his dissertation, is the Gros Ventre term for an illegitimate child, derived from "the term for an unplanned horse pregnancy" (11). He claims to write "from a position of illegitimacy, an exquisite place from which to consider legitimacy": "I have no father, I am part Indian, I am not wealthy, and I choose to live a life of the mind, all 'illegitimacies' in one setting or another" (10). If one accepts the definition of memoir that suggests it must focus on people other than the writer, then *Catch Colt* is closer in nature to autobiography. The autobiographical protagonist that Larson devises possesses slight self-awareness and a general inability, or perhaps unwillingness, to take control over his life, except in the last chapter, when he describes his motive for writing the book: "I believe in writing oneself and the world, not as something better or worse than, say, the practice of law, but as a way of playing a more active role in the process of inventing self" (157).

Born in Seattle in 1949, Sidner Larson reports that his Gros Ventre mother "refused to leave her family for my father" (5). His father then abandoned her. Larson grew up in Shelby, Montana, which he characterizes as a white town of eleven bars, unsympathetic to minorities, "hard-drinking, sports crazy, and probably dysfunctional in some ways by today's standards" (8). Presently the town of Shelby, located on the Hi-Line about 85 miles east of Glacier National Park and 35 miles south of the Canadian border, numbers about 3,100 inhabitants. His alternative home was with his mother's family, particularly his maternal grandparents, on the Gros Ventre reservation at Fort Belknap, about 150 miles east of Shelby. There, he writes, "I learned about ranching, Indian ways, the land, and family values" (8). Similarly, in *The Woman Who Watches over the World* (2001), Denver-born Linda Hogan reiterates her preference for her father's tribal reservation in Oklahoma over her native Colorado: "It was not my birthplace, but it was my home, the place of my heart, my inner world, the place where I lived before I was born."[10]

Although he graduated from high school in Shelby, Larson says he rarely goes back, but he visits the reservation regularly. His memoir tells the story of a mixed-blood: "I am Indian and I am not, as near as I can figure" (9). Identity crises recur throughout, and one is occasionally reminded of the identity motif in the novels of Larson's cousin, the late Blackfeet-Gros Ventre writer James Welch (1940–2003). Predictably, most fiction and memoir written by métis or mixed-blood authors features the identity theme. As his life narratives unravel, it is clear that Larson feels both in and out of several worlds: town and ranch, barroom (as bartender or proprietor) and courtroom (as attorney), and classroom (as both student and teacher). He also portrays himself as alternatively an alienated bachelor and a family man, a brawler and an intellectual.

"Traveling back and forth," Larson writes, "made me independent at a young age, and I still don't like to stay in one place all the time" (6). In 1972, following a year at Eastern Montana College in Billings, he completed his B.A. at Northern Montana College in Havre. He married his high school sweetheart and they soon had a daughter, but already, "the economic struggle that finally did Sally and me in had begun in earnest" (75). After his grandfather and grandmother died, he began what he calls a "self-styled vision quest" (76). Larson tried his hand as proprietor of several bars in Montana before moving to Brookings, South Dakota, where he received his M.A. in English in 1982. Then he went on to the University of Minnesota, taking his law degree in 1985, and returned to Brookings, where he worked three years as a research attorney for banks involved in farm foreclosures. He describes his work as "soul-killing" (personal communication). In 1987 he divorced his wife of eighteen years; they had three children, the oldest of whom had married. The next year, after a brief sojourn at the University of North Dakota, he began work on his doctorate at the University of Arizona, completing it in 1994. By 1992 Larson was teaching at Lewis-Clark State College in Lewiston, Idaho, and he had remarried (they have since divorced). In 1995 he left LCSC for the University of Oregon, where he taught for five years, leaving in 2000 for Iowa State University, where he presently runs the Ethnic Studies Program. In addition to critical essays on Native-American culture in journals like *American Indian Literature* and *MELUS*, Larson has published the book, *Captured in the Middle: Tradition and Experience in Contemporary Native American Writing* (2000), including such essays as "House Made of Cards:

The Construction of American Indians" and "Pragmatism and Indian Thought." He is currently at work on a book-length study of the writings of James Welch.

Writing of his childhood, which entailed frequent moves among relatives and acquaintances, Larson says he never felt "abandoned," but a "distance" opened up between himself and his mother and between himself and other people: "I just developed a taste for being gone at times, and the women of my childhood indulged me in this" (6). In "Constituting and Preserving Self through Writing," Larson observes, "for me, the most effective means of dealing with negative experiences was writing my autobiography."[11] He also discovered in the process of writing what he calls a "meaningful relationship with a place [north-central Montana] that is similar to the most meaningful relationships that exist between people" (*Captured* 76). Throughout his writing, however, one detects an ongoing sense of malaise. Despite his apparent efforts to center himself in the world and to resist his own impulse toward being an "outsider to family, landscape, and tribal identity" (*Catch Colt* 156), Sidner Larson remains distant in some ways. His book prompts several questions, not the least of which concerns his capacity (at least as he presents himself as the protagonist in the story of his own life) to *sustain* lasting relationships with family, with friends and colleagues, with women, or even with place.

Whether because of its origins as a dissertation project or his inexperience as a writer, *Catch Colt* has a rawness about it that drew some less than enthusiastic reviews. In *MultiCultural Review*, Andrew J. Deering noted a "somewhat disjointed" presentation that could be "a little disorienting" for readers, but he rated it "highly recommended."[12] Genevieve Stuttaford, writing for *Publishers Weekly*, was less sanguine: "Unfortunately, this diffuse collection of autobiographical reminiscences contains too much awkward prose, hampering the narrative."[13]

Because Larson's autobiography is most frequently criticized for being somehow "diffuse" or "disjointed," one might consider the construction of the opening chapter, "Meadowhawk, Blackbird, Thorn, Bull Calf," which serves as a prologue. The four nouns in the title pertain to stages of the traditional Gros Ventre coming-of-age process. Larson supplies only ages 12 through 16, which he associates with Bull Calves (61). The word "Meadowhawk" nearly echoes Meadowlark, the name of the grade school Larson and his brother Gary attended in Shelby, but the initial narrative block (a little over two pages) does not much concern the school. Instead, we see Gary as a "tough little guy" who rough-houses with Sidner, the protective big brother who buys him his first two cars (2). Five more narrative or expository blocks, ranging in length from two to seven pages, take the reader on a sometimes erratic ride through his troubled school days and introduce members of his mother's extended family. In general, Larson moves through his entire narrative rapidly and rarely dwells on any particular event or episode; nor does he provide the details that might lead readers to describe his writing as densely textured.

In the second episode of the opening chapter, for example, which runs under two pages, we encounter Sidner in the sixth grade having a run-in with the principal, who grabs him by the shoulder and cautions him about his behavior. Although the principal does not explain his warning, he calls him a "real hard case" and threatens him with a "little surprise." Larson pronounces judgment on himself as he was then: "I didn't say anything, but that mean fuck you of the brain must have crept onto my features" (5). In effect, Larson presents himself as aggressive: a potential troublemaker as a boy who will likely become a troubled man. More than fifty pages of the text will pass before the reader learns that the principal's mean "surprise" is his decision to see to it that the coach drops Sidner from the junior high basketball team.

Some origins of Larson's anger are implicit in the next block of the chapter, a largely expository section that runs about four pages. Shifting away from the narrative mode, Larson portrays his mother's family as large and full of "forceful" personalities, and he conjectures that his father "went his own way" to avoid being "overshadowed" by them (5). Complicating matters, his mother strikes out on her own, leaving Sidner to live a confusing "dual life in white and Indian worlds" (5). Most of the remainder of the section concerns his Indian relatives, particularly his grandmother, who married a white rancher. Never registered as a Gros Ventre, Larson writes, "confusion characterized my relationship with the Bureau of Indian Affairs" (9). One must be one-fourth Gros Ventre or Assiniboine in order to be registered at the Fort Belknap reservation that the two tribes have occupied since the 1870s.[14]

By the time readers reach the sixth and last section of the opening chapter, the longest at about seven pages, they may be suffering from that "epistemological vertigo" to which Brumble has referred. A playground confrontation when he was in the fourth grade leads Larson to reflect on his high school track coach. A comment on his favorite aunt segues into a story about his maternal grandmother, and that leads him to reflect happily on his older "cousin-brothers." The sixth section opens with a quotation from Leslie Silko, which reminds the reader that in some respects this is a "literary memoir." After all, Sidner Larson was writing the initial drafts of this book as a doctoral student in literature preparing for a career as a college professor, and by the time he wrote the final drafts he had become a professor in fact. He recalls a day when he was about five years old, thus reversing, indeed outright disrupting, the overall chronology of the chapter. One is reminded of the free, unpredictable movement in time that is a distinguishing feature of many Native-American oral narratives that can be disconcerting to audiences accustomed to careful transitions and linear or cause-effect structure. His grandmother tells about how her father scouted for the army when the Nez Perce left Idaho in 1877, but young Sidner seemingly ignores the story and coaxes her to let him shoot at magpies with a .22 rifle. His capacity to tease her subtly indicates that he is learning his lessons.

At this point, however, Larson abruptly suspends his narration with the statement, "My mother and Leon came the next day to pick me up" (16). His brother Gary and stepsister Judy accompany them, and they end up at the fair and then in the car outside a bar. The memory appears to be fragmented. Who is Leon? Apparently another of his mother's boyfriends, but we do not learn about him until several pages have elapsed; then we find that he was a Turtle Mountain Chippewa, that as a five-year-old Sidner was afraid of him, and that Leon died in an automobile accident involving the same car they'd ridden to the fair. In the two intervening pages, before he identifies Leon, we are provided an embedded narrative digression about how a man (presumably Indian) named Bobby Gray bloodied the nose of a big cowboy in a barroom brawl.

What are we to make of all this? Is Larson unable to tell the story straight? Or does he have other intentions with his narrative design? Shortly after Leon's death, Larson tells us, his stepsister Judy was taken to an orphanage, and then he writes, "I have known fear in my life" (18). The chapter culminates, in fact, with Larson's realization of this particular sort of "lasting fear" that "has to be learned over a period of time under the right circumstances" (18). He remembers his mother's fear at Leon's death, not her grief, and he fears that like Judy, he will end up in an orphanage. "I saw men trail my mother like hounds," Larson writes, knowing that he "saw some things go seriously wrong" during those years (20). At the end of the chapter, he shifts his focus back to the ranch, which was safe from fear because no one dared to tangle with his mother's family.

The remaining seven chapters that comprise Larson's memoir tend to be more conventional in design and cohesiveness than the first. Larson reminds us of his tribal identity by the titles of the chapters, not all of which are made clear in the text. "Otter Robe Women," however, clearly refers to his grandmother, "an Otter Robe woman, granddaughter of Otter Robe of the Black Lodge, a war clan of the White Clay people" (32). The Gros Ventres (literally, "big bellies," probably because of their perceived appetites) were so named by French Canadian fur trappers; they referred to themselves as the "White Clay People," the northernmost group of the Algonkian speaking Arapaho. The title of the next chapter, "Lame Bull," is never explained, but Larson may intend for it to be self-referential and self-deprecating. Two historical figures, however, are likely candidates for consideration: the powerful head chief of the Piegan Blackfeet, also known as Lone Chief (died 1857), who was the first Indian leader to sign the Treaty of 1855, and a Gros Ventre chief (ca. 1825–1908) mentioned by Regina Flannery in her study of the tribe.[15] A character named Lame Bull appears as the unnamed first-person narrator's stepfather in James Welch's novel, *Winter in the Blood* (1974).

In "Lame Bull" Larson begins with a brief reference to his aunt, which may suggest some desire to sustain cohesiveness in the book, as she also appears in "Otter Robe Women," but the chapter itself, although much of it concerns his school sports activities, features frequent shifts of focus. The rhythm Larson establishes in this chapter, however, creates a sort of shape in the midst of its apparent disarray: school-ranch-school-ranch-school. At school, notably in high school, he concentrates on the athletic activities that for the most part kept him out of trouble; at the ranch he focuses on lessons in being Indian. For example, he recounts a traditional story of Ink'dome, a mythical trickster similar to the Blackfeet Napi (Old Man), who killed his wife but acquired and then lost the magic power to create new women. Why Larson chooses to tell this particular story is open to speculation, but I think the autobiographical implications transcend his casual observation that such stories "were a good diversion" (46).

Larson also tells of going to a Sun Dance ceremony with his mother and of dreaming about the traditional Dog Dance, but as usual, he draws no conclusions from such stories. He simply presents them before turning to his sophomore year in high school, when he subbed into an important football game. One moment we find ourselves in the traditional Indian world; the next moment, we are playing high school football. The abrupt transitions—the lack of any transition at all, in fact, except for a gap in the text—reflect Larson's sense of discontinuity and discord in his life.

Even within an episode he sometimes disrupts his narration, in effect, interrupting himself. Just as he is about to get involved in a critical play, for example, Larson portrays himself as tripping into another zone (the Indian zone instead of the end zone, one might say) as a "movie" seems to run in his head about Melvina Horn, known as "Snake Woman." Then he remembers a day when his grandfather overcame a difficult horse. These digressions run two full pages before Larson returns to the football game, only to spoil a touchdown drive by clipping on the play. From this unfortunate experience, which includes taunting at the end of the game by a local racist businessman, Larson learns a lesson that cycles back to his observations at the conclusion of the opening chapter: "I was afraid, but I was also brave, and I had discovered my fear, too, had a horizon" (55).

In the fourth chapter Larson recounts his time at Eastern Montana College in Billings starting in the fall of 1967, threaded throughout with the deaths of one of his cousin-brothers at age eleven or twelve and of his grandfather. These deaths form the rationale for the chapter's title, "Crying for Pity," which pertains to the young man's plea to "all the powers of sky, earth, and water to have pity upon him" and grant him a vision, and through that vision, power.[16] By other definitions, the phrase might pertain as well to any lone person's crying out for pity in what appears to be an uncaring or hostile world. After burying "the old man" at the ranch, Sidner does not return to Shelby and his pregnant girlfriend (Sally), who is not Indian, until the spring. Throughout the memoir things happen with no apparent cause; that is, Larson does not attempt, as many writers of life narrative do, to show that because he behaved in a certain way, a certain outcome resulted. In some ways he seems to live as Hemingway's Krebs wishes to in "Soldier's Home," "without consequences," and presumably without agency.

Larson's wife appears briefly at the start of the next chapter, "Vision Quest," but she never comes to life in the book, nor do any of their three children, Lorna, Peter, and Sydney. In an Indian's life narrative one might assume that a chapter entitled "Vision Quest" would occupy an important position, placed as it is at the center of the text. The traditional vision quest would involve an intense visionary experience brought on by an ordeal that would include a long period of isolation in nature, fasting, and the discovery of a spirit animal like a raven or bear that would provide the boy or young man insight into himself and a source of power. In his study of their tribal religion and rituals, however, John M. Cooper stresses that not all Gros Ventres went on vision quests, and most who did were unsuccessful: "It seems, therefore, that many men did not go out on hills to seek power (women never did so), and that relatively few even of those who did go were successful."[17] Larson's "self-styled" vision quest (76) amounts to something of a parody of that tradition. Instead of heading for sacred Snake Butte, Larson rambles throughout the Northwest, reads a number of writers he regards as socially alienated (Melville, Woolf, Hemingway), and embarks on a process of self-construction he says has taken him about twenty years to complete.

After graduating from college in 1973, the first of his family to do so, Larson tries teaching high school, but finds the pay "appallingly low" (78). He ends up buying a bar in the small town of Joplin on the Hi-Line, makes a success of it, and then returns to Havre to open a more sizable bar. His stated motives are to make money and at the same time to exact a certain vengeance on those who have mistreated Indians. Larson's barroom encounters are anything but spiritual; however, he demonstrates his physical power, and he succeeds in the white man's world of commerce. But although he emerges as "the light-heavyweight champion of the Montana Bar corner [of Havre]" (94), he ends up selling his holdings and moving his family to California briefly before heading to Brookings, South Dakota, in 1981 to pursue his master's degree in English. Most of the chapter entitled "Crazy Lodge," however, which follows "Vision Quest," pertains to Larson's law school experiences at the University of Minnesota.

The chapter's title pertains to the traditional Crazy Dance (also known as "Lodge," after the temporary lodge constructed for the sacred dance). Most of the details of the Crazy Lodge are not relevant here, but Larson probably does draw on several of its more significant features. The four-day ceremony involved heavy feasting, reverse behavior (if someone says "dance fast," the dancer will dance slowly), a fire test (the "crazy" aspect has its origin in the way moths are attracted to flame), and an unusual sex-test wherein the young men were to submit their wives or substitutes to a number of designated "grandfathers," who were not actually elderly men. Supposedly, the sex act involved the contact of naked bodies, but no sexual penetration, and the intent was to test the husband's confidence in his wife.[18] In "Crazy Lodge" Larson nurtures comically erotic reveries about a barmaid and a classmate, and he confesses his infidelity: "Realizing the strain I was putting on my marriage, I hedged against the possibility that Sally would leave me by spending time and money on other women" (98). The chapter ends with a different kind of craziness when

Larson and a friend escort a suicidal classmate to the county hospital, where the man is pronounced "crazy," after which Larson and his friend head for a bar.

The cynicism Larson feels over his experiences in the crazy lodge of law school comes to a head during his last year and continues into his time practicing law in Brookings after his graduation. The chapter entitled "Ghost Dancer" might suggest the late nineteenth-century movements under Smohalla, a Wanapum, in the Oregon Territory and Wovoka, a Paiute, in Nevada. Both of the messianic leaders preached a return to the old ways, and Wovoka created special songs and a dance that "induced fainting spells among some of the dancers, who would fall out of the circle and thus come into communication with the dead ancestors."[19] The tragic climax of the Ghost Dance rebellion occurred in 1890 when some 150 Indians were killed at Wounded Knee. When in 1973 American Indian Movement leader Russell Means led an occupation of the site on the Pine Ridge Reservation in the southeastern corner of South Dakota two more were killed in a confrontation that remains unresolved.

As a ghost dancer, Larson portrays himself in a very different light, yielding to the basest aspects of late-capitalist Euro-American culture. In "Crazy Lodge" he lashes out against "the pressure monolithic capitalism places on individuals to make money at the expense of their individual identities, their families, and their communities" (98). "Ghost Dancer" opens in a motel room where Larson has taken a woman he picked up at a bar. The bulk of the chapter concerns a minor court case that Larson loses to a prominent attorney, an experience that deepens his cynicism toward the system, and an intramural football game in which he performs poorly. After the game he picks up the barmaid he described in the previous chapter. Everything that happens in "Ghost Dancer" suggests cultural depravity and personal loss. References to the historical Ghost Dances are significant by their absence; the narrator is altogether estranged from history.

In the next chapter, "Sweat Lodge," the ritual alluded to entails a purgation and spiritual or psychological purification from which the individual should emerge with a clear conscience and a renewed sense of self, an assurance of who he is and where he is going. By this time, however, readers will be alert to Larson's method: the values associated with traditional Indian rituals are distorted or outright perverted in the modern white man's world. The first seven pages of the chapter concern his practice in Brookings with an alcoholic and suicidal colleague. When their partnership fails, Larson decides to "move on," this time to a Ph.D. program at the University of North Dakota in Grand Forks, and then on to the University of Arizona. Larson indicates that he has sweated it out in law school, in his law practice, in his marriage: "Leaving the law, my wife, and my family so far behind was an awful chance to take [they divorced in 1987], but it turned out to be the thing I needed to do to finally find my place" (147). Presumably he has also purged himself of the fears that have dogged him, including the fear of loneliness: "It was the first time I had ever been alone in my life, and it was at the same time one of the most difficult things I had ever experienced and the best thing I ever did for myself" (146).

"Sweat Lodge" concludes with a reference to the deaths of Larson's Aunt Sis and Uncle Buck. He feels himself honored to have been asked to deliver Buck's eulogy, and at age 44 he believes that the experience "literally ended my young man days" (149). Larson admits, with some evident pride, to being a grandfather. In the epilogue, which he titles "Nanahax wu, The time of wisdom in Gros Ventre life," he describes himself in the early 1990s, as he was writing this book and teaching at Lewis-Clark State College in northern Idaho. In this chapter Larson takes stock of his life and makes some critical judgments as to his actions: "I allowed myself to become an outsider" (156); "I was, after a while, poorly equipped to cope with challenges that arose" (156); "my success led to a kind of paralysis" (157); "athletic and legal games too easily become just another escape from reality" (157); "When I left Fort Belknap, the features of its familiar landscape no longer centered me, and I became centered upon myself. In doing so, I got lost" (158).

Partly through the act of writing his autobiography, Larson discovers, as many writers of life narrative do, that he "needed to go back" before he could "go forward" and that in embracing his "illegitimacy" he could gain "a kind of freedom" (150). Even his mixed-blood heritage he finds to be valuable: "living in both white and Indian worlds allowed me to pick and choose among those cultures to a certain degree." He insists that he has "always identified more strongly" with his "Fort Belknap background" than with his "white experiences," but that he has "happily adopted a Euro-centric academic lifestyle as well" (159). If Larson's self-analysis were to have ended here, few readers would find it sufficiently self-critical or perceptive. But he clearly sees himself as a work-in-progress: "I feel I have not always fared so well with family relationships"

(159); "there are times when I am tempted to believe I am self-indulgent" (160).

Janet Campbell Hale

At the end of *Catch Colt* Sidner Larson may be said to have attained a significant measure of contentment, but the same cannot be said of Janet Campbell Hale at the end of *Bloodlines: Odyssey of a Native Daughter* (1993). A registered member of the Coeur d'Alene tribe from the Idaho panhandle, Hale introduces herself as one of the "broken-off pieces" of the family of which she once felt a part, and she concludes, "I will remain, as I have long been, estranged from the land I belong to."[20] If Larson's is a life narrative about healing and the coming of self-awareness, Hale's is one of sustained alienation and malaise, and as such, her memoir runs counter to the dominant impulse of the genre toward conciliation. Consider, for example, two closing sentences by other writers:

> We are part of what is sacred. That is our main defense against craziness, our solace, the source of our best politics, and our only chance at paradise [William Kittredge, *Hole in the Sky*].[21]

> Driving the narrow, familiar road back to my parents' ranch, I felt a sense of peace, imagining my house hundreds, thousands of years from now, suspended far below the surface of the shortgrass plains, five stone rooms that hold a part of me, still [Judy Blunt, *Breaking Clean*].[22]

Hale ends her memoir with a negative review of a movie she has just seen in Spokane with her daughter. The movie, *Thunderheart* (1992), concerns a quarter-blood Sioux FBI agent (played by Val Kilmer) sent to the Oglala reservation in Pine Ridge and is based on actual events:

> On the rez, he discovers Who He Is and learns to take pride in His People. After a lot of fancy fights and car chases. It is action-packed and full of clichés like the Indian policeman who's such a good tracker and poetic images having to do with visions of spirits, drums and feathers, shape-shifters and eagles and things [187].

Perhaps it is sufficient to observe here, by way of minimal commentary, that the word "things" has rarely been employed with such a derisive connotation.

Born in Riverside, California, in 1946, Janet Campbell Hale has lived in various locations throughout the inland Northwest, including the Coeur d'Alene reservation in Idaho and the Yakama* reservation town of Wapato, Washington, as well as in San Francisco; Vancouver, British Columbia; and New York City. She currently lives in the reservation town of Plummer, Idaho. By age fifteen she had dropped out of high school, her efforts at finishing having been disrupted by her transient family. In 1964 she married, had a son (Aaron), and was divorced within a year. Struggling to get by on welfare as a single mother, she attended City College of San Francisco in 1968 and procured scholarships and financial aid that helped her earn her B.A. in rhetoric at the University of California at Berkeley in 1974. In 1970 she married Stephen Dinsmore Hale and gave birth to their daughter Jennifer, who has given her two grandchildren and who also lives on the Coeur d'Alene reservation. In 1972 two of Hale's poems appeared in the anthology, *Whispering Wind: Poetry by Young American Indians*, and other poems appeared in such anthologies as *Voices from Wah'Kon-tah* (1974) and *Songs from the Earth on Turtle's Back* (1983). A chapbook of her poems, *Custer Lives in Humboldt County and Other Poems*, was published in 1978. After her graduation from Berkeley, Hale attended law school there and at Gonzaga University in Spokane, Washington, but did not complete a degree. Her first novel, *Owl's Song*, was published by Doubleday in 1974. Hale received her M.A. from the University of California at Davis in 1984, and the next year Random House published her highly acclaimed novel, *The Jailing of Cecilia Capture*. She has occupied several temporary teaching positions in such institutions as Iowa State University, the University of California at Santa Cruz, and the University of Oregon. Following her second divorce, she married Muhammad Ashraf, a Pakistani, and was living in New York City when she completed her memoir in 1993. She has since divorced and returned to Idaho. Her most recent book is a collection of short fiction, *Women on the Run* (1999). A talented painter, one of Hale's oils is featured on the cover of that book. She is currently working on a novel.

Although an occasional concern appeared regarding matters of historical accuracy, reviews of *Bloodlines* were almost unanimously enthusiastic. "A remarkable tale of fortitude," wrote Donna Seaman of what she described as "eight brooding but brave essays."[23] Sherry L. Smith, writing in *Journal of American History*, called it "a depressing book," but also "an important book," and while she pointed out a historical error, she stressed that *Bloodlines* is not primarily history, but "a forceful, intensely personal

*Currently the tribe favors a spelling that replaces the medial [i] with an [a]: Yakama.

statement of an Indian woman's attempt to reconcile a difficult past with an ambiguous future."[24] In his booklet for the Western Writers Series published in 1996, Frederick Hale (no relation) also pointed out historical and factual errors, most of which should have been caught by the editors at Random House, in his largely negative commentary on the book.[25] Julia Watson offers a rebuttal in a perceptive commentary on *Bloodlines*, operating from the premise that Hale "writes against the grain of much contemporary Native American writing" by placing her "stories" (she uses the term "essays" in at least one instance, but she appears to prefer "stories") "paradoxically in a collective cultural past and a world of 'real' experience where that past is lost and irretrievable."[26] *Bloodlines* won an American Book Award in 1994.

Prior to writing *Bloodlines* Hale read not memoirs but essays in the *Best American Essays* series. When she read James Baldwin's *Go Tell It On the Mountain* (1953) at age fourteen, she reports, he "made me able to begin to imagine myself as a writer."[27] But a professor advised Hale that she should stick to novels. The remark "gnawed at me," Hale says, and on a snowy day in May of 1986, when she visited the Bear Paw State Monument in Montana, she sensed that she would write about the experience, and it would not be fiction. Her best friends in her girlhood were descendants of Looking Glass, who is buried at the site, and her own grandmother, a Coeur d'Alene who had been captured by the Nez Perce, accompanied the tribe on their attempt to reach Canada. She survived the battle that occurred there in 1877. "It was like I was closing a circle in visiting Bear Paw," Hale notes. "Never before had I had such a deep emotional understanding of what it means to be an Indian in America" (personal communication).

Bloodlines opens with "Circling Raven: An Introduction," which includes a brief story of the conversion of the Coeur d'Alene tribe to Catholicism in 1740 and observations about her parents and her own early childhood. Hale does not attempt to load her narrative with traditional tribal lore of the Coeur d'Alene, who call themselves Schitsu'umsh ("the ones that were found here"),[28] and whose name in French is usually translated, roughly, as "heart of the awl" (sometimes "heart of steel"). Her father, born in 1892, a full-blood Coeur d'Alene and a veteran of World War I, was of the "first generation to begin to wear shoes instead of moccasins" (xvi). It was a second marriage for both of her parents, and her mother, part Kootenai and "a small part Chippewa," was "light-skinned" and had lived in "white society" until they married in about 1930 (xvi). Her first husband abused Hale's mother and although a mixed-blood herself, she suffered from discrimination because her second husband was Indian. She was in her forties by the time she had Janet in 1946. Her three older sisters (they range from ten to fourteen years her senior) told Janet that her father had been a mean drunkard, but he had reformed by the time she came to know him. Although the violence stopped years before Janet was born, however, her mother never fully forgave him and he returned to his drinking, so Janet grew up in a badly ruptured family haunted by her mother's and three sisters' memories of being abused and by their resentment of her as the youngest sibling partly because she had not shared in their suffering.

The introductory essay features a family photograph taken in Tijuana, Mexico, in 1946, when Janet was an infant, and a dream. The photo shows a happy family of six seated at a photographer's set that features a covered wagon with a little burro hitched to it. Her mother looks "Irish-pretty" (xxix) and her father, wearing a foolish sombrero inscribed "Just Married," is "handsome in a rugged sort of way" (xxx) and appears younger than his age. In her dream, which she says occurred in 1987, she has stepped on a small turtle (her family is the last of the Turtle clan), and she fears she has killed it, but she comes back to the shore of the lake and discovers that the turtle is not only alive, but also is much larger: "The dream was saying that our family only appeared to be dead, stepped on, broken into a million pieces" (xxxi), while in fact it remained whole and strong. But Hale rejects the premise of the dream as only "an expression of my longing," just as she rejects the photographic image of what appeared to be an idyllic family.

While she was writing *Bloodlines* Hale fell ill and spent several weeks in the hospital. During that time some students from Western Washington University interviewed her about "the autobiographical aspects" of her novel, *The Jailing of Cecilia Capture*. Although she submits that she created Cecilia Capture with some similarities to herself (her own age, her residence in California, her two children), Hale considers the character to be only "superficially" kindred. Because she did not feel well enough to be interviewed, Hale wrote the essay "Autobiography in Fiction" for the students. In the often humorous metafiction that ensues, Hale imagines herself writing a "More or Less Autobiographical Story" in which "It won't matter what I say because most people want to believe that it is, indeed, the author's own life that is displayed in such naked, intimate detail for public viewing" (5). The following passage from the essay shows Hale having fun, partly at the expense of critics and scholars who have read her novel from a constricted, autobiographical perspective:

> Either I will make no mention of her race or she is just a white-looking Indian. I don't think race will be an issue ... or maybe it will. Two marriages. One abortion. No children [11].

Stories, Hale insists, are not "written as a series of intellectual decisions"; they are "an intuitive sort of thing": "fiction comes from the deeper, darker places in the writer's soul, the same places that dreams come from" (11).

"Autobiography in Fiction" is followed by a three-page essay entitled "My Half Brother's Mother." This "creative nonfiction," in every sense of the term, involves an imaginative reconstruction of events that occurred more than twenty years before Hale's birth. Around 1920 her father discovered his first wife as she was preparing to elope with her lover, and he shot and killed the man, for which he had to serve a year in prison. The mother subsequently contracted tuberculosis and returned to the reservation, where she died. Hale's half-brother shows up at his (and her) father's funeral in 1969, and again she draws on a photograph, this time of the boy when he was about two years old with his young mother, and she wonders whether he has any memory of that time. The two short paragraphs with which the essay ends are particularly striking:

> We buried my father in his family plot, his grave near the grave of his first wife.
> My mother, who outlived my father by nearly twenty years, always said she preferred to be buried elsewhere. She was [22].

Hale's parents reconciled after their separation, but as these paragraphs attest, that reconciliation did not fully succeed.

The quick essay described above, a sort of "sudden nonfiction," is followed by "Daughter of Winter," the longest essay in the book, running more than sixty pages, and also the one that Hale describes as "the most difficult piece to write." It concerns her relationship with her mother, "whom I loved, whose approval I always wanted but never had, who endured a great deal of pain and suffering in her own life" (xxii). She divides the essay into six sections with a prologue in italics and a labeled epilogue. It opens in Wapato, Washington, on the Yakama reservation with Hale remembering her twelve-year-old self in about 1958 with her mother living in an unheated house and being hungry. In the first section of the essay Hale imagines a video of her earlier years, ages four to ten, "on the run," her mother tells her, "from Dad and his drinkin'" (27) through Idaho, Washington, and Oregon. By the time she is seven, her older sisters have moved out, but her mother often comes back to live with one of them. She records several events in the essay in snapshot fashion. At a Catholic school she is "manhandled by sadistic nuns" (32) and at home her mother swears at her, but when she objects to the swearing, her mother packs her suitcase and sends her away until she comes back and apologizes. Another writer might have retold this story for comic effect: Hale does not. Hale reports having attended 21 schools in three states before dropping out after eighth grade (she did manage several months in the tenth grade later on).

After devoting two sections of the essay to her wanderings throughout the inland Northwest and Portland as a teenager suffering from her mother's psychological and verbal abuse, Hale leaps ahead to 1983, when she was living in Vancouver, British Columbia, one of her favorite places. By then her second marriage had ended, and she thought she might find acceptance by the Indian community in Canada, but she could not bring herself to renounce her U.S. citizenship, so she taught briefly at Northwest Indian College on the Lummi Reservation in Bellingham, Washington, before moving to Seattle in 1985 for a one-year appointment as Distinguished Visiting Writer at the University of Washington. But she does not present herself as "distinguished" at all: "[I]n my soul's darkest corner I am ever the motherless child, the psychologically tortured girl I used to be, the scapegoat of my troubled, troubled family" (55). She senses something "very seriously wrong, intrinsically wrong" with herself. In the most dramatic part of the essay, she drives to Tacoma to visit her sick mother, emaciated, suffering from lupus and other ailments. Ironically, the old woman recalls how she herself was mistreated, but Hale asserts flatly, her mother was "a master, an absolute master, of verbal abuse" (61). Near the end of the fifth section Hale recounts a recurring dream in which she sees herself as a forty-year-old lying in bed with her aged mother, trying to feel secure when her father appears and her parents drive away, refusing to take her with them.

The sixth section of the essay concerns her mother's last days in 1987 when, in her delirium, she thinks Janet has come home from California as a battered wife at age eighteen. In fact, Janet did not return home as promised then, but stuck it out in San Francisco. In her mother's delirium, however, Janet returns and is welcomed. Perhaps this is as close as Hale can come to portraying her mother as a sympathetic person. She recalls that her mother took care of her when she was sick, and she was frequently ill as a child. But although Hale offers some positive elements to the portrait, she still sees herself as "my mother's sacrifice" (74). When her mother dies, Janet, living in Los Angeles, sends her daughter to the funeral (readers may recall a moment in the second section of the essay when her mother screamed at Janet and insisted she promise not to attend her funeral). "In the end," Hale writes, "there are no resolutions. Only an end" (86). In effect, she offers no reconciliation.

Although we observe Janet Campbell Hale from childhood into her forties in "Daughter of Winter," she is nineteen years old and living in a small apartment on Haight Street in San Francisco in the summer of 1965 in the next essay, "Transitions." This sort of chronological disruption or disarrangement has become a staple of the postmodern personal essay. The struggling welfare mother of a one-year-old, Hale is in hiding from her abusive white husband, ironically a psychiatric social worker. This replicates a pattern of behavior that mimics her mother's, whose white husband also abused her. Hale writes flatly, "I have no fond memories of my first brief marriage to a white man who clearly looked down on me" (93). "Transitions," might be described as an essay about survival, the major theme of the book.

Later in the essay Hale visits the reservation in Idaho with her father, and for the first time she thinks seriously of her "ancestral roots," of the possibilities of her own "bloodline continuing down through the ages" (103). Hale records the memory with a snapshot of her father at age seventy-five, still looking healthy and handsome. Her parents surprise her with presents to help her in her first year of college: a hundred dollars and a typewriter. The tribe encourages her indirectly, not by providing scholarship money or a loan, but by approving her application and "never saying they wouldn't" send money (105). The Coeur d'Alene Casino, developed about 1992, has now made the tribe quite prosperous, and it is reputedly capable of providing substantial college scholarship aid to all enrolled members. The name for their new, highly regarded golf course draws on the founding legend of the tribe, Circling Raven.

The title of the essay "The Only Good Indian" refers to the quote usually credited to General Philip Sheridan, "The only good Indians I ever saw were dead" (January 1869).[29] Hale looks back to her twice great grandfather on her mother's side, Dr. John P. McLoughlin, an early factor for the Hudson's Bay Company who founded Oregon City, south of Portland. She prefaces her chapter with a viciously racist passage from

H. H. Bancroft's 1884 history of Oregon deploring the "*degenerate posterity*" that came of McLoughlin's marriage to a Chippewa woman (109). Hale then traces the genealogy and racism within her own family, focusing on her Gram Sullivan's anger at her mother for marrying an Indian, and at Janet herself as the progeny of that union. In effect, Hale relates the familial dysfunction (the cycle of hatred and anger) to race. The rest of Janet's mother's siblings married whites, and her mother, who looked white, "identified very strongly with her Irishness" (120), but Hale suggests that her mother "always felt a strong Indian undercurrent in herself" (122). Hale asks rhetorically whether her grandmother ever hated her "Indianness," and then reflects upon when, at age six or seven, she herself did: in school at Omak, Washington, when other children would not hold her hand during games. She responded by going home and soaking her "hateful brown hands" in bleach (140). Reflecting on her Gram's apparent hatred of her, Hale asks, rhetorically again, in the final sentence of the essay, "Who did I remind Gram of if not herself?" (140).

Hale was living in Seattle in 1986 when Salish-Kootenay Community College in western Montana invited her to undertake an eight-day speaking tour that led to her writing of the climactic essay of the book, "Return to Bear Paw." It was her first visit to the state, and she found herself unprepared for the May snowfall, but she was eager to visit the site where her Coeur d'Alene paternal grandmother, taken captive by the Nez Perce at age fifteen or sixteen, witnessed and survived the combat in the snow. Ironically, the ancestor that Hale seems most to admire died five years before she was born, but in the family photograph she sees an old woman "dressed Indian style" who only appears fragile: "She was strong and tough, full of energy and industry, she kept busy" (149). Her grandmother never learned English, and Hale envies her older sisters' knowledge of the tribal language (Salish). Suffering from illness and not dressed for the cold, Hale does not join her driver when he kneels in the snow at the communal graves, but she feels "with those people" and "part of them":

> I felt the presence of my grandmother there as though two parts of her met each other that day: the ghost of the girl she was in 1877 (and that part will remain forever in that place) and the part of her that lives on in me, in inherited memories of her, in my blood and in my spirit [158].

In effect, Hale reveals that this epiphany prompted her to recognize her own bloodlines and gave rise to the memoir.

In the final essay, "Dust to Dust," Hale looks back not only to the conventional phrase associated with burials, but also to the origins of the family name "Campbell," which she has been told derives from Cole-mannée, which translates as "dust." The essays "The Only Good Indian" and "Return to Bear Paw" celebrate her Indian identity, repudiating the defensive racism and ethnic angst of both her mother and her maternal grandmother. "Dust to Dust," however, offers no genuine healing, no clear answers or resolution. Julia Watson comments on the "narrative crisis" Janet Campbell Hale faces in her memoir as "the dilemma of 'telling' as 'telling on'" (113). Hale cannot tell her story without informing on her parents, but of course this is often the case in memoir. Beyond that, however, Watson argues that a certain paradox cannot be avoided: "To celebrate her Indian identification she must also castigate it" (113).

This memoir is not, as Frederick Hale insists, simply an "exercise in emotional catharsis" (47). We read *Bloodlines* with the sort of trepidation that we read about any family tragedy or calamity. We perceive the high costs of surrendering to feelings of resentment and anger, and we see the necessity of personal agency and responsibility. Certainly *Bloodlines* has therapeutic value, but not just for its writer. As Watson observes, "Only her text can be a site for self-validation, with the reader as a sympathetic audience to coexperience the abuse and validate her critique of its justice" (125). This memoir imposes a considerable burden on the reader as collaborator.

Julia Watson detects three modes or voices in *Bloodlines*: "autobiographical essays primarily on writing and subjectivity where the voice of the present-time narrator predominates ['Circling Raven: An Introduction,' 'Autobiography in Fiction,' 'Transitions']; an extended trauma narrative of Hale's relationship with her mother ['Daughter of Winter']; and three essays on historical and cultural contours of the bloodline ['My Half Brother's Mother,' 'The Only Good Indian,' 'Return to Bear Paw']" (120). Watson does not ascribe the essays, so I have made my own estimates here. The concluding piece, "Dust to Dust," would fall into the first category. The essay opens on a summer day in 1976 with Janet and her two children swimming at Lake Coeur d'Alene. Her twelve-year-old son observes that "Nothing lasts forever" (163), and in fact, by the end of the page it is May of 1992, Hale is living in New York with her third husband, her son lives in California and has fallen out of touch with her, and her daughter attends school in southern Idaho. But most of the essay has to do with Hale's visit with her daughter to the reservation in Idaho: "I stitched together a happy childhood for myself. [...] It had order. It had continuity. And it was not a lie" (169). Of course as readers we know that her story of belonging to a certain place and having a family that valued her is contrived to appeal to her daughter.

In this essay Hale repeats certain passages from the memoir, but I suspect her redundancies are intentional, for they underscore the cyclical or relapsing nature of the narrative. The redundancies bring us back, and they work the way repetition or a refrain works in poetry, for emphasis and rhetorical effect: that day of her father's birth in 1892 when his mother was in the mountains picking huckleberries; the prophecy of the three black ravens and the coming of the three Jesuit missionaries; how her father was forced to speak English, wear shoes, and have his hair cut. Recalling her father's funeral on a cold March day in 1969, Hale reflects on how she had to borrow her niece's coat, but was chastised for draping it on the back of a chair and how no chair was placed for her at the graveside that morning. She laments, "I can never live here, where I came from" (185).

Of course one of the risks of writing memoirs when one is forty-five instead of sixty-five, or perhaps seventy-five, is that one cannot be sure where one will end up. As it happens, Janet Campbell Hale has returned to the reservation and has lived now for several years on tribal land: "When I wrote *Bloodlines* I lived in New York City, was happily married, had a career. I could not imagine I'd ever return to the Coeur d'Alene Reservation, but I have, and, from the looks of things, I'll probably stay here" (personal communication). She has now acquired some sense of her "place" in her own "tribal community," but it would not be accurate to say she feels welcome there, or that she feels contented. Hale has lived much of her life in cities and has enjoyed being part of "an intertribal urban community" (186). Plummer, the largest town on the reservation, numbers under 700 people, and the nearest city is Coeur d'Alene (about 35,000), some 45 miles north. Lacking good literary conversation, Hale feels isolated, even with her daughter and grandchildren living nearby, and she talks sometimes of relocating to New Orleans, or maybe to Vancouver, British Columbia.

The confessional life narrative involves considerable risks, as Kim Barnes's *Hungry for the World* and William Kittredge's *Hole in the Sky* will attest, but memoir or autobiography that takes the form of the complaint takes an even greater risk. In the confessional life narrative the narrator-protagonist makes himself or herself look bad — naïve, self-righteous, vain, even cruel. The writer may depict the errors, or even the downright meanness, of others, but he or she usually intends to take responsibility for the mess his or her life is or was and to express regret. Most readers respond very well to that. We trust those writers who candidly admit their own shortcomings, and we are consequently all the more willing to accept their judgments on others who appear in their life narratives. Perhaps we rather like to be in the godlike role of forgiving the sinner. But in the complaint life narrative the narrator-protagonist perceives herself or himself as the victim, presumably innocent and undeserving of what she or he has suffered. We do not tend to trust that persona so readily, but are inclined to ask what he did to "deserve" that mistreatment, or why she is "whining." As readers of complaint memoir or autobiography we might feel uncomfortable, suspicious that we are being asked to pity or feel sorry for the narrator-protagonist. What *is* requested of us in our collaboration, of course, is understanding and compassion.

Comparison of Sidner J. Larson and Janet Campbell Hale

The life narratives of Sidner J. Larson and Janet Campbell Hale, both mixed-blood (although the "quantum" differs), resemble each other in several ways. Both are narratives of transience and personal malaise; both involve familial dysfunction; both concern estrangement, albeit in different ways, from their tribal origins. Both writers overcame challenges and went on to graduate from college and earn graduate degrees. But if Tolstoy is correct in his famous opening sentence of *Anna Karenina*, that "Happy families are all alike; every unhappy family is unhappy in its own way,"[30] then a comparison of the two should focus on their divergence. For some readers the salient feature might simply come down to the fact that Larson is male, and even though he was also in his late teens when he married and fathered a child, he was not left a single parent after one year, did not suffer spousal abuse, and apparently did not live in poverty. Larson obviously struggled because his father deserted his mother, and his autobiography reveals a distance in his relationship with his mother that never appears to have been resolved, but he developed surrogate mothers in the guise of his maternal grandmother and aunt. Moreover, while he appears to have felt the tension between the white world of Shelby and the Indian world of the ranch, his boyhood years fell into a rhythm of sorts, a predictability that Hale could never count on. While Hale dropped out of school after attending twenty-one schools through her eighth grade year, Larson, despite some harsh memories and racist incidents, graduated from high school with honors in Shelby, where he started in first grade, and he succeeded in athletics.

In fact, in many ways Larson's qualifies as a "success autobiography," while Hale's, despite her considerable achievements as a writer, does not. Julia Watson's description of *Bloodlines* as, at least in part, a "trauma narrative" distinguishes it from Larson's *Catch Colt*. Both writers have undergone multiple marriages and divorces, but Hale has found considerably less financial security than has Larson, who has been successful as an academic. I should perhaps repeat that when Hale wrote her memoir she felt reasonably confident and secure in her future. Larson portrays himself as largely in control of the circumstances of his life and mostly responsible for his shortcomings. He muffs the play in football. He drinks too much and womanizes. He makes the "hard decision" to break up his marriage. Some might read him as a "villain." But as a character he is ultimately the "hero." He breaks all the conference sprint records. He clobbers the punk in the bar. He earns a law degree and a doctorate to boot. He prevails.

Hale portrays herself as neither villain nor heroine. We are made aware of some of her achievements (a novel here, high score on the SAT there; a fellowship here, a speaking engagement or a temporary teaching position there), but we never are prompted to think she has arrived. It would not be altogether accurate to say, however, that Janet Campbell Hale is simply "the victim" of her life story. After all, she does pull herself out of severe poverty, very much by her own bootstraps, and she exposes those who tormented her and her people (her mother and sisters, various white racists) for what they are, in effect exacting what Julia Watson calls "a kind of literary revenge" (124).

In most respects both *Catch Colt* and *Bloodlines* qualify as autobiographies rather than memoirs, inasmuch as both lead the reader from the writer's birth through early childhood to the present time of the writing, although the route is not easily chronological in either book. Neither writer shifts the focus from himself or herself for long. That is, neither writer concentrates primarily on other persons or "characters," as do Edmund Gosse in *Father and Son* (1907) or Geoffrey Wolff in *The Duke of Deception* (1979), where they focus on their fathers. Nor do they shift their attention to various other family members, as do Ivan Doig, Teresa Jordan, and Mary Clearman Blew. Considered as ethnic autobiographies, particularly from the perspective of the critical context that has developed over the past twenty years for the examination of Native-American life narrative, both *Catch Colt* and *Bloodlines* defy expectation. Neither writer waxes poetic or spiritual about nature, and while Larson makes some effort to celebrate communal and tribal (as opposed to individualistic) values, neither writer can be said to feel fully connected with their tribal community and its cultural legacy or with their native place.

Ironically, while Sidner Larson writes affirmatively about the Gros Ventre reservation at Fort Belknap, he has never been a permanent resident there, nor is he an enrolled member of the tribe. Janet Campbell Hale has lived on the Coeur d'Alene reservation in northern Idaho for several years now and is an enrolled member of the tribe, but she remains dissatisfied and estranged. In various ways, both of these life narratives reflect the potential cost to Native Americans of their cultural identity and of their centeredness in the world when they enter the Euro-American mainstream.

Chapter Seven

The Ecomemoirs of William Kittredge and Terry Tempest Williams

Sidonie Smith and Julia Watson propose the term "ecobiography" for life narratives that "interweave the story of the protagonist with the story of the fortunes, conditions, geography, and ecology of a region, and reflect on their connection (and perhaps its failure) as a significant feature of the writing."[1] For my purposes a neologism like "ecomemoir" may be more apt. In this hybrid of autobiography three features usually vie for the reader's attention: details of the speaker's life story, scientific data (from agrology to zoology), and political pronouncements. One might hypothesize that the best ecomemoirs maintain some equilibrium among the three aspects, but perfect balance would be impossible to sustain. Moreover, if the text should shift strongly in the direction of either science or politics, it would no longer qualify, as I see it, as ecomemoir. Despite its personable tone, for example, Aldo Leopold's classic *A Sand County Almanac and Sketches Here and There* (1949) would qualify only loosely as ecomemoir, as does Anne Zwinger's personally infused nature writings, which I have mentioned in my first chapter. The Pulitzer Prize–winning meditations of Annie Dillard's *Pilgrim at Tinker Creek* (1974), however, would qualify fully. Neither Leopold nor Zwinger invest enough in the self, in self-probing or self-revelation, as I see it, to be attempting ecologically focused memoir: the self is there, but it remains rigorously subordinated to the environment.

The origins of ecomemoir in the northern Rockies could be said to go back to the Lewis and Clark journals or to such texts as John Wesley

Powell's journals of his 1869 expedition on the Colorado River, first published in 1874. Such writings, however, clearly subordinated the personal and political elements to the scientific. A more recent analogue would be *Desert Solitaire* (1968), set in southeastern Utah, in which Edward Abbey adheres to the balance among the three key aspects of ecomemoir fairly closely. One might go so far as to argue that the proper balance should create a tension of sorts for readers, who might find themselves wondering whether they are engaged most by the environmental politics, the science, or the personality of the narrator. Generally, academicians might regard the science in such memoirs as "soft," what used to be called "natural history," and the writers might more properly be called "naturalists" than "botanists" or "geologists."

In his introduction Abbey asserts "there is a kind of poetry, even a kind of truth, in simple fact,"[2] and many "hard" scientists would probably agree. No hard core botanist, however, would likely get a combo poetry-science sentence like the following published in an issue of the *Journal of Experimental Botany* or *New Phytologist*: "Loveliest of all, however, gay and sweet as a pretty girl, with a fragrance like that of orange blossoms, is the cliffrose, *Cowania stansburiana*, also known — by the anesthetic — as buckbrush or quinine bush" (27). *Desert Solitaire* tells a personal story about a summer in the late 1950s Abbey spent as a seasonal park ranger in the Arches National Monument. "Down the River," the longest chapter at nearly sixty pages, concerns the Colorado River that Powell wrote of a century earlier, before the Glen Canyon Dam was built, creating the irony of a lake named after Powell. Abbey writes with considerable vitriol:

> This reservoir of stagnant water will not irrigate a single square foot of land or supply water for a single village; its only justification is the generation of cash through electricity for the indirect subsidy of various real estate speculators, cottongrowers and sugarbeet magnates in Arizona, Utah and Colorado [188].

The foregoing offers perhaps a sufficient taste of Abbey's political sentiments, which are thoroughly familiar to those who have read his novels, the most renowned and notorious of which is *The Monkey Wrench Gang* (1975).

In chapters like "Polemic: Industrial Tourism and the National Parks" Abbey lines out what he believes are "constructive, practical, sensible proposals for the salvation of both parks and people" (65), beginning with the advice that cars be banished from national parks and that no new roads be built in them (64). Abbey's appeals throughout the book for the cause of wilderness: "No, wilderness is not a luxury but a necessity of the human spirit, and as vital to our lives as water and good bread" (211). He leavens his political bread with passages of vivid descriptive prose like the following:

> The flowers that graced the red dunes in April and May have withered now, all gone to seed except for a few drooping sunflowers. The cliffrose has faded, the yucca stalks have bloomed, blown, died, cracked and dried, the seedpods now only empty husks. Under the daily sweep of the parching May winds almost everything that was green has been turned to soft, sere tones of saffron and auburn [166].

But Abbey's ecomemoir also involves personal encounters and stories, like that of the doomed uranium prospector Albert Husk and his son, Abbey's own flings at riding the range as a pro tem cowboy, and his involvement in a search for a missing man in the desert, "The Dead Man at Grandview Point." By the end of the book, what we have learned about the wildlife, plant forms, and geology of southeastern Utah is less likely to stay with us than a powerful statement of environmental politics and a sharply etched image of Abbey's personality.

More recently the prolific writer of both fiction and nonfiction, Rick Bass, has produced at least half a dozen books that often verge on ecomemoir from his vantage point in the Yaak Valley that borders northwestern Montana and Idaho. Educated as a petroleum geologist at Utah State University, the Texas native moved to Idaho from Mississippi in 1987 with his artist wife Elizabeth. His books of nonfiction include *The Ninemile Wolves* (1992), *The Last Grizzlies: A Search for Survivors in the Wilderness of Colorado* (1997), and an anthology entitled *The Roadless Yaak: Reflections and Observations about One of Our Last Great Wild Places* (2003). His books of short fiction, including *Platte River* (1994) and *The Lives of Rocks* (2006), feature characters living "in nature," often in the wilderness. Bass comes closest to the ecomemoir with *Winter: Notes from Montana* (1991), which recounts his and his wife's first winter (1987–1988) in the Yaak Valley through a series of journal entries.

Abbey's spirit and vision directly inform Colorado naturalist and outdoor writer David Petersen's *The Nearby Faraway* (1997), a collection of personal essays including such titles as "A Hunter's Heart," "Where Phantoms Come to Brood and Mourn: A Tribute to Edward Paul Abbey:

1927–1989," "Yellowstone Death Watch," and "Good Times in the Owyhee Badlands." These titles indicate the nature of the contents. Petersen hunts (elk, for example) in order to acknowledge his "evolutionary roots, countless millennia deep, as a predatory omnivore" and for many other reasons: "To participate actively in the grand play of nature. [...] To learn the lessons, about nature and myself, that only hunting can teach. To accept personal responsibility for at least some of the deaths that nourish my life" (79). Coincidentally, Petersen's book on the possible survival of the grizzly in Colorado, *Ghost Grizzlies: Does the Great Bear Still Haunt Colorado* (1998), appeared just one year after Bass's *The Last Grizzlies*. Petersen's most recent book of nonfiction, *On the Wild Edge: In Search of a Natural Life* (2005), which deals with his and his wife's life in a remote cabin in the Colorado Rockies, also embodies the characteristics of the ecomemoir.

A similar hunting ethic to Petersen's is implicit in Montana writer Pete Fromm's *Indian Creek Chronicles* (1993), set in the Selway-Bitterroot wilderness of the Idaho panhandle. In this ecomemoir the twenty-year-old Fromm, envisioning life as a mountain man, takes a break from his studies in wildlife biology at the University of Montana to tend to a salmon hatchery. Unlike Petersen's or Abbey's books, *Indian Creek Chronicles* is a short, cohesive narrative laced with humor and sustaining something of a plot or narrative arc, a term sometimes used to describe the plotlike shape that governs many life narratives. Although Fromm's job will likely appeal to most environmentalists, his enthusiasm for pot-shooting grouse, trapping (he stops after taking a raccoon), and bagging a moose, not to mention his camaraderie with elk and cougar hunters, would alienate the affections of those who oppose hunting.

Outdoorsmen like Petersen and Fromm can wax as lyrical about nature as a naturalist like Ann Zwinger, but an implicit line of demarcation separates the environmental camps. Idaho writer John Rember's memoir *Traplines* (2003) concerns memories of hunting, fishing, and trapping (his father was a fishing and hunting guide) along with an environmental message, for even more than most anglers, hunters know the necessity for maintaining wilderness. At age 39 Rember resumes hunting big game: "I consciously accepted my father's ethic that you ought to kill the meat you eat and began killing deer and elk again."[3] In *The Solace of Open Spaces* (1985), however, Wyoming writer Gretel Ehrlich depicts the elk as part of the scenery: "Already, the elk have started moving out of the mountains toward sheltered feed-grounds. Their great antlers will soon fall off like chandeliers shaken from ballroom ceilings."[4]

William Kittredge's *Hole in the Sky* (1992), one of the most renowned ecomemoirs to come out of the West in recent years, includes apologetic reflections on the excesses of fishing and hunting in which he was involved during his boyhood and young manhood. Reflecting on how he and his relatives would gather hellgrammites for bait, he refers to "our main business of the outdoor day, which was killing fish."[5] In one of the more memorable episodes in his book a teenaged Kittredge joins his buddies in slaughtering jackrabbits, shooting them from a jeep with his .22, "thrilled by the sound of it and my ability to send jackrabbits twitching and dying into the dust" (97). He also laments the overkilling of waterfowl near his family's ranch in southeastern Oregon, describing his father as "the crown prince of shotgunning" for killing 123 ducks for the Elks Club feed (173). By way of contrast, one of the most memorable moments in Terry Tempest Williams's *Refuge* (1991), which Smith and Watson cite as an example of "ecobiography," occurs early in the book, when she flips off a couple of good-old-boys at a ruined nesting site of the burrowing owls near Great Salt Lake.[6]

What connects all of these ecomemoirists, from Leopold and Abbey to Fromm and Bass, is a conviction that, as Williams phrases it in an aphorism, "Wilderness courts our souls" (148). Or, as she elaborates later in her book: "A blank spot on the map is an invitation to encounter the natural world, where one's character will be shaped by the landscape. To enter wilderness is to court risk, and risk favors the senses, enabling one to live well" (244).

William Kittredge

Although *Hole in the Sky* takes place largely in southeastern Oregon, where his family ran a huge ranch and agribusiness going back three generations, Kittredge ends his memoir in Missoula, where he began teaching at the University of Montana in the fall of 1969, and his perspective in the memoir and in his other fiction and nonfiction is clearly from the northern Rockies. Moreover, the ecology of southeastern Oregon, unlike that of the Willamette Valley, for example, has much in common with that of the northern Rockies. By the time his memoir appeared, Kittredge had developed a reputation as a writer of short stories, mostly set in Montana, several of which were collected in *We Are Not in This Together* (1984). *The Best Short Stories of William Kittredge* appeared in 2003; his novel, *The Willow Field*, was published in 2006. He had already coauthored with his University of Montana colleague Steven M. Krauzer under the pseudonym Owen Rountree a series of genre Westerns, and more important, he had published his first volume of nonfiction, *Owning It All* (1987), a collection of essays in which he lays out what have become his predominant themes and gives voice to a mantra repeated with some variations in several of his books:

> We baited the coyotes with 1080, and rodents destroyed our alfalfa; we sprayed weeds and insects with 2-4-D Ethyl and Malathion, and Parathion for clover mite, and we shortened our own lives. [...] We had reinvented our valley according to the most persuasive ideal given us by our culture, and we ended with a landscape organized like a machine for growing crops and fattening cattle, a machine that creaked a little louder each year, a dreamland gone wrong.[7]

At the heart of this misusage of land lurks what Kittredge calls "a pastoral story of agricultural ownership" that is at heart "a racist, sexist, imperialist mythology of conquest; a rationale for violence — against other people and against nature" (63).

In *Hole in the Sky*, among other things, Kittredge accepts responsibility for his own part in that violence. Like Sidner Larson in *Catch Colt*, Kittredge writes a confession memoir, but it is also a kind of ecomemoir. In an interview conducted while he was writing the book, Kittredge described it as "a chronological, autobiographical book, but it ends up being an ecological book; it's a story about taking care of ourselves and taking care of the world and how to conduct ourselves in what I conceive to be proper ways."[8] He begins his narrative in the spring of 1938 when, about to turn six years old, he was recovering from polio. Reflecting on the "luminous" world of his childhood, he argues in his introductory essay that we are all looking for "a set of stories to inhabit" that will help explain the world and our place in it and that we are all seeking "a place to care about" (10). Kittredge draws the title of the book from a Tsimshian house pole; the hole cut through the base of the pole functioned as a "doorway to heaven." But Kittredge also cautions that the "simple emptiness" may be taken as "a modernist idea of God" (10), and in that sense of the term he looks back to a "breakdown" he suffered in April of 1961, after he had finished a tour of duty in the U.S. Air Force and returned to the family ranch as farming boss. He offers a few details of this personal crisis about 170 pages later, a vague sense of the meaninglessness of the world that he fights off by withdrawing into himself and distancing himself from others: "In the theory of life I was closing in on, selfishness was pure and necessary. It became an excuse for whatever you wanted to do" (189).

In the opening essay from *Owning It All* Kittredge concludes that "Stories are valuable precisely to the degree that they are for the moment useful in our ongoing task of finding coherency in the world" (19). At the end of his prefatory chapter to *Hole in the Sky* he asserts, "This is meant to be a book that is useful" (11). Kittredge has been a leader in the assault on the popular Western myth of the rugged (male) individualist and loner who tames or civilizes the savages, eradicates the outlaws, establishes law and order (often with gun in hand), and conquers the rugged land. In such books as *Who Owns the West?* (1996), *Taking Care: Thoughts on Storytelling and Belief* (1999), and *The Nature of Generosity* (2000) he moves toward an ethical stance aimed at the arrogance that comes of land ownership, and he celebrates stewardship, community, social responsibility, and kindness toward others and toward the environment. In effect, he has set himself up as something of a moralist, and his memoir plays a central role in this regard because in it he analyzes, perhaps even deconstructs, himself. Such self-scrutiny and self-culpation (to coin a term) may be expected by a modern readership. We have no confident, self-assured Cato the Moralist in the United States today and one may dispute whether we have ever had one since the likes of Ralph Waldo Emerson. Modern American readers tend to distrust the easy self-assurance of the aphorism. As I have noted in my booklet on Kittredge written for the Western Writers Series, he is capable of a remarkable "self-reflexivity" whereby he is not only self-critical, but also capable of being "critical of himself for being critical of himself."[9] Partly because of this stance Kittredge acquires considerable credibility from most readers.

Hole in the Sky comprises nine essays and two interludes presented in chronological order. Kittredge uses a sort of freely associative montage technique, telling his stories in patches set apart by breaks in the text, an approach that seems to typify contemporary creative nonfiction. "The Promise of Generations," for example, is built of fourteen such patches running from slightly under a page to six pages. The chapter opens in 1940, when eight-year-old Kittredge had begun to work on the ranch under his grandfather's supervision, and it covers a wide range of events, usually presented as miniature stories, running through 1949. During those years he was being trained as a horseman, particularly during the summers, but he proves to be an uneasy buckaroo. He finds himself bored and given to "goldbricking" (77). As a boy in a world of horses, Kittredge appears to be a sort of polar opposite to Mark Spragg as he presents himself in *Where Rivers Change Direction*. Kittredge devotes much of the chapter to small portraits of and tributes to the men who worked for his father and grandfather, but he is typically unwilling to make himself look good. When, just after VJ Day, a hand named Cecil Dixon commends him, Kittredge writes, "You, he was saying, have earned your own way. Not that I had actually. Cecil was drunk and I was still the shit-for-brains kid whose grandfather owned the MC" (88). In this chapter Kittredge recounts a painful tale of hunting jackrabbits, after which he pronounces a hard judgment on himself: "I felt like an asshole, and pitied myself. [...] I still feel the excitement of those hapless boys. We didn't know anything" (97).

During the 1940s the family ranch prospered and his father was making "a lot of money farming grain"; however, his father was also becoming estranged from William's grandfather and namesake, whom he describes earlier as "the most powerful figure in my life" (15) but also as a man who "came to feel he didn't have to discuss anything with anybody" (27). As they bought increasingly sophisticated equipment, pumped the lakes dry, and created diversion canals for irrigation, Kittredge sees his family as "reinventing the land and the water-flow patterns of the valley on a model copied from industry, and irrevocably altering the ecology of everything, including our own lives; moving into the monied technology which is agribusiness" (91). In an earlier chapter he writes, "We worked hard to be analytic and coldhearted. The places around us were not alive with history but they could be useful. It was another way for the world to be dead" (27). Kittredge describes the destructive nature of the family business as a function of his grandfather's "imperious and heedless" personality: "Accumulation was my grandfather's game. [...] He was not so much cruel as indifferent to purposes other than his own" (39). The point, Kittredge stresses, is "abundance, an overwhelming property thronging with natural life, and what my family did with it" (41). His father, who was educated as an engineer, Kittredge presents as "a more generous kind of animal" (51) who made the mistake of turning away from his goal of studying law and joining Grandfather William in the family business. Of himself and his siblings he writes regretfully, "We have lived reckless and haphazard lives" (56).

The dysfunction Kittredge illustrates differs considerably from that of Janet Campbell Hale's family, which was rooted in poverty and transience. The Kittredge family's dysfunction is rooted in prosperity and place. But in both cases the inability or unwillingness to communicate creates distance, resentment, and eventual dissolution. One form of that dissolution appears to be divorce: Kittredge's parents divorce, and William records the failure of his two marriages in this memoir. In the longest chapter, "The Beautiful House," located at the center of the book, Kittredge recounts his college days at Oregon State University, where he received a B.S. in general agriculture in 1954; his marriage in 1951 at age nineteen; and his four years in the air force.

In 1958 his grandfather died, and at that point Kittredge describes himself as making "a mistake that cost me a decade" (150) by returning to the family business as farming boss. Soon, "bursting with self-importance" (160), the twenty-six-year-old Kittredge finds himself coldheartedly firing several hired hands and following his father's alcoholic pace (it is as much a hectic rhythm as it is a pathway). The pathetic workers named in this chapter, "Who Owns the West?" balance those whom he praises in "The Promise of Generations." Confronted with the death of one old worker, he comments flatly, "I learned to look away" (167). At the end of the chapter Kittredge tells of dancing with a crop duster's wife, who scolds him for his indifference to others in terms he can now conceptualize, although he could not at the time: "Failures of sympathy, she was saying, if I read her correctly, originate in failures of the imagination, which is a betrayal of self" (175).

In "Sleeping Alone" Kittredge tells of his breakdown in April of 1961 and of his increasing bouts of drinking and infidelity. In "Selling Out" his wife and two children leave him as his cousin Jack makes plans to sell the ranch. At the age of 35, as he puts it, his "boyhood" was finally "finished" (206). His confession of late maturation is similar to Sidner Larson's and recalls the comment by Wilson, the white hunter in Hemingway's "The Short, Happy Life of Francis Macomber," about the "great American boy-men." Reflecting on his former life on the ranch, Kittredge concludes, "I have a new life, which is mine. I invented it. That other life belonged to someone else, to somebody's son or grandson" (204). The remaining thirty pages of the memoir quickly account for Kittredge's second, short-lived marriage, his return to college to study creative writing (he completed his M.F.A. at the University of Iowa in 1969), and the start of his teaching career at the University of Montana, where he was to meet writer and film producer Annick Smith. The last chapter of the book, "Paradise All Around," offers resolution as he finds himself at home in the northern Rockies. In what might be described as a prose poem Kittredge celebrates Montana and the proposed Buffalo Commons. He reconciles with his children and celebrates his capacity to tell his stories as he feels himself moving "a little closer toward feeling at home in the incessant world" (238).

The first of Kittredge's books to be released by a major trade publisher, *Hole in the Sky* was reviewed enthusiastically, and it won the PEN West Literary Award for Nonfiction. By the time the paperback edition appeared in 1993, the book had acquired an array of blurbs that one might associate with a highly successful novel, and the writers of those blurbs read like a who's who of Western letters: "One of the few thoroughly honest accounts of a western upbringing [...] the kind of book I have been hoping to see come out of the West in greater and greater profusion, as the West at large discovers the sort of honesty that Kittredge has discovered in himself" (Wallace Stegner); "If there's a literary New West, growing crazywild and green and true right out of the Old one, Bill Kittredge is it. Compared to him, the rest of us are pavement." (David Quammen); "*Hole in the Sky* is the Rape of Eden recalled first as an idyll and then as a family curse. [...] Out of the pain and glory of growing up in a dying dream, Bill Kittredge has produced a great book." (Thomas McGuane); "Bill Kittredge's *Hole in the Sky*, about a man's long, stumbling passage from fear and selfishness to compassion and communality, is honest, wise, and immensely human" (Barry Lopez); "*Hole in the Sky* is a heartbreaking masterpiece of a lifetime of growing self-knowledge, and Kittredge is one of the best writers around — anywhere" (James Welch).

This memoir is painfully and candidly self-revelatory, as any good confession memoir must be, so unless we doubt the writer's honesty, we must concede that Kittredge does regret the errors of his life, particularly his egocentricity. Clearly, however, he felt himself constrained by the powerful figure of his grandfather, whose influence also compromised his father's life. Finally, Kittredge is less concerned with self-realization than he is with examining the relationship between character and the environment. In effect, choices others make do influence our own, and when those others occupy the privileged position of the patriarch, particularly one noted for "stiff-lipped silences" (113), we are not likely to come to grips with ourselves with any ease. The arguments against the mute patriarchs we encounter in the memoirs of Mary Clearman Blew and Kim Barnes come to mind here. Kittredge holds that there is a connection between the breakdown of human relations and the degradation of the environment.

His relatively rare descriptions of the near-paradise he knew as a boy resemble those of the landscapist rather than the naturalist: "the reek of damp sage and greasewood and the raw odor of the apple orchard" (5). But even as a prose "landscapist" Kittredge is something of a minimalist:

> Think of afternoons on Crump Lake Bar, amid the rosebushes, the waterbirds clattering as they come and go. At that latitude and elevation there are days in the fall when the sunlight lies like glory over the dying red-orange reeds of the tule-beds and the muddy soft water [18].

Here he does not identify the "waterbirds" as many nature writers would have done, and later in the paragraph he refers rather diffidently to "the singular beauty at the heart of a desert flower" and to "long-legged insects" that "walk the surface tension of the water."

Nature writers like Edward Abbey, Annie Dillard, or Ann Zwinger almost certainly would have named the flowers and insects, perhaps supplying the scientific names in Latin for good measure. And most nature writers would offer frequent and often lengthy forays into descriptive prose, but Kittredge is not a "nature writer" per se, even though his writing does concern the natural world. He admires his father, for example, because he protected the sandhill cranes (78), even though he later learned they were not an endangered species. But as he observes, "We were not people who sat and studied animals in their wildness," and what he learned ultimately was "the art of keeping intimacy at some distance, and living with power" (69). As the RD-6 Caterpillars give way to the D-7's, the family contrived what Kittredge sees as a "vision": "We were doing God's work, and thought we were making a paradise on earth, a perfection of fields" (171). In retrospect, however, he realizes they were driven by a "self-absorption" that made them unable to "cherish" themselves and "the native actualities of the place where we lived" (171). What happened to his world, therefore, entailed a flawed vision and a failure of comprehension: "The ecology of the valley was complex beyond our understanding" (171).

Terry Tempest Williams

William Kittredge's environmental views are stated clearly, but his memoir leans strongly toward the personal. Although his political stance is obvious, we rarely detect the role of science in *Hole in the Sky*, and so it lacks the equilibrium or balance among the three elements (personal, scientific, political) that I hypothesize one might expect to encounter in most ecomemoirs. Perhaps because Terry Tempest Williams has served as Naturalist-in-Residence at the Utah Museum of Natural History, her renowned memoir, *Refuge* (1991), features a decidedly scientific focus while at the same time it incorporates a moving personal narrative centered on her mother's deadly struggle with cancer. Unlike Kittredge, Williams has no personal guilt to assuage, having played no role herself in the destruction of the environment. In fact, in a way, it could be said that while Kittredge's family was involved in the devastation of the environment, albeit unintentionally through their misuse of technology, Williams's family has suffered because of a technologically impaired or infected environment, as she makes clear in her epilogue essay, "The Clan of One-Breasted Women," which fixes the blame for the high incidence of breast cancer in her family on the Nevada above-ground nuclear tests conducted between 1951 and 1962. In an interview published in 1993, Williams reiterated what she says in *Refuge*, that she wrote the book "to explore the idea of how one finds refuge in change."[10] But finding refuge in change is no simple matter, for as she puts it in her memoir, even though that refuge exists in her "capacity to love," it necessarily involves the embracing of death: "If I can learn to love death then I can begin to find refuge in change" (178). She read books like Elisabeth Kübler-Ross's *On Death and Dying* (1975) before writing *Refuge*.

Born and raised in Salt Lake City to "a Mormon family with roots in Utah since 1847" (281), Terry Tempest Williams became a birdwatcher at age ten when her paternal grandmother gave her binoculars and a field guide. An avid hiker and camper, she received her B.A. in English in 1979 and her master's degree in environmental science in 1984 from the University of Utah. She married Brooke Williams, an environmental consultant, in 1975. They have no children, an issue that comes up more than once in her memoir, most notably when her mother asks her what she fears. Her response is of interest: "I am afraid of losing my solitude, my time to retreat and my time to create. [...] My ideas, Mother, are my children" (220–221). Although she considers herself an orthodox Mormon and claims to see the world through the lenses of the Latter-Day Saints, Williams remains a controversial figure. Certainly, her attitude toward motherhood opposes tradition, and her arguments against her faith's patriarchal values render her something of a renegade. Nevertheless, *Refuge* was named book-of-the-year by the Association of Mormon Letters, perhaps because she remains faithful to her religion's commitment to family and community, and also to its long-standing traditions of education and storytelling.

Williams's first book, *The Secret Language of Snow* (1984), which she co-authored with Ted Major, applies a different Inuit term for snow to each chapter. Also written for children is *Between Cattails* (1985), which Williams has described as "a celebration of my childhood obsession with the Bear River Migratory Bird Refuge," where she first "fell in love with birds."[11] Her second book, *Pieces of White Shell* (1984), deals with her experiences as a teacher among the Navajo between 1977 and 1985 and concerns Navajo myths and sense of place. Inspired by Annie Dillard's *Pilgrim at Tinker Creek* (1974), her own voice developed with *Coyote's Canyon* (1989), which also involves Navajo lore. Since the publication of *Refuge* her books have included *An Unspoken Hunger: Stories from the Field* (1994); *Desert Quartet: An Erotic Landscape* (1995); *Leap* (2001), an unusual and in many ways profound meditation on Hieronymus Bosch's painting, "The Garden of Earthly Delights" (ca. 1500); *Red: Passion and Patience in the Desert* (2001), essays, poems, and journal entries on the canyon lands of southern Utah; and *The Open Space of Democracy* (2004), which concerns the politics and ethics of the environment.

We do not read many pages into *Refuge* before encountering the sort of textured descriptive prose as common to her book as it is rare to Kittredge's: "What is distinctive about these owls is their home. It rises from the alkaline flats like a clay-covered fist. If you were to peek inside the tightly clenched fingers, you would find a dark-holed entrance" (8–9). Following her introduction of the entrance to the bird's "home" (in preference to the more distancing term "den" or "habitat"), Williams imitates the "distress cries" of the burrowing owl's young ("*Tttss! Tttss! Tttss!*") before elaborating with additional details: "The entrance is littered with bones and feathers. I recall finding a swatch of yellow feathers like a doormat across the threshold — meadowlark, maybe. These small owls pursue their prey religiously at dusk" (9). Williams's use of similes is one striking feature of her ecomemoir that helps sustain the tension between what might be called her observations-as-naturalist and her perceptions-as-poet. She heightens the domesticity of the scene, for example, by likening the feathers to a doormat. In the latter sentence of the passage cited above we encounter a homonymic pun (prey/pray) that surely must be intentional, given the qualifying adverb.

The second person (you) in the passage above immediately locates the reader in the scene in a personal, even intimate way. At times Williams moves from the expository mode (conveying information) to what one might call the familiar, essentially through the shift into the second-person pronoun:

> When a curlew is near, the air is stirred; they are anxious and aggressive. Godwits are serene. They demand little from you except the patience to observe. Curlews cause guilt. You are reminded of your intrusion, that you do not belong [151].

Throughout *Refuge* Williams moves easily through the range of personal pronouns, often abandoning the first-person singular for the first-person plural when she joins her husband Brooke, as she does in the next paragraph: "Two ravens hover with eyes on the eggs. We leave quickly, so the heron can return."

As with Kittredge's ecomemoir, reviewers greeted Williams's book enthusiastically, and the paperback edition of 1992 is accompanied by blurbs from notable western writers: "There isn't a page in *Refuge* that doesn't whistle with the sound of wings" (Wallace Stegner); "*Refuge* is an almost unbearably intense and skillful essay on mortality, our own and that of the creative world. It is isolated from nearly all others of the genre by Ms. Williams's 'greatness of soul'—there is no other way to express the dense beauty and grace of this book" (Jim Harrison); "The courage, the passion, and the purity of motive in Terry Tempest Williams's voice are remarkable. Her demonstration of how deeply human emotional life can become intertwined with a particular landscape could not be more relevant to our lives" (Barry Lopez); "A record of loss, healing grace, and the search for a human place in nature's large design. [Her] courage is matched by the earnest beauty of her language and the keen compassion of her observations" (Louise Erdrich). In effect, one way any book becomes a "classic" is *who* says it is good. But this is not to say that the majority doesn't count for something. Twenty-four of the 28 "Spotlight Reviews" (from readers) on Amazon.com rated the book the maximum five stars.

Most of the Spotlight Reviews, which I surveyed in the fall of 2004, were unsigned. Typically, professional book reviewers point to possible flaws. For example, while she commended Williams's prose as "clear, strong and vivid," Margaret B. Guthrie found her interrogation of Mormonism "not smoothly interwoven" with other major themes, and she considered the epilogue "disruptive" and "contrived."[12] Similarly, Marilyn R. Chandler, writing for *Women's Review of Books*, while she obviously admired the memoir suggested that the "bimodal narrative" appears sometimes "forced and interruptive."[13] Structurally, the book is unusual and perhaps lends itself to criticism because it is built (a critic might say "cobbled together") of so many pieces: a prologue and an epilogue with no fewer than 36 essays in between, these ranging in length from just under two to about twenty pages. Moreover, the narrative is arguably more than simply "bimodal," so we encounter what those who dislike the book prefer to describe as thematic confusion, while those who admire the book consider it thematic complexity.

Writing of Terry Tempest Williams's *Refuge*, Brooke Libby proposes that the book's "marriage of the ecological with the autobiographical crystallizes what is the general though perhaps unstated aim of most nature writing: to write about the natural world and about oneself simultaneously, to look mutually outward and inward."[14] The chronology of the memoir follows the rising and flooding of Great Salt Lake (the lake level is indicated with each chapter) between the first of June 1983 (4203.25') and the latter part of June in 1989. The lake reaches its highest point (4211.85') in April of 1987. By that point in the narrative, Williams's mother has died of breast cancer, but that theme is sustained by the diagnosis of her paternal grandmother with the return of the same disease (operated on a year earlier, she died about two years later). Of her mother's struggle with cancer Williams writes, "A person with cancer dies in increments, and a part of you slowly dies with them" (173). Most of the pathos that figures so powerfully in this memoir concerns Williams's painful efforts to cope with her mother's progress toward death, which at times appears to be in sync with the rising of Great Salt Lake and the threat to the bird sanctuaries: "I could not separate the Bird Refuge from my family. Devastation respects no boundaries" (40). As the flooding continues, Williams finds the refuge "unusually silent" (96). Both the species count and the individual numbers drop, and she finds that like the birds of Bear River, she has been "displaced" (96). This unsettling context sets up the section "White Pelicans" that takes as its point of departure the removal of a benign cyst from Williams's breast. Her maternal grandmother had a mastectomy, and she has also seen her mother's scars, so she fears for herself.

But what has that to do with the "gregarious" white pelicans of Gunnison Island in Great Salt Lake? And what have the pelicans to do with Brigham Young and the Mormon apostle Lorenzo Snow back in 1864? Snow, we are told, set up a successful cooperative "based on an ecological model" (100), but when the cooperative failed to tolerate the "critical component" of "diversity," it declined. "History," Williams concludes, "has shown us that exclusivity in the name of empire building eventually fails. Fear of discord undermines creativity. And creativity lies at the heart of adaptive evolution" (102). Williams next demonstrates how the white pelicans, with their "highly synchronized" reproductive activities, have succeeded as a colony (105). The connection between the Mormon's utopian United Order and the pelican's colony becomes clear enough, but how do those elements connect with Williams's appeal to her husband, after she returns from the hospital, to hold her breasts? I think the connection appears tenuous, but credible. Like the birds at the refuge, Williams feels "displaced," but her thoughts about her connections with her mother and grandmother, and then with her husband, reassure her of her adaptability. The white pelicans have thrived because they have adapted by adopting an "asynchronous" reproductive cycle. Williams establishes a connection between her personal life story and scientific observation; her conclusions amount to a political pronouncement about the necessity of diversity.

The theme of loss, almost universal in the memoir, dominates the text, but the environmental theme, which also involves loss, carries almost equal weight. Each chapter bears the name of a bird, from burrowing owls to screech owls, from whimbrels and barn swallows to snowy plovers and the great blue heron. Williams provides a list of birds associated with Great Salt Lake, not all of them mentioned in the text, at the end of the book. A good birdwatcher's field guide would seem as essential to reading this book as a good dictionary is to reading the poems of Wallace Stevens. A dictionary may offer a definition of a whimbrel (a kind of curlew) or a Wilson's phalarope (similar to a sandpiper), but not of a burrowing owl, which Williams describes as one of those bird "you gauge your life by" (8). Sometimes, as in the essay entitled "Ravens," the bird appears in the text only tangentially, in the raven's case as a simile describing the burned pier of the old Saltair pavilion, a "few charred posts" of which "still stand, looking like ravens" (79). In other places, as in "Whistling Swan," where, after a friend's funeral, Williams encounters a dead swan on the beach "like an abandoned lover" (121), the bird lies at the very heart of the meditation, and in fact the meditative mode is common (although not universal) to the book. In this instance Williams undertakes an elaborate funeral ritual and then stretches out by the body "imagining the great white bird in flight" (121). When she departs at dusk, she leaves the swan "like a crucifix on the sand" and does not look back (122). Kim Barnes points to this passage as risky in its pathos, apparently non–Western in its emotionality, but ultimately powerful and persuasive: "It gave me permission to make something precious in a very positive sense."[15]

A third variety of bird reference occurs in the chapter entitled "Peregrine Falcon," in which Williams tells of going birding at the municipal dump, where the garbage attracts starlings and gulls. Her commentary in this chapter mostly pertains to the noisome starlings, infamously introduced around 1890 by a fan of Shakespeare's plays who wished to transport all of the birds found therein to the United States. She describes the ubiquitous black bird, notorious for robbing the nests of other species and crowding them out of their habitat, admires their "adaptability" and their predation on clover weevils, but laments their threat to species diversity. In one of her most memorable passages on what might be called the birding theme, she writes, "Perhaps we project on to starlings that which we deplore in ourselves: our numbers, our aggression, our greed, and our cruelty. Like starlings, we are taking over the world" (56). The peregrine falcon of the essay's title appears only at the end, when one of the birds dives on a flock of starlings "and plucks its body from mid-air" (57). Of course as the title implies, she has been waiting for the rarer peregrine falcon. This is one of the few chapters in which Williams does not take a "bimodal" approach. We see nothing here of her mother's ongoing struggle with cancer, although some might read the falcon's attack as metaphoric.

Bird enthusiasts surely will find the book more amenable than those who are ambivalent or altogether uninterested in the subject. As a writer, however, Williams rarely allows ornithological details to get in the way of the story or the meditation; rather, such details are employed to enhance or to create reader interest. For example, in "Pink Flamingoes," which begins with her mother's moving letter to a friend who has been operated on for a brain tumor, Great Salt Lake has fallen by more than a foot, and Williams speculates they might be given a "reprieve" (82). Presumably, that reprieve would apply both to the lake level and to her mother's cancer. Then she reflects on a walk with her biologist husband Brooke on the salt flats near Wendover, Nevada, where they observe a mirage, which he explains scientifically, but she prefers to interpret as "hope on a hot day" (86). This single-page episode is followed by an upbeat letter to Williams from her mother, vacationing in Switzerland, that begins, "More and more, I am realizing the natural world is my connection to myself" (86). More than halfway through the chapter the flamingo finally makes its appearance, and then, more or less like the mirage, it is in the context of three "accidental" sightings.

Nor does Williams hesitate to provide us with a statistic when apposite: "In 1985, over 450,000 plastic flamingos were purchased in the United States" (89). From that point in the apparently loosely strung essay she leads us to other "accidentals" sighted in Utah, like a flock of five roseate spoonbill seen in 1919. "How can hope be denied," Williams asks, when such accidentals can occur, "how can we rely solely on the statistical evidence and percentages that would shackle our lives [...]?" (90). Obviously, she is thinking here not only of the birds, but also of the doctor's prognosis for her mother's recovery. She ends the chapter with a metaphoric and conceptual leap by citing Emily Dickinson's poem that begins, "'Hope' is the thing with feathers —/ That perches in the soul." These lines remind us, Williams says, "as birds do, of the liberation and pragmatism of belief" (90).

Both professional and more casual reviewers reiterate certain key words when they comment on Terry Tempest Williams's *Refuge*: lyrical/poetic, spiritual/visionary, intimate/passionate, moving/elegiac, courageous/brave, powerful, honest, beautiful. These qualifiers pertain to the texture and voice of the book. But the texture and voice vary more than such qualifiers might suggest. Numerous historical and scientific references figure throughout the text: "By 1896, all that remained of Brigham City's hive of industry was the unused honey stored on the shelves of the new general store" (103); "In 1979, the Utah ibis population was estimated at 8690 pairs" (111); "The pathologist's report defined Mother's tumor as Stage III epithelial ovarian cancer" (38). Williams maintains a fine balance between such hard data and perceptive, personally derived insights, sometimes offered with aphoristic flair: "Peace is the perspective found in patterns. [...] We are no more and no less than the life that surrounds us. My fears surface in my isolation. My serenity surfaces in my solitude" (29); "A museum is a good place to be quietly subversive on behalf of the land" (44); "Dying doesn't cause suffering. Resistance to dying does" (53); "To spend a night at the marsh is to wax and wane with birdsong" (151).

But while these conceptual passages move toward a cool and rational, aphoristic sort of wisdom, another kind of voice makes first-personal (perhaps even egocentric) emotional statements that strike us quite differently: "Mother is living in the heart of each day. I am not" (52); "I have refused to believe that Mother will die" (75); "'How do you find refuge in change,' I asked softly" (119); "But this time I was not crying for Mother. I was crying for me. I wanted my life back" (164); "I wept silently for all I had lost. I reentered my own landscape of grief with perfect recall" (277). Against the wisdom of the apparently objective (third-person or usually muted first-person) aphorism, Williams voices the pain of the personal.

In effect, the success of *Refuge* depends on the delicate balance of these three voices (the historic/scientific, the rational/aphoristic, and the personal/emotional), and perhaps a fourth as well that might be called mystical or esoteric, perhaps even occult, although Williams herself would most likely prefer "spiritual." Early in the book she declares herself with a sort of credo:

> I was raised to believe in a spirit world, that life exists before the earth and will continue to exist afterward, that each human being, bird, and bulrush, along with all other life forms had a spirit life before it came to dwell physically on earth [14].

Williams provides several such glimpses into her inner life. For example, she portrays her family at prayer over her mother in conventional Mormon fashion, and then she depicts herself praying, in somewhat less orthodox fashion, with her hand on her mother's belly. As her mother's disease advances, they have their astrological charts read and her mother begins to study "Zen, Krishnamurti, and Jung [...] as personal revelation replaces orthodoxy" (136). But as Williams observes later, "Mormon religion has roots firmly planted in a magical worldview," and she loves "knowing that Joseph Smith was a mystic who ascribed magical properties to animals and married his wives according to astrological 'mansions of the moon'" (195–196).

Following her mother's death, Williams goes to her "secret den of healing," a "holy place [...] where egrets hover like angels" (237), and after her Grandmother Mimi's death (it was she who introduced Williams to bird-watching), she has something of a mystical vision involving a pair of circling screech owls: "Mimi and I shared a clandestine vision of things" (273). "If I am to survive," Williams concludes, "I must let my secrets out like white doves held captive too long. I am a woman with wings." In the next essay she recounts a mystical experience recalled from her participation in a Mexican celebration of the *Día de los Muertos* in which "The voices of my Dead came back to me" (278).

For some readers Williams's spirituality may seem New Age; others may have a difficult time negotiating the realms of the spiritual and the scientific. In the epilogue, "The Clan of One-Breasted Women," she inquires into the "anomaly" of her family's high incidence of breast cancer, observing that Mormons traditionally "have a low rate of cancer" (282). When her father tells her that a recurring dream of a "flash of light in the night in the desert" (282) is actually a memory of a nuclear blast the family witnessed in 1957, when Terry was a baby, she realizes that they have been victims of the down-winder effects of eleven years of atmospheric nuclear tests. At this point she unleashes her anger not only at the U.S. government, but also at her own religion in what are probably her most courageous and risky statements: "In Mormon culture, authority is respected, obedience is revered, and independent thinking is not" (285). No doubt this sentiment is more objectionable to Latter-Day Saint orthodoxy than are her scattered complaints about the patriarchy and women's diminished authority: "I must question everything, even if it means losing my faith. [...] Tolerating blind obedience in the name of patriotism or religion ultimately takes our lives" (286).

After publication of the book rumors circulated to the effect that Williams might face excommunication. In the last pages of her epilogue she joins in a demonstration of civil disobedience, empowered by having watched women in her family "die common, heroic deaths" (285). With nine other Utahans she trespasses on the Nevada Test Site, and when an officer frisks her and finds a pen and note pad tucked into her boot, Williams tells her they are "weapons" (290). The protestors are arrested, driven out of town, and released in the desert, but Williams has elsewhere described the desert as a sacred place, and in her closing sentence she celebrates the moment: "What they didn't realize was that we were home, soul-centered and strong, women who recognized the sweet smell of sage as fuel for our spirits" (290).

Although some reviewers and readers have complained about the disjunctive nature of *Refuge*, Kip Clark and Deb Thornton, in their entry in the *Dictionary of Literary Biography*, praise "the seamless structure of the book."[16] They observe that "Each section is named for a bird (the symbol that unites heaven and earth), and each marks the water level of the rising Great Salt Lake, which corresponds with the rising salt of her grief." They conclude that *Refuge* has become "a powerful ecofeminist manifesto" (308). In fact, in a 1997 interview Williams commented that "it wasn't the scientific mind or the poetic mind, but the feminine mind that I wanted to embrace" (9). John Tallmadge compares the book favorably with *Pilgrim at Tinker Creek*, suggesting that Annie Dillard's memoir "opens the door, and *Refuge* shows us the way."[17] He notes, in Williams's memoir, "Nature's lessons apply to pressing personal issues that are also politically charged" (202). The natural world, as seen through a scientist's exacting eyes, is balanced by a personal world that involves apparently (but not actually) trivial and domestic intimacies like the shopping trip at Nordstrom's, and the whole is leavened with political statements sometimes directly asserted and other times implied. As Brooke Libby has observed,

"'Care,' 'empathy,' 'compassion'—long dismissed as women's essential biological excess—in these accounts gain political clout" (256). Moreover, Libby suggests, Williams addresses "the ambivalence of being both human and natural, demonstrating the utility of such disorientation. [...] In other words, it is the cognitive and physically empty or invisible space between individuals in nature that is itself volatile, sympathetic, and ultimately productive. Living in and writing about the natural world, in this sense, we must negotiate our shared between-ness" (261).

Comparison of William Kittredge and Terry Tempest Williams

William Kittredge almost certainly would not say of himself what Terry Tempest Williams said in an interview conducted in 1988: "I will tell you that I am a naturalist first and a writer second, that the landscape came before the words."[18] While Kittredge's writing makes an important contribution to ecocriticism, he is not a naturalist by training, and he does not present himself as expert on fauna or flora. In effect, he does not claim to be a "nature writer," even though I think his book should be regarded as an ecomemoir. On the other hand, Cheryll Glotfelty has observed that Williams presents herself as a naturalist in several ways, from the short biographical note to the prefatory map of Great Salt Lake.[19]

One of my students in a paper for a graduate seminar on Western memoir saw the differences between Kittredge's and Williams's memoirs as largely a matter of gender, beginning with the observation that Kittredge starts his book with the image of himself as a boy recovering from polio, whereas Williams opens with observations on the Great Salt Lake flooding in 1983. Kittredge, she observed, used "the self-centered, phallic 'I,' which draws us into a memoir and allows the author to take center stage," while "Willliams focuses on the lake, symbolic of the womb."[20] If we disregard her two-page prologue, as my student did, we read, in fact, nearly eleven pages into Williams's memoir before she identifies herself as the oldest child of a Mormon family. Jeanette E. Riley in an essay published in *Women's Studies* observes that when Williams travels in the desert or elsewhere, she is almost always accompanied by someone else, and "In integrating her social connections with her connections to the environment, Williams creates a social geography; thus the Western self is not only a self emergent in the soul of the terrain, but also from a web of social relations."[21]

In a provocative essay that touches upon several potential issues that arise if we read Williams through the lenses of ecofeminism, however, Cassandra Kircher takes her to task for her "problematic" tendency to resort to stereotypical "dichotomies" in her portrayal of "women with nature and men with culture."[22] Kircher does not acknowledge Cheryll Glotfelty, whose essay appeared two years earlier, but she observes similar problems of polarized gender portrayal and goes so far as to wish that Williams's "invoking gender were done in the spirit of bridging differences rather than exaggerating them" (166). On the other hand, Williams composes one of the most elaborate and generous sections of acknowledgments I have ever encountered, and in the process she celebrates the many men in her family and otherwise for whose direct or indirect assistance she expresses her gratitude. Moreover, she portrays her relationship with her husband and her father with considerable affection.

By contrast, Kittredge feels distance between himself and others, including fellow workers and members of his family, and from the natural world, and he claims to write from his "most grievous isolations" (11). He describes his love-making as "brutal, but quick. And isolated, more than anything; isolated, and actually alone" (198). Even when he attempts to reestablish relations with his brother after his first divorce, he phrases it hesitantly: "I began to ease my way toward a guarded friendship with my brother" (207). To the extent that he has been a type of the "rugged individualist," then, we can only conclude that that old paradigm has failed him. Not until the end of his memoir, in part because of his relationship with writer Annick Smith, "the luck of my later life" (230), does Kittredge visit the natural world for solace and the kind of healing that Williams finds in the desert and the Bear River Migratory Bird Refuge from the outset.

Both memoirs involve efforts at self-healing through writing. When he writes of killing mice and stabbing to death a tame duck, Kittredge concludes that something is wrong with himself (49), and later he creates a word to describe what he sees as his malady: "'antidysthanasia' [...] failure to take positive efforts to preserve life" (68). Elsewhere he describes himself as "sick with anomie" (218). Williams, however, never appears to suffer from the identity and existential crises that beset Kittredge. At one point in her ordeal she feels she has "hit rock-bottom" (135), but she is sustained by her mother's strength, her husband's support, and her own kinship with the land. She feels herself connected, as Kittredge never can, through her family, community, religion, and the natural world. As Riley observes, "the sense of belonging to a community of people and nature [...] nurtures one's self-identity. [...] The individual ventures out amidst an interrelated web of influences that include both the land and people. As such, Williams navigates a terrain that has an inbuilt support system that sustains her" (592).

Williams's family's struggle with cancer dominates the text of *Refuge*. The diseases in *Hole in the Sky*, some of which are psychological or perhaps spiritual, in fact pervade the text more than may at first reading seem apparent. In addition to his own illness with polio as a child, Kittredge's second wife suffers an ulcerated colon, and he exposes his readers to the deaths of his father and grandfather and of hired hands like Henry Nicol and Bill Gouldin from heart disease; Vance Beebe from emphysema; Vernon Wasson and Uncle Hank presumably, among others, from drinking. Alcoholism is easily the prevalent disease among the "heartbroken souls" in Kittredge's memoir. While Williams carefully follows the unraveling plot of her mother's fight with cancer, Kittredge tends simply to tick off the deaths as they happen. Death is more prevalent and more widespread, in fact, in Kittredge's memoir than in Williams's, but in *Refuge* death is more intimate. Williams speculates at the end of her prologue, "Perhaps, I am telling this story in an attempt to heal myself" (4). Of his psychological "terror" over feeling "utterly alone," Kittredge writes, "That dis-ease took decades to cure, if it is cured" (11).

The theme of change is important to both of these ecomemoirs, but in very different ways. "An ancient world was changing," Kittredge writes, "and my people were on the leading edge of the conversion" (40). He and his family glory in change, which they regard as "improvement," making what they think proper "use" of the natural world. Kittredge and his family have been avid participants in the myth of the American West that he describes in *Owning It All*:

> The story begins with a vast innocent continent, natural and almost magically alive, capable of inspiring us to reverence and awe, and yet savage, a wilderness. A good rural people come from the East, and they take the land from its native inhabitants, and tame it for agricultural purposes, bringing civilization [63].

When he returns to the ranch from military service, Kittredge sees that everything is "changing" and he embraces his role in the future (*Hole in the Sky* 151). The changes in the Warner Valley are mostly contrived by humans: "[W]e began to reshape the place, following a dream of machinelike perfection, a corps of engineers/ag school mirage of remaking the world" (171).

Williams's natural world is also changing as the rising Great Salt Lake threatens her beloved wildlife refuge, and her personal world is changing as cancer spreads through her mother's body. Presumably because the changes in Williams's environment are natural, she can adapt, just as her mother does. Kittredge and his family do not think of adapting their own behavior because they erroneously believe they control change in their world. Terry Tempest Williams and her family are not deluded: they *must* adapt, and it is not easy. "I am not adjusting," Williams observes midway through her memoir. "I keep dreaming the Refuge back to what I have known" (140). But a few pages later a "wedge of long-billed curlews" reminds her that "the only thing we can expect is change" (146). Eventually, she watches a lone great blue heron and observes that "[s]he has weathered the changes well" (266), and she concludes that like the heron, "I am adapting as the world is adapting" (267). The State of Utah takes steps to control what is happening through the West Desert Pumping Project, an action the Kittredge family would likely have approved, but it proves to be an almost comical waste of money, as the flood waters subside before it can be fully activated. Lest the reader suspect that Williams means to propose a program of acquiescence, however, she portrays herself as an activist in the epilogue to the book, and she has built her credentials as a conservationist in recent years, witness her testimony before the U.S. Senate Subcommittee on Forest & Public Lands Management on 13 July 1995.

Among the terms most often used to describe *Refuge* is the word "spiritual," and in fact the last words of the book are "our spirits" (290). She regards her Grandmother Mimi as her "spiritual mentor" (246) and she asserts her belief that "the Holy Ghost is female" (241). As a teenager she reports having once "felt the presence of angels" (197). She prays not only for the birds (152), but to them: "I pray to the birds because I believe they will carry the messages of my heart upward" (149). Williams, Cassandra Kircher concludes, "considers the landscape religiously charged" (162). William Kittredge, on the other hand, declares, "I am as irreligious as a stone" (237). But although he does not regard himself as a spiritual or religious person, he considers the world at hand to be "sacred," and "luminous," and at least a potential "paradise," which is the last word in his memoir (238).

Conclusions and Speculations

> Memoir is the speaking "I" of a trusting author, walking hand in hand with the reader down a path both know well.
> —Thomas Larson, *The Memoir and the Memoirist*

Writers from the northern Rockies are likely to continue turning out their life narratives, either as autobiography or as memoir, as personal essays or as environmental commentaries infused with autobiographical elements. One might conjecture that as fewer writers of life narrative from the region are able to look back to a childhood centered in the woods, farm, or ranch, the nature of northern Rockies memoir will change. The region boasts a spectacular, lightly inhabited landscape marked by sometimes forested and sometimes barren rock mountains flanked by thousands of acres of semi-arid sagebrush-scattered land economically useful only for marginal grazing except for occasional oil and gas or mineral deposits. Although "outsiders" are buying up much of that land, large acreage will likely stay under federal control, so it will remain available; but, increasingly, I think, residents of the region will visit such sites as tourists in their own country to hunt, fish, and backpack. Their life narratives may well become more like those of writers from other regions, more reflective of life in corporate America and less inclined to reveal the intimacy with the landscape that growing up *inside* it affords. The place will remain; where the writers locate themselves in the context of that place will change. Their life narratives will likely exhibit increased concern over political issues that threaten the northern Rockies with environmental degradation and exploitive development.

The memoirs surveyed in this study testify, on the one hand, to a lingering nostalgia for rural life, particularly for life on the ranch, and on the other hand, to an awareness that that way of living has become untenable for most people, including the writers themselves. Of the ten writers on whose work I have concentrated my attention, only one, Sidner Larson, has left the West (for the university town of Ames, Iowa), and only one, Ivan Doig, has settled in a large metropolitan area (Seattle). Four of the writers live in university towns (Missoula, Montana, or Moscow, Idaho): Judy Blunt, William Kittredge, Mary Clearman Blew, and Kim Barnes. Only Mark Spragg (rural south central Montana), Teresa Jordan (a ranch in northern Nevada), Terry Tempest Williams (Castle Valley, a town of about 350 in eastern Utah near Arches National Park), and Janet Campbell Hale (Plummer, on the Coeur d'Alene Indian Reservation, a town of about 800) live in rural areas or in very small towns. Five of the ten books, those of Doig, Spragg, Blunt, Blew, and Jordan, are essentially ranch or rural memoirs, and another three, those of Barnes, Larson, and Kittredge, involve a sort of blending of life in the forest or on the farm with small-town or city life. Although we encounter Terry Tempest Williams most memorably when she visits Great Salt Lake and the Bear River Wildlife Refuge, she is the only one of the ten memoirists to write from a consistently urban point of view. Barnes's *Hungry for the World* (2000), her sequel to *In the Wilderness*, also takes place mostly in urban settings.

At the end of the second chapter of this book I outlined several "topics" I intended to visit throughout, one of which concerned the tendency of memoirists to focus on characters other than themselves (see page 54). I was curious as to how that inclination might apply to the ten writers I was dealing with, and how self-critical these writers would be. Six of the writers (Spragg, Barnes, Blunt, Hale, Kittredge, Larson) maintain the focus largely, though of course not exclusively, on themselves, and like most autobiographers, they portray themselves maturing from childhood into adulthood, ending pretty much with some portrait of the person they have become at the time of writing. Kittredge's *Hole in the Sky* comes closest to the conventional autobiography, inasmuch as he traces the family ancestry back to the seventeenth century. But in fact all but Spragg and Blunt of the six introduce us not only to their parents, aunts, and uncles, but also to their grandparents, whether they ever knew them personally or not. Ancestry remains an important part of their identity, and for the two ethnic memoirists, Hale and Larson, it appears to be especially significant. The four writers who focus largely, though of course not exclusively, on others (Doig, Blew, Jordan, Williams) also acquaint us with their ancestors, particularly with grandparents they have known. Of the ten writers, Williams maintains the closest balance in her attention to others in tandem with herself; Blew scarcely appears at all in six of the eleven essays that comprise *All But the Waltz*. Only rarely does Blew hold herself up to direct scrutiny or self-criticism. In fact, rigorous self-examination with an eye, perhaps, toward the expression of regrets over past folly and bad choices would not seem to define these life narratives. Only Kittredge verges on the confessional and is inclined toward some degree of self-blame and remorse. Larson, Hale, and Spragg delve into some serious self-interrogation, but neither they nor the other writers appear to regard the choices they have made with much regret.

This is not to say that the capacity to be self-questioning and perhaps even self-judgmental necessarily defines the quality or success of a memoir, but that issue does influence in some ways the roles the writers adopt for themselves as "characters" in their life stories. And the roles they play are connected with the fourth of my topics, the apparent authorial intention. Of course it is not as simple as a game of victims and villains, but clearly Blew, Barnes, Blunt, and Hale are victimized in various ways by the traditional patriarchy or by familial dysfunction. Only Kittredge, part victim himself, puts himself forward as a villain of sorts, a difficult role to adopt. Barnes, Blunt, and Hale are all at least to some degree sympathetic characters; Kittredge, and to some degree Sidner Larson, is not. Blew hardly develops her role as a character in her memoir. She criticizes the behavior of her great-grandfather Abraham and of her father early in the book, and toward the end, notably in the title essay, she rebels against the role of submissive wife that two husbands attempt to impose on her. But Mary Blew tends to keep the camera's lens aimed away from herself. Barnes, Blunt, and Hale also revolt against those who have thwarted their efforts at self-actualization and personal autonomy. Their refusal of the identity their parents and culture attempt to impose on them transforms them, even Hale to some degree, from victim to rebel as their memoirs evolve; indeed, their memoirs serve as expressions of their rebellion.

Both Teresa Jordan and Terry Tempest Williams come of age under fairly prosperous circumstances, and they provide no indication that they have significant problems accepting the patriarchal world into which they were born, although they do question it, and ecofeminist critics have noted that Williams connects nearly all of the misconduct in her memoir with male characters, from the good-old-boys in the blue pickup to Thomas Murray, the atomic energy commissioner, who asserts, "'Gentlemen, we must not let anything interfere with this series of tests, nothing.'"[1] Ivan Doig and Mark Spragg portray themselves in the role of boy-coming-of-age in the rugged outdoors. Their maturation process involves undergoing a series of ordeals. Coincidentally, the deaths of their mother figure prominently for the latter four memoirists. In effect, Doig, Spragg, Jordan, and Williams emerge triumphant; they appear variously as the heroes or heroines of their life stories. Jordan's memoir ends with her marriage. These four writers do nothing wrong, and much of what they do is admirable. Even Spragg's divorce is adverted to simply in passing, and he is happily remarried at the end of his memoir. Although Larson's is ultimately a success story, he presents himself as a flawed character, as do Barnes, Blunt, and Hale in certain ways. Barnes and Blunt appear confident and content at the end, but Hale portrays herself as alone, and her issues with her family remain unresolved. Blew's status at the end of her memoir remains perhaps the most ambiguous of the ten. The "technical widow" and single parent, she seems haunted as she and her daughter leave her former husband's windswept grave; when she goes home, it will not be to the section of Montana she has celebrated throughout her memoir, but to her new residence in northern Idaho.

Regarding the subject of place, I found myself uncertain as to just what I was looking for in these life narratives. Was it simply a matter of finding out who wrote lyrically and passionately, as did such pioneer memoirists as Annie Pike Greenwood, of their portion of the northern Rockies landscape? Or was I pursuing some ecological or environmental agenda? I knew of the cliché notion of place-as-character and was alert to the issues of gendered landscape, but having commented on such matters, so what? In his review of *All But the Waltz* Ivan Doig admires as Mary Clearman Blew's "gut-feeling for the land."[2] Most although not all of these writers demonstrated some of that feeling. Predictably, most of the memoirists sustained something of a love affair with their particular landscape, even when, or perhaps particularly when, as in Blunt's case, it was harsh and apparently unhandsome; moreover, they state sometimes quite explicitly their belief that they have been shaped by the land, even though they do not so explicitly indicate just how. On the other hand, in *Bloodlines* Hale struggles to escape the various sites where she finds herself, largely because her transient life drew her away from the reservation in northern Idaho where she now lives and left her in an economic struggle wherever she moved, from central Washington to San Francisco. When she does visit Idaho or Montana, she finds the places easier to name than to describe. Her relationship to her native landscape remains one of love-hate.

At the other end of the spectrum Williams's *Refuge* tells a story of place even more than it does of the inhabitants. Heavily laden with birds and similes, with several wildlife refuges and archaeological sites as well as the Great Salt Lake itself, the book runs thick with images, and both the lake and the Bear River Wildlife Refuge do become "characters" in her story, objects of her affection. Although I have described Kittredge's book as an ecomemoir, he does not often depict the landscape, either of the ranch in Oregon or of the part of Montana he now calls home. The place he describes near the end of *Hole in the Sky* seems at first an idyllic one of cattle grazing "belly-deep in meadows by the river," "Rain-Bird sprinklers [...] throwing rainbows over the alfalfa benchlands"; but it becomes an almost apocalyptic world of "roadsides [...] built up with shops and parlors — beauty, plumbing, welding, fencing, chain saw, ranchette realtor, taxidermy."[3] Larson rarely describes the landscape of the northern Montana Hi-Line, and much of his narrative reflects on his experiences as owner of various bars and as a law student. In short, although he argues at the end of his book that a person should remain close to his or her "place of origin," Larson does not devote much attention to the details of that place. After Williams, the sense of place figures most prominently in the memoirs of Doig, Spragg, Blunt, and Jordan.

Someone might argue, however, that a Diaspora has affected the American population since World War II, so the "axial centeredness" of which Harold P. Simonson has written may be something of an illusion.[4] What if, as is sometimes the case, the writer has lived in several regions during his or her lifetime? Wyoming memoirist Jeffe Kennedy, for example, begins her book, *Wyoming Trucks, True Love, and the Weather Channel: A Woman's Adventure* (2004) with her air force pilot father's death in a plane crash in North Carolina. Her family then moves to Denver, where her mother grew up and where Jeffe goes to school. Kennedy ends her book in Wyoming, where she is presently employed by an environmental consulting firm that does contract work for the Environmental Protection Agency. Place, she argues, offers one way of working through the "deeper meanings" of events, and she writes, "I think this place influences me in the light and the way the thunderstorms march across huge sky for hours to reach me."[5] On the other hand, Kennedy continues, "I also love the glow of magnolias while the cicadas grind in the tropical heat of the South, and the putrid smell of gingko fruits in Midwestern cobblestones, and the sloping fogs and rounded islands of the Pacific Northwest." Ought we to regard this as some form of regional apostasy? While this study focuses on writers from a very particular region, it would be disingenuous of me to imply that the writers whose works I am examining are committed solely to the place of their birth or upbringing, even when that landscape dominates the text under consideration. Increasingly, as the saying goes, we are all from somewhere else.

Motivated partly by the growing critical argument to the effect that writers of life narrative, autobiography, memoir, whatever it is, cannot help writing fiction, I have also been attracted to the question of what kind of fiction these books most resemble. In all cases, even those in which the structure was that of a collection of essays, which I often found to be story like in nature, the organization tended to be at least loosely chronological. For example, even though Spragg carefully disrupts the chronology of his early chapters so that he is fourteen years old in the first, twelve in the second, fourteen again in the fifth, and so on, the overall pattern is chronological. In the first ten essays he ranges in age from twelve to sixteen, in the eleventh he is apparently about twenty-one, having just graduated from college, and in the remaining three essays he is an adult (aged thirty-six in the last one). Similarly, although the first chapter of Blunt's *Breaking Clean* concerns her engagement, the next chapter begins with a pre-natal "memory," after which the chronology remains linear, and she sustains a narrative arc although she skips several years between her first years of marriage in "Learning the Ropes" and her daughter's bout with fever in "Winter Kill." The texts that work most like books of short stories are Blew's *All But the Waltz*, Jordan's *Riding the White Horse Home*, and Hale's *Bloodlines*, which might be described as structured like a central novella, "Daughter of Winter," accompanied by seven related short stories. Kim Barnes's *In the Wilderness* features numbered chapters and by that gesture seems to emphasize its novel-like nature. But even though portions of his memoir were published in more than half a dozen periodicals, Kittredge's novel-like memoir follows the plot of his life with its climax occurring with his "breakdown" and subsequent divorce. By the end of the book he has reached what most readers would call a clear resolution.

This having been said — this analogy to fictional genres having been advanced — I do not in the final analysis feel altogether at ease with the views by two influential spokespersons as to the fundamentally, or inescapably, fictional nature of life narrative writing. To recap my earlier citations, Wallace Stegner forcefully blurs the generic distinctions: "If there is a sense in which every piece of fiction is autobiographical, it is just as true that every autobiography is a fiction."[6] Later he describes autobiography and fiction as "variant means to the same end" (220), but I do not read such assertions as hedged bets. And surely Jill Ker Conway pulls no punches when she opens her book with a rhetorical question: "Why is autobiography the most popular form of fiction for modern readers?"[7] In his scholarly study, *Fictions in Autobiography* (1985), Paul John Eakin agrees that "the self that is the center of all autobiographical narrative is necessarily a fictive structure," but he maintains that he does not intend "to expel truth from the house of autobiography and to install fiction in its stead. One could conflate autobiography with other forms of fiction only by willfully ignoring the autobiographer's explicit posture *as autobiographer* in the text."[8] And vice versa, I am inclined to add, when it comes to the fiction writer's explicit posture (think Hemingway, Norman Maclean) as *writer of fiction*.

The thematic concerns of these memoirs vary and are implicit in the way I have presented them. Both Kittredge and Williams pursue manifest environmental agendas, and in both cases (although in very different ways) their own lives and those of their families are interwoven with the landscape. Both Larson and Hale speak not only to their Native American ethnicity, but also to issues of transience. It is perhaps the supreme irony of their life narratives that they portray themselves as the least "at home" of all the memoirists in their native landscape. Both Barnes and Blunt offer coming-of-age stories gendered female, emphasizing considerable tension with the patriarchal values of their family and place. The male coming-of-age narratives of Doig and Spragg manifestly reflect, albeit quite differently, the supportive role of the father who wishes to see his son grow to maturity and independence doing physical labor in the outdoors. Blew and Jordan offer family memoirs in which the persona of the narrator is modulated in various ways. The generation that separates the two at least partially accounts for the difference in their presentation of family history and personalities, but although both writers can be said to have feminist agendas, an equally apparent theme in their memoirs concerns the passing of a way of life that has traditionally been thought to define the interior West.

Although no single theme may be said to be essential to the memoir, we might reflect briefly on loss and death in these books. Having opened his memoir with the death of his mother, Doig might have chosen to conclude with his departure from Montana for college, but instead he takes us through the deaths of his father and grandmother. Spragg's memoir culminates in the death of his mother. Blew leads us from the death of her father to the death of her second husband. Jordan writes only after going through therapy that helped her deal with her mother's death and the loss of the family ranch. The death of her estranged mother constitutes the centerpiece of Hale's memoir, and Larson apparently comes to full self-awareness only with the deaths of his Aunt Sis and other relatives. Although the deaths of his father and both grandfathers do not appear to have had so momentous an impact on Kittridge, he records those along with the death of numerous hired hands and friends. And while Williams's memoir celebrates survival and renewal, she portrays courageous, spiritual meditations on death that are reminiscent in some ways of the seventeenth-century British minister Jeremy Taylor's *Holy Dying* (1651). Only the memoirs of Barnes and Blunt, while they do concern loss, do not deal significantly with death, although both writers encounter it, Barnes in her dramatic story of Matthew Lang and Blunt in her comments on the deaths of animals.

But while death may be an inevitable ingredient in memoir, these life narratives never strike the reader as gloomy or morbid, for they tell stories of survival and sometimes of triumph as they celebrate the landscape and people of a particular, beloved place. Obviously, the writers have themselves survived, sometimes after enduring hardships, and their books reflect something of the triumph of art. Ultimately, any memoir testifies to survival. All writers of life narrative no doubt hope for readers to say of their books what Ivan Doig wrote in his review of Mary Clearman Blew's *All But the Waltz*: "This is a brave and an enduring book" (X6).

Chapter Notes

Preface

1. Arthur Hugh Clough, "Introduction," *Plutarch's Lives* (New York: Modern Library, 1942) xvii.

2. Betty Bergland, "Postmodernism and the Autobiographical Subject: Reconstructing the 'Other,'" in *Autobiography & Postmodernism*, ed. Kathleen Ashley et al. Amherst: University of Massachusetts Press, 1994.

3. Mary Clearman Blew, *Writing Her Own Life: Imogene Welch, Western Rural Schoolteacher* (Norman: University of Oklahoma Press, 2004) 8.

4. T. S. Eliot, "Tradition and the Individual Talent," *The Sacred Wood: Essays on Poetry and Criticism* (London: Methuen, 1960; rpr. of 1920) 49.

5. Kim Barnes, personal communication (29 October 2004).

6. Judy Blunt, personal communication (25 August 2004).

7. Janet Campbell Hale, personal communication (29 June 2004).

8. Jeffe Kennedy, personal communication, (27 August 2004).

9. Annie Dillard, *Pilgrim at Tinker Creek* (New York: Harper, 1974) 139.

10. Julia Watson, "'I Have Never Been Myself': Introducing Mary MacLane," *The Story of Mary MacLane* (Helena, MT: Riverbend, 2002) vi; see also "Engendering Montana Lives: Women's Autobiographical Writing," in *Writing Montana: Literature under the Big Sky*, ed. Rick Newby (Helena: Montana Center for the Book, 1996) 141–142.

11. Krista Comer, *Landscapes of the New West: Gender and Geography in Contemporary Women's Writing* (Chapel Hill: University of North Carolina Press, 1999) 11.

12. Gretel Ehrlich, *The Solace of Open Spaces* (New York: Penguin 1985) 11.

13. Ernest Hemingway, *Selected Letters, 1917–1961*, ed. Carlos Baker (New York: Scribner's, 1981) 355.

14. *http://www.powells.com/authors/blunt.html*.

Chapter One

1. Laura Marcus, *Auto/biographical Discourses* (Manchester: Manchester University Press, 1994) 8

2. Mary Clearman Blew, "Introduction," *When Montana and I Were Young*, by Margaret Bell (Lincoln: University of Nebraska Press, 2002) xxiv; the announcement of the 1990s as "the decade of the memoir" likely can be traced to William Zinsser's essay, "How to Write a Memoir," first published in 1999.

3. Kathleen Boardman and Gioia Woods, "Western Autobiography and

Memoir: A Panel of Writers," *Western American Literature* 37.2 (Summer 2002) 164.

4. Sidonie Smith and Julia Watson, *Reading Autobiography: A Guide for Interpreting Life Narratives* (Minneapolis: University of Minnesota Press, 2001) 183–207. I have found this text to be the most valuable single volume of commentary on the genre.

5. Jerome Bruner, "The Autobiographical Process," *The Culture of Autobiography: Construction of Self-Representation*, ed. Robert Folkenflik (Stanford, CA: Stanford University Press, 1993) 38.

6. Philippe Lejeune, *On Autobiography*, trans. Katherine Leary (Minneapolis: University of Minnesota Press, 1989) 4.

7. Elizabeth W. Bruss, *Autobiographical Acts: The Changing Situation of a Literary Genre* (Baltimore: Johns Hopkins University Press, 1976) 11.

8. Robert Folkenflik, "Introduction: The Institution of Autobiography," *The Culture of Autobiography: Constructions of Self-Representation* (Stanford, CA: Stanford University Press, 1993) 5.

9. Paul de Man, "Autobiography as De-facement," *Modern Language Notes* 94 (1979) 919.

10. Georges Gusdorf, "Conditions and Limits of Autobiography," trans. James Olney, *Autobiography: Essays Theoretical and Critical* (Princeton, NJ: Princeton University Press, 1980) 28.

11. Northrup Frye, *The Anatomy of Criticism* (Princeton, NJ: Princeton University Press, 1957) 307.

12. Georg Misch, *A History of Autobiography in Antiquity*, Vol. 1, trans. E. W. Dickes (Cambridge, MA: Harvard University Press, 1951) 4–5.

13. C. G. Jung, *Memories, Dreams, Reflections* ed. Aniela Jaffé, trans. Richard and Clara Winston (New York: Random House, 1963) 3.

14. Francis R. Hart, "Notes for an Anatomy of Modern Autobiography," *New Literary History* 1 (1970) 486.

15. William Zinsser, "Introduction," *Inventing the Truth: The Art and Craft of Memoir*, rev. ed. (Boston: Houghton Mifflin, 1998): 14–15.

16. Linda K. Karell, *Writing Together/Writing Apart: Collaboration in Western American Literature* (Lincoln: University of Nebraska Press, 2002) 119.

17. Vivian Gornick, *The Situation and the Story* (New York: Farrar, Straus & Giroux, 2001) 91.

18. Annie Dillard, "To Fashion a Text," *Inventing the Truth: The Art and Craft of Memoir* (Boston: Houghton Mifflin, 1998): 143.

19. William Gass, "The Art of Self: Autobiography in an Age of Narcissism," *Harper's* (May 1994): 45, 49.

20. Patricia Hampl, *I Could Tell You Stories: Sojourns in the Land of Memory* (New York: Norton, 1999) 33.

21. Wallace Stegner, *Where the Bluebird Sings to the Lemonade Springs: Living and Writing in the West* (New York: Penguin, 1992) 220.

22. James Goodwin, *Autobiography: The Self Made Text* (New York: Twayne, 1993): 6.

23. Paul John Eakin, *How Our Lives Become Stories* (Ithaca, NY: Cornell University Press, 1999) 69.

24. Mary Clearman Blew, "The Art of Memoir," *Bone Deep in Landscape: Writing, Reading, and Place* (Norman: University of Oklahoma Press, 1999) 6–7.

25. Andrew Hudgins, "An Autobiographer's Lies," *American Scholar* 65 (Autumn 1996) 542, 553.

26. Thomas Larson, *The Memoir and the Memoirist: Reading & Writing Personal Narrative* (Athens: Swallow/Ohio University Press, 2007) 112.

27. Fern Kupfer, "Everything But the Truth?" *The Fourth Genre: Contemporary Writers of/on Creative Nonfiction*, ed. Robert R. Root, Jr. and Michael Steinberg (Boston: Allyn and Bacon, 1999) 327.

28. Suzanne Nalbantian, *Aesthetic Autobiography* (New York: St. Martin's, 1994) 11.

29. William C. Spengemann, *Forms of Autobiography: Episodes in the History of a Literary Genre* (New Haven, CT: Yale University Press, 1980) xi.

30. Jill Ker Conway, *When Memory Speaks: Reflections on Autobiography* (New York: Knopf, 1998): 3.

31. Barrett J. Mandel, "Full of Life Now," *Autobiography: Essays Theoretical and Critical* (Princeton, NJ: Princeton University Press, 1980): 52, 55.

32. Robert Folkenflik, "Introduction,"

The Culture of Autobiography: Constructions of Self-Presentation (Stanford, CA: Stanford University Press, 1993): 13–14.

33. William Kittredge, *Hole in the Sky: A Memoir* (New York: Vintage, 1993) 5.

34. Mark Spragg, *Where Rivers Change Direction* (New York: Riverhead Books, 1999) 3.

35. Ann Zwinger, *Wind in the Rock: The Canyonlands of Southeastern Utah* (Tucson: University of Arizona Press, 1978) 26.

36. Janet Varner Gunn, *Autobiography: Toward a Poetics of Experience* (Philadelphia: University of Pennsylvania Press, 1982) 13.

37. James Olney, *Memory & Narrative: The Weave of Life-Writing* (Chicago: University of Chicago Press, 1998) xv.

38. Norman Maclean, *A River Runs through It and Other Stories* (Chicago: University of Chicago Press, 1976) 104.

39. Annick Smith, *Homestead* (Minneapolis: Milkweed Editions, 1995) 56.

40. Gretel Ehrlich, *The Solace of Open Spaces* (New York: Penguin, 1986) 4; Annie Pike Greenwood, *We Sagebrush Folks* (Moscow: University of Idaho Press, 1988) 14.

41. Richard Freadman, *Threads of Life: Autobiography and the Will* (Chicago: University of Chicago Press, 2001) 284.

42. Friedrich Schlegel, *The Culture of Autobiography*, ed. Robert Folkenflik (Stanford, CA: Stanford University Press, 1993) 3. From *Athenaeum* fragments (1798).

Chapter Two

1. Sidonie Smith and Julia Watson, *Reading Autobiography: A Guide for Interpreting Life Narratives* (Minneapolis: University of Minnesota Press, 2001) 58.

2. James C. Work, ed., *Prose and Poetry of the American West* (Lincoln: University of Nebraska Press, 1990) vi–vii.

3. Susan Armitage, "Through Women's Eyes: A New View of the West," *The Women's West*, ed. Susan Armitage and Elizabeth Jameson (Norman: University of Oklahoma Press, 1987) 14.

4. Sidonie Smith, *A Poetics of Women's Autobiography* (Bloomington: Indiana University Press, 1987) 176.

5. Krista Comer, *Landscapes of the New West: Gender and Geography in Contemporary Women's Writing* (Chapel Hill: University of North Carolina Press, 1999), 62.

6. Wallace Stegner, *Where the Bluebird Sings to the Lemonade Springs* (New York: Penguin, 1992) 46.

7. William Kittredge, "Introduction: West of Your Town: Another Country," *The Portable Western Reader*, ed. William Kittredge (New York: Penguin, 1997) xvi.

8. Linda K. Karell, *Writing Together/Writing Apart: Collaboration in Western American Literature* (Lincoln: University of Nebraska Press, 2002) xxviii.

9. Andrew Garcia, *Tough Trip through Paradise (1878–1879)* (New York: Houghton Mifflin, 1967) 5.

10. Bennett H. Stein, "Introduction," *Tough Trip through Paradise (1878–1879)* (New York: Houghton Mifflin, 1967) xiv.

11. James Willard Schultz, *My Life as an Indian* (New York: Beaufort Books, 1983) 19. I have altered the British spellings in this edition to conform with American conventions.

12. Anonymous, *London Times* 6 (July 12, 1907) 222.

13. Nannie T. Alderson and Helena Huntington Smith, *A Bride Goes West* (New York: Farrar & Rinehart, 1942) 221.

14. Anne Ellis, *The Life of an Ordinary Woman* (Boston: Houghton Mifflin, 1990; rpr. of 1929 ed.) 268.

15. Anne Ellis, *Plain Anne Ellis* (Lincoln: University of Nebraska Press, 1984; rpr. of 1931 ed.) 207.

16. Paul John Eakin, *How Our Lives Become Stories* (Ithaca, NY: Cornell University Press, 1999) 50.

17. Annie Dillard, "To Fashion a Text," in *Inventing the Truth: The Art and Craft of Memoir*, rev. ed., ed. William Zinsser, (Boston: Houghton Mifflin, 1998) 155.

18. Mary Clearman Blew, "The Art of Memoir," *Bone Deep in Landscape: Writing, Reading, and Place* (Norman: University of Oklahoma Press, 1999) 6.

19. Jill Ker Conway, "Points of Departure," *Inventing the Truth*, 50.

20. Annie Pike Greenwood, *We Sagebrush Folk* (Moscow: University of Idaho Press, 1988; rpr. of 1934 ed.) 17.

21. Carol Bly, "Foreword," *The Life of an Ordinary Woman* (Boston: Houghton Mifflin, 1990) ix.

22. E. F. Kelly, *New York Times* (August 30, 1931) 9.
23. Margaret Wallace, *Bookman* 74 (October 1931) 204.
24. C. B. Sherman, "Books," *New York Herald Tribune* (November 18, 1934) 21.
25. E. F. Kelly, *New York Times* (November 18, 1934) 21.
26. F.B., Review of *We Sagebrush Folks*, *Boston Tribune* (5 December 1934); cited in Maralyn Morton, Compiler, *Idaho Writers: Biographical and Critical Information* (Pocatello: Idaho State College Library, 1952) 181.
27. Jo Ann Ruckman, "Afterword," *We Sagebrush Folks* 485.
28. William Kittredge, *Owning It All* (Saint Paul: Graywolf, 1987) 64.
29. William Kittredge, *Taking Care: Thoughts on Storytelling and Belief* (Minneapolis: Milkweed Editions, 1999) 12, 73. Kittredge elaborates these principles in *The Nature of Generosity* (New York: Knopf, 2000).
30. Rodman W. Paul, "Introduction," *A Victorian Gentlewoman in the Far West* (San Marino, CA: Huntington Library, 1972) 3.
31. Mary Hallock Foote, *A Victorian Gentlewoman*, 262.
32. Paul, "Introduction," *A Victorian Gentlewoman*, 26.
33. Laura L. Bush, *Faithful Transgressions in the American West: Six Twentieth-Century Mormon Women's Autobiographical Acts* (Logan: Utah State University Press, 2004) 59.
34. Annie Clark Tanner, *A Mormon Mother*, Tanner Trust Fund (Salt Lake City: University of Utah Press, 1976) 61.
35. Mary Clearman Blew, 'Introduction," *When Montana and I Were Young: A Frontier Childhood* (Lincoln: University of Nebraska Press, 2002) xix.
36. Norman Maclean, *A River Runs through It and Other Stories* (Chicago: University of Chicago Press, 1976) 127.
37. Elinore Pruitt Stewart, *Letters of a Woman Homesteader* (New York: Houghton Mifflin, 1982, rpr. of 1914 ed.) 10.
38. Mary MacLane, *The Story of Mary MacLane* (Helena, MT: Riverbend, 2002) 7.
39. Cathryn Halverson, *Maverick Autobiographies: Women Writers and the American West, 1900–1936* (Madison: University of Wisconsin Press, 2004) 80.
40. Julia Watson, "'I Have Never Been Myself': Introducing Mary MacLane," *The Story of Mary MacLane* (Helena, MT: Riverbend, 2002) x.
41. "Mary MacLane, "The Second *Story of Mary MacLane*," *Butte Evening News* (3 April 1910) 9–10; cited in Watson xxi, Halverson 71.
42. Mary Clearman Blew, *All But the Waltz: A Memoir of Five Generations in the Life of a Montana Family* (Norman: University of Oklahoma Press, 1991) 22.
43. Ivan Doig, personal communication (30 March 2002).
44. Enos A. Mills, *Wild Life on the Rockies* (Boston: Houghton Mifflin, 1909) 32. At least a dozen of Mills's books, including *Wild Life on the Rockies*, have been reprinted within the past fifteen years by the University of Nebraska Press and the Temporal Mechanical Press, which is connected with the Enos Mills' Cabin Museum.
45. John Dotson, "Enos Mills," *American Nature Writers*, II (New York: Scribner's, 1996) 621.
46. Jackson J. Benson, *Wallace Stegner: His Life and Work* (New York: Viking, 1996) 35.
47. Leigh Gilmore, *The Limits of Autobiography: Trauma and Testimony* (Ithaca, NY: Cornell University Press, 2001) 12–13.
48. Barry Lopez, *Arctic Dreams: Imagination and Desire in a Northern Landscape* (New York: Scribner's, 1986) xxvii.

Chapter Three

1. William Stafford, *Stories That Could Be True: New and Selected Poems* (New York: Harper & Row, 1977) 84.
2. William W. Bevis, "Region, Power, Place," in *Reading the West: New Essays on the Literature of the American West*, ed. By Michael Kowalewski (Cambridge: Cambridge University Press, 1996) 21.
3. Frank Trippett, Review of *This House of Sky*, *Time* 112 (11 September 1978) 90.
4. Nicholas O'Connell, *At the Field's End: Interviews with Twenty Pacific Northwest Writers* (Seattle: Madrona, 1987) 304.
5. Linda K. Karell, *Writing Together/*

Writing Apart (Lincoln: University of Nebraska Press, 2002) 120.

6. Harold P. Simonson, *Beyond the Frontier: Writers, Western Regionalism and a Sense of Place* (Fort Worth: Texas Christian University Press, 1989) 14.

7. Ivan Doig, *This House of Sky: Landscapes of a Western Mind* (New York: Harcourt Brace Jovanovich, 1978) 3.

8. Mark Spragg, *Where Rivers Change Direction* (New York: Penguin Putnam, 1999) 1.

9. Pete Hamill, *A Drinking Life: A Memoir* (Boston: Little, Brown, 1994) 3.

10. Elizabeth Simpson, *Earthlight, Wordfire: The Work of Ivan Doig* (Moscow: University of Idaho Press, 1992) 10.

11. Anonymous, review of *This House of Sky*, *Christian Science Monitor* (23 October 1978) B15.

12. Ivan Doig, "Introduction," *This House of Sky* (New York: Harcourt, 1992) x.

13. William W. Bevis, *Ten Tough Trips: Montana Writers and the West* (Seattle: University of Washington Press, 1990) 167.

14. Ivan Doig, personal communication (30 March 2002).

15. James P. Degnan, "Cowboys and Crazies: The West, Then and Now," *Hudson Review* 33 (Spring 1980) 146–150.

16. A. Carl Bredahl, *Ivan Doig* (Boise, ID: Boise State University Western Writers Series no. 140, 1999) 17.

17. William Zinsser, *Inventing the Truth: The Art and Craft of Memoir*, ed. (Boston: Houghton Mifflin, 1998) 15.

18. Bill Ott, Review of *Unfinished Life*, *Booklist* 100 (1 August 2004) 1901.

19. Mark Spragg, *Where Rivers Change Direction* (New York: Riverhead, 1999) 3.

20. Mark Spragg, personal communication (1 May 2004).

21. Roripaugh's publications include a Western novel, *Honor Thy Father* (1963) and several books of poetry, including *Learn to Love the Haze* (1976) and *Ranch: Wyoming Poetry* (reprinted 2001).

22. Mark Spragg, personal communication (1 May 2004).

23. Brian Dillon, "Closure in Mark Spragg's *Where Rivers Change Direction*," *Western American Literature* 40.2 (Summer 2005) 157.

24. Edmund Gosse, *Father and Son* (New York: Penguin, 1982) 224.

25. Gretel Ehrlich, *The Solace of Open Spaces* (New York: Penguin, 1985) 8.

26. Martin Padget, Review of *Where Rivers Change Direction*, *Times Literary Supplement* no. 5071 (9 June 2000) 36.

27. Paul Gediman, Review of *Where Rivers Change Direction*, *Publishers Weekly* 246, no. 37 (13 September 1999) 70.

28. http://pdxbooks.com/compare.

29. Melody Graulich, review essay on *Where Rivers Change Direction*, *Western American Literature* 37.2 (Summer 2002) 270, 271.

Chapter Four

1. William Kittredge, *Hole in the Sky: A Memoir* (New York: Vintage, 1992) 8, 11.

2. John Rember, *Traplines: Coming Home to Sawtooth Valley* (New York: Pantheon Books, 2003) xii.

3. Thomas Larson, *The Memoir and the Memoirist: Reading & Writing Personal Narrative* (Athens: Swallow/Ohio University Press, 2007) 9.

4. Paul John, Eakin, *How Our Lives Become Stories* (Ithaca, NY: Cornell University Press, 1999) 185.

5. Mark Spragg, *Where Rivers Change Direction* (New York: Riverhead Books, 1999) 50.

6. Ivan Doig, *This House of Sky: Landscapes of a Western Mind* (New York: Harcourt Brace Jovanovich, 1978) 222.

7. Mary Clearman Blew, *Writing Her Own Life: Imogene Welch, Western Rural Schoolteacher* (Norman: University of Oklahoma Press, 2004) 8, 9.

8. Teresa Jordan, *Riding the White Horse Home: A Western Family Album* (New York: Pantheon Books, 1993) 195.

9. Barbara Howard Meldrum, "Creative Cowgirl: Mary Clearman Blew's Herstory," *South Dakota Review* 31 (Spring 1993) 63.

10. Ivan Doig, "Bone-Deep in Landscape," *Washington Post Book World* (29 September 1991) X6.

11. Krista Comer, *Landscapes of the New West: Gender and Geography in Contempo-*

rary Women's Writing (Chapel Hill: University of North Carolina Press, 1999) 224.

12. Mary Blew, personal communication (19 May 2004).

13. Victoria Amador, Review of *All But the Waltz* and *Runaway*, *Bloomsbury Review* (July/August 1992) 8.

14. Mary Clearman Blew, *All But the Waltz: A Memoir of Five Generations in the Life of a Montana Family* (Norman: University of Oklahoma Press, 1991) 3.

15. Linda K Karell, *Writing Together/Writing Apart: Collaboration in Western American Literature* (Lincoln: University of Nebraska Press, 2002) 133.

16. Thomas Dow Adams, *Light Writing & Life Writing: Photography in Autobiography* (Chapel Hill: University of North Carolina Press, 2000) 226.

17. Mary Clearman Blew, "The Art of Memoir," *Bone Deep in Landscape: Writing, Reading, and Place* (Norman: University of Oklahoma Press, 1999) 7.

18. Ernest Hemingway, *By-line: Ernest Hemingway*, ed. William White (New York: Bantam, 1967) 190.

19. Margot Liberty, Review of *Riding the White Horse Home*, *Western Historical Quarterly* 25 (Summer 1994) 219.

20. Teresa Jordan, personal communication (2 September 2004).

21. Norman Maclean, "The Hidden Art of a Good Story: Wallace Stegner Lecture," in *Norman Maclean*, ed. Ron McFarland and Hugh Nichols (Lewiston, ID: Confluence Press, 1988) 27.

22. In a review of Fairchild's *The Art of the Lathe* (1998), published in *New Criterion* 21.4 (December 2002), poet William Logan is sharply critical of the "deskbound" poet for romanticizing his past as a manual laborer.

23. Carolyn Heilbrun, *Writing a Woman's Life* (New York: Ballantine Books, 1988) 18.

24. Roland Wulbert, Review of *Riding the White Horse Home*, *Booklist* 89 (15 March 1993) 1294.

Chapter Five

1. Sidonie Smith, *A Poetics of Women's Autobiography: Marginality and the Fictions of Self-Representation* (Bloomington: Indiana University Press, 1987) 175.

2. Sidonie Smith, *Subjectivity, Identity, and the Body: Women's Autobiographical Practices in the Twentieth Century* (Bloomington: Indiana University Press, 1993) 12.

3. Patricia Meyer Spacks, "Female Rhetorics," *The Private Self: Theory and Practice of Women's Autobiographical Writing*, Ed. Shari Benstock (Chapel Hill: University of North Carolina Press, 1988) 178.

4. Susan Stanford Friedman, "Women's Autobiographical Selves: Theory and Practice," *The Private Self: Theory and Practice of Women's Autobiographical Writing*, Ed. Shari Benstock (Chapel Hill: University of North Carolina Press, 1988) 40.

5. Paul John Eakin, *How Our Lives Become Stories* (Ithaca, NY: Cornell University Press, 1999) 50.

6. Mary Clearman Blew, *Balsamroot: A Memoir* (New York: Viking, 1994) 75.

7. Carolyn G. Heilbrun, *Writing a Woman's Life* (New York: Ballantine Books, 1988) 13.

8. Kim Barnes, personal communication (29 October 2004).

9. Roberta Bernstein, Review of *Hungry for the World*, *New York Times Book Review* 105, no. 14 (2 April 2000) 23.

10. Kim Barnes, *In the Wilderness: Coming of Age in Unknown Country* (New York: Doubleday, 1994) 4.

11. Kim Barnes, "Prayer, Piety, Passion, and Prose: One Writer's Quest for the Sacred," *Connections* (Summer 2000) n.a.

12. Kim Barnes, *Hungry for the World: A Memoir* (New York: Villard, 2000) 102.

13. Elizabeth Gilbert, "Even Cowgirls Get the Blues," *New York Times Book Review* 107 (3 March 2002) 6.

14. Mary Zeiss Stange, "Little Joy on the Prairie," *Women's Review of Books* 19 (April 2002) 13.

15. Blaine Harden, "Suffering and Creativity," *New York Times* 151 (28 May 2002) E3.

16. Judy Blunt, *Breaking Clean* (New York: Knopf, 2002) 3, 4.

17. Mary Clearman Blew, "The Art of Memoir," *Bone Deep in Landscape: Writing, Reading, and Place* (Norman: University of Oklahoma Press, 1999) 6–7.

18. Andrew Hudgins, "An Autobiographer's Lies," *American Scholar* 65 (Autumn 1966) 552; reprinted as "The Glass Anvil: 'The Lies of an Autobiographer" in *The Glass Anvil* (Ann Arbor: University of Michigan Press, 1997): 92–106.

19. Sidonie Smith and Julia Watson, *Reading Autobiography: A Guide for Interpreting Life Narratives* (Minneapolis: University of Minnesota Press, 2001) 10.

20. http://www.powells.com.

21. http://www.bookbrowse.com.

Chapter Six

1. Brian Swann and Arnold Krupat, "Introduction," *I Tell You Now: Autobiographical Essays by Native American Writers* (Lincoln: University of Nebraska P, 1987) ix.

2. Arnold Krupat, *For Those Who Come After: A Study of Native American Autobiography* (Berkeley: University of California Press, 1985) 30.

3. A. LaVonne Ruoff's 29-volume series, American Indian Lives, provides new and reprinted biographies of Native American writers, including Sarah Winnemucca. Mariela Hristova's Pathfinder website is devoted specifically to American Indian autobiography: http://www.ischool.utexas.edu/~hrsitova/portfolio/research/papers/autobiography.html.

4. Paul John Eakin, *How Our Lives Become Stories* (Ithaca, NY: Cornell University Press, 1999) 174, 181.

5. Jay Miller, "Introduction," *Mourning Dove: A Salishan Autobiography* (Lincoln: University of Nebraska Press, 1990) xxxi.

6. G. Thomas Couser, *Altered Egos: Authority in American Autobiography* (New York: Oxford University Press, 1989) 207.

7. Hertha D. Wong, *Sending My Heart Across the Years: Tradition and Innovation in Native American Autobiography* (New York: Oxford University Press, 1992) 6.

8. Sidner Larson, personal communication (28 June 2004).

9. Sidner J. Larson, *Catch Colt* (Lincoln: University of Nebraska Press, 1995) 92.

10. Linda Hogan, *The Woman Who Watches over the World: A Native Memoir* (New York: Norton, 2001) 116.

11. Sidner J. Larson, *Captured in the Middle: Tradition and Experience in Contemporary Native American Writing* (Seattle: University of Washington Press, 2000) 75.

12. Andrew J. Deering, Review of *Catch Colt*, *MultiCultural Review* 4 (December 1995) 68.

13. Genevieve Stuttaford, Review of *Catch Colt*, *Publishers Weekly* 242 (24 April 1995) 57.

14. Loretta Fowler, *Sacred Symbols, Contested Meanings: Gros Ventre Culture and History, 1778–1984* (Ithaca, NY: Cornell University Press, 1987) 14.

15. Regina Flannery, *The Gros Ventres of Montana: Part I, Social Life*, Catholic University of America Anthropological Series no. 15 (Washington, DC: Catholic University of America Press, 1953) xi.

16. John C. Ewers, *The Blackfeet: Raiders of the Northwestern Plains* (Norman: University of Oklahoma Press, 1959) 163.

17. John M. Cooper, *The Gros Ventres of Montana: Part II, Religion and Ritual*, ed. Regina Flannery (Washington, DC: Catholic University of America Press, 1957) 274.

18. Cooper 200–221; see also A. L. Kroeber, "Ethnology of the Gros Ventre," *Anthropological Papers of the American Museum of Natural History* 1, no. 4 (April 1908): 241–250.

19. Edward H. Spicer, *A Short History of the Indians of the United States* (New York: Van Nostrand Reinhold, 1969) 90.

20. Janet Campbell Hale, *Bloodlines: Odyssey of a Native Daughter* (New York: Random House, 1993) 185.

21. William Kittredge, *Hole in the Sky: A Memoir* (New York: Vintage, 1992) 238.

22. Judy Blunt, *Breaking Clean* (New York: Knopf, 2002) 303.

23. Donna Seaman, Review of *Bloodlines*, *Booklist* 89 (15 May 1993) 1669.

24. Sherry L. Smith, Review of *Bloodlines*, *Journal of American History* 81 (September 1994) 836.

25. Frederick Hale, *Janet Campbell Hale*, Western Writers Series no. 125 (Boise, ID: Boise State University Press, 1996) 50.

26. Julia Watson, "Writing in Blood: Autobiography and Technologies of the

Real in Janet Campbell Hale's *Bloodlines,*" *Haunting Violations: Feminist Criticism and the Crisis of the "Real,"* ed. Wendy Hesford and Wendy Kozol (Champaign-Urbana: University of Illinois Press: 2000) 111.

27. Janet Campbell Hale, personal communication (29 June 2004).

28. Rodney Frey, *Landscape Traveled by Coyote and Crane: The World of the Schitsu'umsh (Coeur d'Alene Indians)* (Seattle: University of Washington Press, 2001) 3.

29. John Bartlett, *Familiar Quotations,* 14th ed. (Boston: Little, Brown, 1968) 742a.

30. Leo Tolstoy, *Anna Karenina,* trans. Joel Carmichael (New York: Bantam Books, 1960) 1.

Chapter Seven

1. Sidonie Smith and Julia Watson, *Reading Autobiography: A Guide for Interpreting Life Narratives* (Minneapolis: University of Minnesota P, 2001) 194.

2. Edward Abbey, *Desert Solitaire: A Season in the Wilderness* (New York: Ballantine, 1971) x.

3. John Rember, *Traplines: Coming Home to Sawtooth Valley* (New York: Pantheon Books, 2003) 202.

4. Gretel Ehrlich, *The Solace of Open Spaces* (New York: Penguin, 1985) 131.

5. William Kittredge, *Hole in the Sky: A Memoir* (New York: Vintage, 1992) 52.

6. Terry Tempest Williams, *Refuge: An Unnatural History of Family and Place* (New York: Vintage, 1991) 13.

7. William Kittredge, *Owning It All* (Saint Paul, MN: Graywolf, 1987) 61.

8. Gregory L. Morris, *Talking Up a Storm: Voices of the New West* (Lincoln: University of Nebraska Press, 1994) 173.

9. Ron McFarland, *William Kittredge,* Western Writers Series no. 152 (Boise, ID: Boise State University Press, 2002) 40.

10. Mickey Pearlman, *Listen to Their Voices: Twenty Interviews with Women Who Write* (New York: Norton, 1993) 122.

11. Jocelyn Bartkevicius and Mary Hussmann, "A Conversation with Terry Tempest Williams," *Iowa Review* 27 (Spring 1997) 8.

12. Margaret B. Guthrie, Review of *Refuge, New York Times Book Review* 97 (19 January 1992) 18.

13. Marilyn B. Chandler, Review of *Refuge, Women's Review of Books* 9 (March 1992) 10.

14. Brooke Libby, "Nature Writing as *Refuge*: Autobiography in the Natural World," in *Reading under the Sign of Nature: New Essays in Ecocriticism,* ed. John Tallmadge and Henry Harrington (Salt Lake City: University of Utah Press, 2000) 252.

15. Kim Barnes, personal communication (29 October 2004).

16. Kip Clark and Deb Thornton, "Terry Tempest Williams," *Dictionary of Literary Biography: Twentieth-Century American Western Writers, First Series* 206 (Detroit: Gale Group, 1999) 306.

17. John Tallmadge, "Beyond the Excursion: Initiatory Themes in Annie Dillard and Terry Tempest Williams," in *Reading the Earth: New Directions in the Study of Literature and Environment,* ed. Michael P. Branch, et al. (Moscow: University of Idaho Press, 1998) 207.

18. Edward Lueders, ed., *Writing Natural History: Dialogues with Authors* (Salt Lake City: University of Utah Press, 1989) 41.

19. Cheryll Glotgelty, "Flooding the Boundaries of Form: Terry Tempest Willams's Ecofeminist *Unnatural History,*" in *Change in the American West: Exploring the Human Dimension,* ed. Stephen Tchudi (Reno: University of Nevada Press, 1996) 158.

20. Cynthia J. Hollenbeck, unpublished paper (Moscow, University of Idaho, 2 December 2003). Used with permission of the writer.

21. Jeanette E. Riley, "Finding One's Place in the 'Family of Things': Terry Tempest Williams and a Geography of Self," *Women's Studies* 32 (July/August 2003) 591.

22. Cassandra Kircher, "Rethinking Dichotomies in Terry Tempest Williams's *Refuge,*" in *Ecofeminist Literary Criticism,* ed. Greta Gaard and Patrick D. Murphy (Urbana: University of Illinois Press, 1998) 158.

Conclusions and Specualtions

1. Terry Tempest Williams, *Refuge: An Unnatural History of Family and Place* (New York: Vintage, 1992) 284.
2. Ivan Doig, "Bone-Deep in Landscape," *Washington Post Book World* (29 September 1991) X6.
3. William Kittredge, *Hole in the Sky* (New York: Vintage, 1993) 236.
4. Harold P. Simonson, *Beyond the Frontier: Writers, Western Regionalism and a Sense of Place* (Fort Worth: Texas Christian University Press, 1989) 4.
5. Jeffe Kennedy, personal communication (27 August 2004).
6. Wallace Stegner, *Where the Bluebird Sings to the Lemonade Springs: Living and Writing in the West* (New York: Penguin, 1992) 218.
7. Jill Ker Conway, *When Memory Speaks: Reflections on Autobiography* (New York: Knopf, 1998) 3.
8. Paul John Eakin, *Fictions in Autobiography: Studies in the Art of Self-Invention* (Princeton, NJ: Princeton University Press, 1985) 3, 4.

Works Consulted

As a rule, this listing omits reference to book reviews and anonymous entries; however, these are cited at the end of relevant chapters. Where appropriate I have indicated the date of the first publication of memoirs of historical interest.

Abbey, Edward. *Desert Solitaire: A Season in the Wilderness.* New York: Ballantine Books, 1971.
Adams, Thomas Dow. *Light Writing & Life Writing: Photography in Autobiography.* Chapel Hill: University of North Carolina Press, 2000.
Alderson, Nannie T., and Helena Huntington Smith. *A Bride Goes West.* New York: Farrar & Rinehart, 1942.
Arenas, Reinaldo. *Before Night Falls.* New York: Penguin, 1994.
Armitage, Susan. "Through Women's Eyes: A New View of the West." In *The Women's West.* Ed. Susan Armitage and Elizabeth Jameson, 9–18. Norman: University of Oklahoma Press, 1987.
Ashley, Kathleen, Leigh Gilmore, and Gerald Peters. *Autobiography & Postmodernism.* Amherst: University of Massachusetts Press, 1994.
Axtell, Horace, and Margo Aragon. *A Little Bit of Wisdom: Conversations with a Nez Perce Elder.* Lewiston, ID: Confluence, 1997.
Baker, Russell. *Growing Up.* New York: Signet, 1982.
Barnes, Craig S. *Growing Up True: Lessons from a Western Boyhood.* Golden, CO: Fulcrum, 2001.
Barnes, Kim. *Hungry for the World: A Memoir.* New York: Villard, 2000.
———. *In the Wilderness: Coming of Age in Unknown Country.* New York: Doubleday, 1996.
———. Personal Communication. 29 October 2004.
———. "Prayer, Piety, Passion, and Prose: One Writer's Quest for the Sacred." *Connections* (Summer 2000): n.p.; online version: http://www.washington.edu/

uwired/outreach/cspn/Website/Hist%20n%20Lit/Part%20Five/Texts/Barnes%20Prayers.html.
Bartkevicius, Jocelyn, and Mary Hussmann. "A Conversation with Terry Tempest Williams." *Iowa Review* 27 (Spring 1997): 1–23.
Bass, Rick. *Winter: Notes from Montana*. Boston: Houghton Mifflin, 1991.
Bell, Margaret. *When Montana and I Were Young: A Frontier Childhood*. Lincoln: University of Nebraska Press, 2002.
Benson, Jackson. *Wallace Stegner: His Life and Work*. New York: Viking, 1996.
Benstock, Shari, ed. *The Private Self: Theory and Practice of Women's Autobiographical Writing*. Chapel Hill: University of North Carolina Press, 1988.
Bevis, William W. "Region, Power, Place." In *Reading the West: New Essays on the Literature of the American West*. Ed. Michael Kowaleski, 21–43. Cambridge, UK: Cambridge University Press, 1996.
———. *Ten Tough Trips: Montana Writers and the West*. Seattle: University of Washington Press, 1990.
Blew, Mary. *All But the Waltz: A Memoir of Five Generations of a Montana Family*. Norman: University of Oklahoma Press, 2002. Reprint, New York: Penguin, 1991.
———. *Balsamroot*. New York: Viking, 1994.
———. *Bone Deep in Landscape: Writing, Reading, and Place*. Norman: University of Oklahoma Press, 1999.
———. "Introduction." In Margaret Bell, *When Montana and I Were Young*, ix–xxx. Lincoln: University of Nebraska Press, 2002.
———. Personal Communication. 19 May 2004.
———. *Writing Her Own Life: Imogene Welch, Western Rural Schoolteacher*. Norman: University of Oklahoma Press, 2004.
Blunt, Judy. *Breaking Clean*. New York: Knopf, 2002.
———. Interview. http://www.powells.com/authors/blunt.html.
———. Personal Communication. 25 August 2004.
Bly, Carol. "Foreword." *The Life of an Ordinary Woman*, vii–xii. Boston: Houghton Mifflin, 1990.
Boardman, Kathleen, and Gioia Woods. "Western Autobiography and Memoir: A Panel of Writers." *Western American Literature* 37.2 (Summer 2002): 147–169.
Bredahl, A. Carl. *Ivan Doig*. Western Writers Series no. 140. Boise, ID: Boise State University Press, 1999.
Bruner, Jerome. "The Autobiographical Process." In *The Culture of Autobiography: Construction of Self-Representation*. Ed. Robert Folkenflik, 38–56. Stanford, CA: Stanford University Press, 1993.
Bruss, Elizabeth. *Autobiographical Acts: The Changing Situation of a Literary Genre*. Baltimore: Johns Hopkins University Press, 1976.
Bush, Laura L. *Faithful Transgressions in the American West: Six Twentieth-Century Mormon Women's Autobiographical Acts*. Logan: Utah State University Press, 2004.
Clark, Kip, and Deb Thornton. "Terry Tempest Williams." *Dictionary of Literary Biography: Twentieth-Century American Western Writers*. First Series, vol. 206, 303–309. Detroit: Gale Group, 1999.
Clough, Arthur Hough. "Introduction." *Plutarch's Lives*, ix–xxiv. New York: Modern Library, 1942.
Comer, Krista. *Landscapes of the New West: Gender and Geography in Contemporary Women's Writing*. Chapel Hill: University of North Carolina Press, 1999.

Conway, Jill Ker. "Points of Departure." In *Inventing the Truth*. Ed. William Zinsser, 41–59. Boston: Houghton Mifflin, 1998.
_____. *The Road from Coorain*. New York: Knopf, 1989.
_____. *When Memory Speaks: Reflections on Autobiography*. New York: Knopf, 1998.
Cooper, John M. *The Gros Ventres of Montana: Part II, Religion and Ritual*. Ed. Regina Flannery. Washington, DC: Catholic University of America Press, 1957.
Couser, G. Thomas. *Altered Egos: Authority in American Autobiography*. New York: Oxford University Press, 1989.
Davis, Nell Portrey. *Stump Ranch Pioneer*. Moscow: University of Idaho Press, 1942, 1990.
Degnan, James P. "Cowboys and Crazies: The West, Then and Now," *Hudson Review* 33 (Spring 1980): 146–150.
de Man, Paul. "Autobiography as De-facement," *Modern Language Notes* 94 (1979): 919–930.
Dillard, Annie. *An American Childhood*. New York: Harper & Row, 1974.
_____. *Pilgrim at Tinker Creek*. New York: Harper & Row, 1987.
_____. "To Fashion a Text." *Inventing the Truth: The Art and Craft of Memoir*. Ed. William Zinsser. Boston: Houghton Mifflin, 1998.
_____, and Cort Conley, eds. *Modern American Memoirs*. New York: HarperCollins, 1995.
Dillon, Brian. "Closure in Mark Spragg's *Where Rivers Change Direction*." *Western American Literature* 40.2 (Summer 2005): 148–172.
Doig, Ivan. "Bone-Deep in Landscape." *Washington Post Book World*. 29 September 1991, X6.
_____. *Heart Earth*. New York: Penguin, 1993.
_____. *This House of Sky*. New York: Harcourt, 1978, 1992.
_____. Personal Correspondence. 30 March 2002.
Dotson, John. "Enos Mills." *American Nature Writers*, II. New York: Scribner's, 1996.
Eakin, Paul John. *Fictions in Autobiography: Studies in the Art of Self-Invention*. Princeton, NJ: Princeton University Press, 1985.
_____. *How Our Lives Become Stories*. Ithaca, NY: Cornell University Press, 1999.
Eggers, Dave. *A Heartbreaking Work of Staggering Genius*. New York: Vintage, 2001.
Ehrlich, Gretel. *The Solace of Open Spaces*. New York: Penguin, 1985.
Eire, Carlos. *Waiting for Snow in Havana*. New York: Simon & Schuster, 2003.
Eliot, T.S. "Tradition and the Individual Talent." *The Sacred Wood: Essays on Poetry and Criticism*. London: Methuen, 1960. Reprint of 1920.
Ellis, Anne. *The Life of an Ordinary Woman*. Boston: Houghton Mifflin, 1929, 1990.
_____. *Plain Anne Ellis*. Lincoln: University of Nebraska Press, 1931, 1984.
Ewers, John C. *The Blackfeet: Raiders of the Northwestern Plains*. Norman: University of Oklahoma Press, 1959.
Flannery, Regina. *The Gros Ventres of Montana: Part I, Social Life*. Catholic University of America Anthropological Series no. 15. Washington, DC: Catholic University of America Press, 1953.
Folkenflik, Robert. "Introduction: The Institution of Autobiography." *The Culture of Autobiography: Constructions of Self-Representation*. Stanford, CA: Stanford University Press, 1993.
Foote, Mary Hallock. *A Victorian Gentlewoman in the Far West*. San Marino, CA: Huntington Library, 1972.

Fowler, Loretta. *Sacred Symbols, Contested Meanings: Gros Ventre Culture and History, 1778–1984*. Ithaca, NY: Cornell University Press, 1987.
Freadman, Richard. *Threads of Life: Autobiography and the Will*. Chicago: University of Chicago Press, 2001.
Frey, Rodney. *Landscape Traveled by Coyote and Crane: The World of the Schitsu'umsh (Coeur d'Alene Indians)*. Seattle: University of Washington Press, 2001.
Friedman, Susan Stanford. "Women's Autobiographical Selves: Theory and Practice." In *The Private Self: Theory and Practice of Women's Autobiographical Writing*. Ed. Shari Benstock, 34–62. Chapel Hill: University of North Carolina Press, 1988.
Fromm, Pete. *Indian Creek Chronicles: A Winter Alone in the Wilderness*. New York: St. Martin's, 1993.
Frye, Northrup. *The Anatomy of Criticism*. Princeton, NJ: Princeton University Press, 1957.
Garcia, Andrew. *Tough Trip through Paradise (1878–1879)*. New York: Houghton Mifflin, 1967.
Gass, William. "The Art of Self: Autobiography in an Age of Narcissism." *Harper's Magazine* (May 1994): 43–52.
Gilmore, Leigh. *The Limits of Autobiography: Trauma and Testimony*. Ithaca, NY: Cornell University Press, 2001.
Glotgelty, Cheryll. "Flooding the Boundaries of Form: Terry Tempest Williams's Ecofeminist *Unnatural History*." In *Change in the American West: Exploring the Human Dimension*. Ed. Stephen Tchudi, 158–167. Reno: University of Nevada Press, 1996.
Goodwin, James. *Autobiography: The Self Made Text*. New York: Twayne, 1993.
Gornick, Vivian. *The Situation and the Story*. New York: Farrar, Straus & Giroux, 2001.
Gosse, Edmund. *Father and Son*. New York: Penguin, 1907, 1982.
Greenwood, Annie Pike. *We Sagebrush Folks*. Moscow: University of Idaho Press, 1934, 1988.
Gunn, Janet Varner. *Autobiography: Toward a Poetics of Experience*. Philadelphia: University of Pennsylvania Press, 1982.
Gusdorf, Georges. "Conditions and Limits of Autobiography." In *Autobiography: Essays Theoretical and Critical*. Ed. James Olney, 28–48. Princeton, NJ: Princeton University Press, 1980.
Guthrie, A.B., Jr. *The Blue Hen's Chick: An Autobiography*. Lincoln: University of Nebraska Press, 1965, 1993.
Hale, Frederick. *Janet Campbell Hale*. Western Writers Series no.125. Boise, ID: Boise State University Press, 1996.
Hale, Janet Campbell. *Bloodlines: Odyssey of a Native Daughter*. New York: Random House, 1993.
———. Personal Communication. 29 June 2004.
Halverson, Cathryn. *Maverick Autobiographies: Women Writers and the American West, 1900–1936*. Madison: University of Wisconsin Press, 2004.
Hamill, Pete. *A Drinking Life: A Memoir*. Boston: Little Brown, 1994.
Hampl, Patricia. *I Could Tell You Stories: Sojourns in the Land of Memory*. New York: Norton, 1999.
Harden, Blaine. "Suffering and Creativity." *New York Times*, 28 May 2002, E3.
Hart, Francis R. "Notes for an Anatomy of Modern Autobiography." *New Literary History* 1 (1970): 485–511.

Heilbrun, Carolyn. *Writing a Woman's Life*. New York: Ballantine Books, 1988.
Hemingway, Ernest. *By-line: Ernest Hemingway*. Ed. William White. New York: Bantam, 1967.
_____. *The Complete Short Stories of Ernest Hemingway*. Finca Vigía Edition. New York: Scribner's, 1987.
_____. *Selected Letters, 1917–1961*. Ed. Carlos Baker. New York: Scribner's, 1981.
Hogan, Linda. *The Woman Who Watches over the World: A Native Memoir*. New York: Norton, 2001.
Hudgins, Andrew. "An Autobiographer's Lies," *American Scholar* 65 (Autumn 1996): 541–55. Reprint, "The Glass Anvil: 'The Lies of an Autobiographer." *The Glass Anvil*, 92–106. Ann Arbor: University of Michigan Press, 1997.
Jordan, Grace. *Home Below Hell's Canyon*. Lincoln: University of Nebraska Press, 1954.
Jordan, Teresa. Personal Communication. 2 September 2004.
_____. *Riding the White Horse Home: A Western Family Album*. New York: Pantheon Books, 1993.
Jung, C. G. *Memories, Dreams, Reflections*. Ed. Aniela Jaffé. Trans. Richard Winston and Clara Winston. New York: Random House, 1963.
Karell, Linda K. *Writing Together/Writing Apart: Collaboration in Western American Literature*. Lincoln: University of Nebraska Press, 2002.
Karr, Mary. *The Liar's Club*. New York: Viking Penguin, 1995.
Kennedy, Jeffe. Personal Communication. 27 August 2004.
_____. *Wyoming Trucks, True Love, and the Weather Channel: A Woman's Adventure*. Albuquerque: University of New Mexico Press, 2004.
Kircher, Cassandra. "Rethinking Dichotomies in Terry Tempest Williams's *Refuge*." In *Ecofeminist Literary Criticism*. Ed. Greta Gaard and Patrick D. Murphy. Urbana: University of Illinois Press, 1998.
Kittredge, William. *Hole in the Sky: A Memoir*. New York: Vintage, 1993.
_____. "Introduction: West of Your Town: Another Country.' In *The Portable Western Reader*. Ed. William Kittredge, xv–xxi. New York: Penguin, 1997.
_____. *The Nature of Generosity*. New York: Knopf, 2000.
_____. *Owning It All*. St. Paul, MN: Graywolf, 1987.
_____. *Taking Care: Thoughts on Storytelling and Belief*. Minneapolis: Milkweed Editions, 1999.
Kroeber, A. L. "Ethnology of the Gros Ventres." *Anthropological Papers of the American Museum of Natural History* 1.4 (April 1908): 241–250.
Krupat, Arnold. *For Those Who Came After: A Study of Native American Autobiography*. Berkeley: University of California Press, 1985.
Kupfer, Fern. "Everything but the Truth?" *The Fourth Genre: Contemporary Writers of/on Creative Nonfiction*. Ed. Robert R. Root, Jr. and Michael Steinberg, 327–329. Boston: Allyn and Bacon, 1999.
Larson, Sidner. *Captured in the Middle: Tradition and Experience in Contemporary Native American Writing*. Seattle: University of Washington Press, 2000.
_____. *Catch Colt*. Lincoln: University of Nebraska Press, 1995.
_____. Personal Communication. 28 June 2004.
Larson, Thomas. *The Memoir and the Memoirist: Reading & Writing Personal Narrative*. Athens: Swallow/Ohio University Press, 2007.
Lejeune, Philippe. *On Autobiography*. Trans. Katherine Leary. Minneapolis: University of Minnesota Press, 1989.

Leopold, Aldo. *A Sand County Almanac and Sketches Here and There*. New York: Oxford University Press, 1949, 1989.

Libby, Brooke. "Nature Writing as *Refuge*: Autobiography in the Natural World." In *Reading under the Sign of Nature: New Essays in Ecocriticism*. Ed. John Tallmadge and Henry Harrington, 251–264. Salt Lake City: University of Utah Press, 2000.

Logan, William. "Verse Chronicle: The Real Language of Men." *New Criterion* 21.4 (December 2002): 73–80.

Lopez, Barry. *Arctic Dreams: Imagination and Desire in a Northern Landscape*. New York: Scribner's, 1986.

Lueders, Edward, ed. *Writing Natural History: Dialogues with Authors*. Salt Lake City: University of Utah Press, 1989.

MacLane, Mary. *The Story of Mary MacLane*. Helena, MT: Riverbend, 1902, 2002.

Maclean, Norman. "The Hidden Art of a Good Story: Wallace Stegner Lecture," In *Norman Maclean*. Ed. Ron McFarland and Hugh Nichols, 23–38. Lewiston, ID: Confluence Press, 1988.

———. *A River Runs through It and Other Stories*. Chicago: University of Chicago Press, 1976.

Mandel, Barrett J. "Full of Life Now." In *Autobiography: Essays Theoretical and Critical*. Ed. James Olney. Princeton, NJ: Princeton University Press, 1980.

Marcus, Laura. *Auto/biographical Discourses*. Manchester, UK: Manchester University Press, 1994.

McCourt, Frank. *Angela's Ashes*. New York: Simon & Schuster, 1996.

———. *Teacher Man*. New York: Scribner's, 2005.

———. *'Tis: A Memoir*. New York: Scribner's, 1999.

Meldrum, Barbara Howard. "Creative Cowgirl: Mary Clearman Blew's Herstory." *South Dakota Review* 31 (Spring 1993): 63–72.

Miller, Jay. "Introduction." *Mourning Dove: A Salishan Autobiography*, xi–xxxix. Lincoln: University of Nebraska Press, 1990. .

Mills, Enos. *Wild Life on the Rockies*. Boston: Houghton Mifflin, 1909.

Misch, Georg. *A History of Autobiography in Antiquity*. Vol. 1. Trans. W. E. Dickes. Cambridge, MA: Harvard University Press, 1951.

Momaday, N. Scott. *The Way to Rainy Mountain*. Tucson: University of Arizona Press, 1996.

Morris, Gregory L. *Talking Up a Storm: Voices of the New West*. Lincoln: University of Nebraska Press, 1994.

Nalbantian, Suzanne. *Aesthetic Autobiography*. New York: St. Martin's, 1994.

O'Connell, Nicholas. *At the Field's End: Interviews with Twenty Pacific Northwest Writers*. Seattle: Madrona, 1987.

Offutt, Chris. *The Same River Twice*. New York: Simon & Schuster, 1993.

Olney, James, ed. *Autobiography: Essays Theoretical and Critical*. Princeton, NJ: Princeton University Press, 1980.

———. *Memory & Narrative: The Weave of Life-Writing*. Chicago: University of Chicago Press, 1998.

———. *Metaphors of Self: The Meaning of Autobiography*. Princeton, NJ: Princeton University Press, 1972.

Paul, Rodman W. "Introduction." In Mary Hallock Foote. *A Victorian Gentlewoman in the Far West*, 1–44. San Marino, CA: Huntington Library, 1972.

Pearlman, Mickey. *Listen to Their Voices: Twenty Interviews with Women Who Write.* New York: Norton, 1993.
Rainer, Tristine. *Your Life as Story: Discovering the "New Autobiography" and Writing Memoir as Literature.* New York: Penguin Putnam, 1998.
Rember, John. *Traplines: Coming Home to Sawtooth Valley.* New York: Pantheon Books, 2003.
Riley, Jeanette E. "Finding One's Place in the 'Family of Things': Terry Tempest Williams and a Geography of Self." *Women's Studies* 32 (July/August 2003): 585–602.
Ruckman, Jo Ann. "Afterward." In Annie Pike Greenwood, *We Sagebrush Folks,* 485–489. Moscow: University of Idaho Press, 1988.
Russell, Osborne. *Journal of a Trapper (1834–1843).* Ed. Aubrey L. Haines. Lincoln: University of Nebraska Press, 1955, 1968.
Sandoz, Mari. *Old Jules.* 2d rev. ed. Lincoln: University of Nebraska Press, 1935, 2005.
Schultz, James Willard. *My Life as an Indian.* New York: Beaufort Books, 1907, 1983.
Schwantes, Carlos. *The Pacific Northwest: An Interpretive History.* Lincoln: University of Nebraska Press, 1989.
Simonson, Harold P. *Beyond the Frontier: Writers, Western Regionalism, and a Sense of Place.* Fort Worth: Texas Christian University Press, 1989.
Simpson, Elizabeth. *Earthlight, Wordfire: The Work of Ivan Doig.* Moscow: University of Idaho Press, 1992.
Smith, Annick. *Homestead.* Minneapolis: Milkweed Editions, 1995.
_____. *In This We Are Native.* Guilford, CT: Lyons, 2001.
Smith, Sidonie. *The Poetics of Women's Autobiography.* Bloomington: Indiana University Press, 1987.
_____. *Subjectivity, Identity, and the Body: Women's Autobiographical Practices in the Twentieth Century.* Bloomington: Indiana University Press, 1993.
Smith, Sidonie, and Julia Watson. *Reading Autobiography: A Guide for Reinterpreting Life Narratives.* Minneapolis: University of Minnesota Press, 2001.
Spengemann, William C. *Forms of Autobiography: Episodes in the History of a Literary Genre.* New York: Yale University Press, 1980.
Spicer, Edward H. *A Short History of the Indians of the United States.* New York: Van Nostrand Reinhold, 1969.
Spragg, Mark. Personal Communication. 1 May 2004.
_____. *Where Rivers Change Direction.* New York: Riverhead Books, 1999.
Stafford, William. *Stories That Could Be True: New and Selected Poems.* New York: Harper & Row, 1977.
Stegner, Wallace. *Where the Bluebird Sings to the Lemonade Springs: Living and Writing in the West.* New York: Penguin, 1992.
_____. *Wolf Willow: A History, a Story, and a Memory of the Last Plains Frontier.* Lincoln: University of Nebraska Press, 1980.
Stein, Bennett H. "Introduction." *Tough Trip through Paradise (1878–1879),* xiii–xix. New York: Houghton Mifflin, 1967.
Stewart, Elinore Pruitt. *Letters of a Woman Homesteader.* New York: Houghton Mifflin, 1914, 1982.
Swann, Brian, and Arnold Krupat. "Introduction." *I Tell You Now: Autobiographical Essays by Native American Writers,* ix–xv. Lincoln: University of Nebraska Press, 1987.

Tallmadge, John. "Beyond the Excursion: Initiatory Themes in Annie Dillard and Terry Tempest Williams." In *Reading the Earth: New Directions in the Study of Literature and Environment*. Ed. Michael P. Branch et al. Moscow: University of Idaho Press, 1998.

Tanner, Annie Clark. *A Mormon Mother*. Salt Lake City: University of Utah Press, 1941, 1976.

Tolstoy, Leo. *Anna Karenina*. Trans. Joel Carmichael. New York: Bantam, 1960.

Watson, Julia. "Engendering Montana Lives: Women's Autobiographical Writing." In *Writing Montana: Literature under the Big Sky*. Ed. Rick Newby and Suzanne Hunger. Helena: Montana Center for the Book, 1996.

———. "'I Have Never Been Myself': Introducing Mary MacLane." *The Story of Mary MacLane*, v–xxii. Helena, MT: Riverbend, 2002.

———. "Writing in Blood: Autobiography and Technologies of the Real in Janet Campbell Hale's *Bloodlines*." In *Haunting Violations: Feminist Criticism and the Crisis of the "Real."* Ed. Wendy Hesford and Wendy Kozol, 111–136l. Champaign-Urbana: University of Illinois Press, 2000.

Williams, Terry Tempest. *Refuge: An Unnatural History of Family and Place*. New York: Vintage, 1991.

Wolff, Geoffrey. *The Duke of Deception: Memories of My Father*. New York: Vintage, 1979.

Wolff, Tobias. *This Boy's Life*. New York: Grove, 1989.

Wong, Hertha. *Sending My Heart across the Years: Tradition and Innovation in Native American Autobiography*. New York: Oxford University Press, 1992.

Work, James C., ed. *Prose and Poetry of the American West*. Lincoln: University of Nebraska Press, 1990.

Zinsser, William, ed. *Inventing the Truth: The Art and Craft of Memoir*. Rev. ed. Boston: Houghton Mifflin, 1998.

———. *Writing about Your Life: A Journey into the Past*. New York: Marlowe, 2004.

Zwinger, Ann. *Wind in the Rock: The Canyonlands of Southeastern Utah*. Tucson: University of Arizona Press, 1978.

Index

Abbey, Edward 9, 153–154, 155, 156, 162
Absalom 105
Adams, Ansel 81
Adams, Thomas Dow 82
Alaska 5, 51
Alberta 3
Albuquerque, NM 40
Alderson, Nannie 3, 5, 38, 61, 89
Alexander the Great 1
Alexie, Sherman 7
Algonkian language 134
All But the Waltz 2, 12, 25, 51, 77–92, 94–95, 97–99, 122, 181
Amador, Victoria 80, 87
Amazon.com 165
Ames, Iowa 177
Anderson, Sherwood 40
Aragon, Margot 94, 125
Arapaho Indian tribe 9, 134
Arches National Monument (Utah) 153, 177
Arenas, Eeynaldo 87
Aristotle, Aristotelian 13
Arizona 153
Arkansas 48
Armitage, Susan 32
Arnold, Matthew 43
Assiniboine Indian tribe 132
Augustine, St. 5, 19, 20
Austin, Mary 40
The Autobiography of Malcolm X 5
Axtell, Horace 94, 125

Bacon, Sir Francis 7, 15
Bair, Julene 4
Baker, Russell 5, 12, 16
Baldwin, James 5, 141

Balsamroot 2, 25, 94, 101
Bancroft, H.H. 146
Barnes, Craig S. 77
Barnes, Kim 1, 4, 8, 11, 12, 16, 66, 80, 119, 161, 167, 177, 178, 179, 182, 183; *Hungry for the World* 33, 103, 111–112, 114, 148, 177; *In the Wilderness* 4, 12, 56, 102–114, 120, 122–123, 181
Bashkirtseff, Marie 50
Bass, Rick 9, 154, 155, 156
Bataille, Gretchen 124
Bear Paw State Monument (Montana) 141, 146, 147
Bear River Migratory Bird Refuge (Utah) 164, 166, 173
Bear River Wildlife Refuge 177, 180
Beards, JoAnn 4
The Beatles 106
Beauvoir, Simon de 108
Beecher, Henry Ward 44
Bell, Margaret 4, 44, 46–47, 48, 49, 53, 54
Bellingham, WA 144
Benson, Jackson J. 52
Beowulf 127
Bergland, Betty 2
Bernstein, Roberta 103
Bevis, William 4, 56, 61–62, 63, 76
Billings, MT 6, 130, 135
Black Elk 125, 127
Black Hawk 125
Blackfeet Indian tribe 9, 34, 35, 36, 75, 130, 134
Blew, Mary Clearman 1, 2, 3, 4, 5, 6, 11, 18, 39, 47, 101, 103, 115, 116, 150, 161, 177, 178, 179, 182, 183; *All But the Waltz* 2, 12, 25, 51, 77–92, 94–95, 97–99, 122, 181;

204 Index

Balsamroot 2, 25, 94, 101; *Writing Her Own Life: Imogene Welch, Western Rural Schoolteacher* 2, 78, 85
Bloodlines 4, 12, 139–151, 181
Blunt, Judy 1, 4, 5, 9, 92, 103, 177, 178, 179, 180, 182, 183; *Breaking Clean* 9, 12, 102, 113–123, 139, 181
Boardman, Katherine 11
Boise, ID 6, 31, 44
Boise River (Idaho) 45
Bonanza, CO 38
Bosch, Hieronymus 164
Boulder, CO 6
Bozeman, MT 34
Breaking Clean 9, 12, 102, 113–123, 139, 181
Bredahl, A. Carl 63, 64
Bridger Range (Montana) 58, 59
Brigham City, UT 169
Brigham Young Academy (later University) 41, 45, 46
British Columbia 3
Brookings, SD 130, 136, 137, 138
Brooklyn, NY 57
Brumble, H. David, III 124, 125–127, 128, 132
Bruner, Jerome 13
Bruss, Elizabeth 13
Bullock, Thomas 30
Bush, George W. 9
Bush, Laura L. 45, 46
Butte, MT 8, 49, 50, 53, 89
Byron, George Gordon, Lord 50

California 7, 45, 55, 91, 107, 136, 142, 144, 147
Canada, Canadian 113, 129, 141, 144
Cannon, Hal 89, 97
Carey Act (1894) 31, 41
Casper, WY 89
Castañeda, Pedro de 29, 30
Castle Valley, UT 177
Catch Colt 12, 128–139, 149–151
Cather, Willa 8
Cato the Moralist 158
Cellini, Benvenuto 20
Chandler, Marilyn R. 165
Chateaubriand, René de 23
Chaucer, Geoffrey 7
Chelan Lake (Washington) 55
Cher 106
Chesterfield, ID 51
Cheyenne, WY 6, 76, 89, 90
Chicago 23, 24, 50
Chippewa Indian tribe 141, 146
Chodorow, Nancy 101
Chugwater Creek (Wyoming) 97
Chugwater, WY 90, 95
Church of Jesus Christ of Latter-Day Saints 45; *see also* Mormons

City College of San Francisco 140
Clark, Kip 171
Clark, William 29
Clearwater River (Idaho) 102, 103, 106, 109, 110
Cleaveland, Agnes Morley 89
Clough, Arthur Hugh 1
Coates, Grace Stone 47
Coeur d'Alene, ID 109, 148
Coeur d'Alene Casino (Idaho) 145
Coeur d'Alene Indian Reservation, ID 140, 148, 151
Coeur d'Alene Indian tribe 7, 9, 139, 141, 146, 151
Coeur d'Alene Lake 147
collaborations 2, 15, 23, 65, 74, 81, 90, 94, 96, 125, 126, 147, 149
Colorado 5, 6, 8, 25, 26, 31, 43, 48, 51, 54, 77, 129, 153, 154, 155
Colorado River 153
Colorado State University 89
Colville Indian tribe 125
Comer, Krista 6, 7, 8, 33, 79, 88
Continental Divide 67
Conway, Jill Ker 5, 20, 39, 182
Cooper, John M. 135
Cooper Institute (later Union) 44
Coronado, Francisco Vázquez de 31
Couser, G. Thomas 125
Crews, Harry 113
Crow Indian tribe 9, 36

David 105
Davis, Claire 103
Davis, Nell Portrey 51, 53, 54
Dawes Severalty Act (1887) 31
Deering, Andrew J. 131
Degnan, James P. 63
de Man, Paul 14
Denver, CO 6, 9, 31, 40, 48, 89, 129, 180
Desser, Robin 115
Detroit, MI 91
Dickens, Charles 20, 40, 87
Dickinson, Emily 169
Dillard, Annie 5, 12, 16, 17, 28, 39, 56, 66, 152, 162, 164, 171
Dillon, Brian 72
Doig, Ivan 1, 3, 9, 11, 51, 66, 77, 79, 81, 86, 87, 91, 97, 150, 177, 178, 179, 182, 183; *This House of Sky* 3, 11, 17, 44, 55–69, 73–76, 80, 84
Dos Passos, John 8
Dotson, John 52
Doty, Mark 113
Douglass, Frederick 44
dreams 15, 16, 20, 25, 27, 32, 54, 60, 61, 68, 80, 95–96, 98, 106, 127, 134, 142, 143, 144, 157, 161, 170, 174, 175
Druker, Phil 80

Dryden, John 1
Dworshak Dam (Idaho) 106

Eakin, Paul John 17–18, 39, 77, 101, 125, 126, 182
Eastend, Saskatchewan 52
Eastern Montana College (Billings) 130, 135
Eggers, Dave 47
Ehrlich, Gretel 9, 90; *The Solace of Open Spaces* 5, 8, 25, 26, 27, 72, 74, 89, 155
Eliot, George 40
Eliot, T.S. 2
Elko, NV 90
Ellis, Anne 3, 4, 30, 38–43, 44, 46, 48, 49, 50, 51, 52, 53, 54
Emerson, Ralph Waldo 158
Environmental Protection Agency 180
Erdrich, Louise 165

Fairchild, B.H. 91
Faulkner, William 55, 64
Fergus County (Montana) 97
Ferris, Warren Angus 30, 34, 38
Fields, W.C. 90
Fitzgerald, John D. 51
Flannery, Regina 134
Flathead (Kutenai) Indian tribe 34, 36
Florida 9, 92
Folkenflik, Robert 13, 21
Foote, Arthur 44
Foote, Mary Hallock 3, 44–45, 48, 50, 53, 54
Fort Belknap Indian Reservation (Montana) 129, 132, 138, 151
Fort Peck, MT 85
Franklin, Benjamin 5, 20
Franks, Dan 89
Freadman, Richard 27
Freeman, Morgan 65
Frémont, John C. 29
Friedan, Betty 92
Friedman, Susan Stanford 101
Fromm, Pete 9, 25, 155, 156
Frost, Robert 20, 93
Frye, Northrup 14

Gallagher, Tess 91
Garcia, Andrew 3, 30, 34–37, 38, 40, 42, 43, 46, 47, 48, 49, 51, 52, 53
Garden City, KS 41
Gary, IN 91
Gass, William 16, 17, 28
Gediman, Paul 73
Geronimo 125
Ghost Dance 137
Gilbert, Elizabeth 114
Gilmore, Leigh 53
Glacier National Park 31, 129
Glen Canyon Dam (Utah) 153

Glotfelty, Cheryll 172, 173
Gonzaga University (Washington) 140
Goodwin, James 17
Gordon, Rose 61, 62
Gordon, Taylor 58, 62
Gornick, Vivian 15–16, 20
Gosse, Edmuhnd 5, 69, 150
Gould, Steven J. 4
Graham, Katherine 12
Grand Forks, ND 138
Grant, Ulysses S. 17
Graulich, Melody 72, 74
Great Salt Lake 156, 166, 167, 168, 171, 172, 177, 180
Greeley, CO 6
Greeley, Horace 30
Greenwood, Annie Pike 26, 27, 30, 38–43, 44, 45, 46, 48, 50, 51, 53, 54, 179
Greenwood, Charles 41
Greer, Germaine 92
Griffin, Karol 4
Gros Ventre Indian tribe, White Clay people 9, 36, 128, 129, 130, 131, 132, 134, 135, 138, 151
Gunn, Janet Varner 22, 23
Gunnison Island (Utah) 166
Guthrie, A.B., Jr. 3, 51, 61
Guthrie, Margaret B. 165

Haggard, Rider 40
Hale, Frederick 141, 147
Hale, Janet Campbell 1, 4, 9, 124, 159, 177, 178, 179, 182, 183; *Bloodlines* 4, 12, 139–151, 181
Hale, Stephen Dinsmore 140
Hallström, Lasse 65
Halverson, Cathryn 49, 50
Hamill, Pete 56, 57–58
Hampl, Patricia 16
Harden, Blaine 115, 116
Harrison, Jim 165
Hart, Francis R. 15
Hasselstrom, Linda 12
Hatfield Mountain (Montana) 59
Havre, MT 79, 130, 136
Hawthorne, Nathaniel 20
Hazelton, ID 41, 43
Heartland (film) 3, 48
Heilbrun, Carolyn G. 96, 101–102, 111
Helena, MT 23
Hemingway, Ernest 8, 16, 17, 28, 73, 87, 135, 136, 160, 182
Hendrix, Jimi 107
Hill, Carol 63
Hogan, Linda 128, 129
Hole in the Sky 12, 21, 77, 139, 148, 156–162, 172–175, 180, 181
Homestead 24

Homestead Act of 1862 31, 110
Hoover, Herbert 42
Hudgins, Andrew 18, 23, 116
Hudson's Bay Company 145
Hugo, Victor 40
Hungry for the World 33, 103, 111–112, 114, 148, 177
Hutterite/s 84

Iacocca, Lee 17
Idaho 3, 5, 6, 8, 9, 25, 26, 30, 31, 41, 42, 43, 44, 45, 48, 51, 53, 54, 56, 77, 79, 80, 102, 103, 113, 133, 138, 139, 140, 144, 145, 147, 151, 154, 155, 179, 180
In the Wilderness 4, 12, 56, 102–114, 120, 122–123, 181
In This We Are Native 24
independence 2, 5, 32, 33, 78, 81, 88, 101, 117, 123, 130, 171, 182
individualism 17, 19, 21, 27, 31, 32, 33, 34, 39, 72, 76, 101, 102, 108, 124, 126, 127, 137, 151, 158, 172, 173, 174
International Workers of the World 31
intimacy 8, 25, 36, 57, 68, 69, 83, 88, 114, 127, 142, 162, 164, 169, 171, 174, 176
Inuit Indian tribe 164
In-who-lise (White Feather) 35
Iowa State University 130, 140
Iron Mountain (Wyoming) 90, 97
isolation 7, 8, 32, 94, 121, 135, 148, 169, 173
Israel 105

Jackson, WY 9
James, Henry 16
Jezebel 108
Jocko Indian tribe 83, 84
Jonson, Ben 79
Jopline, MT 136
Jordan, Grace 51, 53, 54
Jordan, Michael 17
Jordan, Teresa 1, 4, 5, 82, 101, 122, 150, 177, 178, 179, 180, 182, 183; *Riding the White Horse Home* 5, 12, 77–78, 88–99, 181
Joyce, James 17
Judith Mountains (Montana) 34, 97
Judith River 80, 97
Julius Caesar 1
Jung, C.G. 15, 170
Juvenal 79

Kansas 91, 98
Kansas City, KS 9
Karell, Linda K. 15, 34, 56, 62, 64, 74, 80, 81, 82
Karr, Mary 5, 12
Keats, John 50
Kelly, E.F. 40–41
Kennedy, Jeffe 4, 5, 180–181

Kingsolver, Barbara 4
Kircher, Cassandra 173, 175
Kittredge, William 1, 3, 4, 24, 33, 43–44, 65, 90, 91, 164, 177, 178, 182, 183; *Hole in the Sky* 12, 21, 77, 139, 148, 156–162, 172–175, 180, 181; *Owning It All* 43, 79, 157, 158, 174; *Taking Care* 44
Kootenai, Kutenai (Flathead) Indian tribe 141
Krupat, Arnold 124, 126
Kübler-Ross, Elisabeth 163
Kuna, ID 44, 45
Kupfer, Fern 19, 23, 25

labor 20, 31, 66, 78, 91, 95, 119; *see also* work
landscaping 6, 17, 23, 26, 29, 33, 34, 37, 40, 46, 49, 51, 53, 54, 56, 57, 62, 63, 67, 69, 72, 75, 78, 79, 83, 114, 122, 131, 138, 156, 157, 161–162, 164, 165, 169, 172, 176, 179, 180, 181, 182, 183
Laramie, WY 65, 90
Larson, Sidner J. 1, 4, 5, 124, 157, 160, 177, 178, 179, 180, 182, 183; *Catch Colt* 12, 128–139, 149–151
Larson, Thomas 18–19, 20–21, 27–28, 77, 80, 176, 177
Las Vegas, NV 72
Lawrence, D.H. 40
Leadville, CO 44
LeClaire, Antoine 125
Lee, John D. 30
Lejeune, Philippe 13, 15
Lenore, ID 110
Leopold, Aldo 152, 156
Levine, Philip 91
Lewis, Meriwether 29
Lewis and Clark Expedition, Journals 9, 29, 31, 152
Lewis-Clark State College (Lewiston, ID) 79, 99, 102, 103, 130, 138
Lewiston, ID 9, 33, 79, 102, 106
Lewistown, MT 79
Libby, Brooke 166, 171–172
Lives of the Noble Grecians and Romans (Plutarch's Lives) 1
Lolo Creek, ID 9
loneliness 32, 34, 36, 49, 52, 55, 62, 83, 90, 135, 138, 158, 160, 175
Looking Glass 141
Lopez, Barry 54, 161, 165
Lopez, Jennifer 65
Los Angeles, CA 145
loss 56, 78, 90, 94, 98, 109, 119, 137, 165, 167, 182–183
Lummi Indian Reservation (Washington) 144

MacLane, Mary 4, 8, 44, 49–50, 53, 54
Maclean, Norman 23, 24, 47, 60, 79, 91, 182

Mailer, Norman 73
Maine 9
Major, Ted 164
Malta, MT 113, 114, 119
Mandel, Barrett J. 20, 23
Mann, Horace 125
Mann, Mary Peabody 124
Marcus, Laura 24–25
Maryland 90
McCourt, Frank 5, 47, 87
McGuane, Thomas 161
McKinnon, WY 48
McLoughlin, Dr. John P. 145, 146
McWhorter, Lucullus Virgil 124
Means, Russell 137
Meldrum, Barbara Howard 79
Melville, Herman 136
memory 2, 9, 16, 19, 28, 41, 56, 60–61, 63, 78, 80–81, 87, 110, 111, 115–116, 117, 125, 133, 143, 145, 146, 149, 155, 170
Merriam, Hart 35
Merrill, Julius 30
Mesa Verde National Park 31
Mexico 92, 170
Miles City, MT 38
Miller, Jay 125
Mills, Enos A. 51–52, 53
Milton, John 15, 107
Milton, NY 44
Minidoka Mountains (Idaho) 41
Misch, Georg 14, 15, 19
Mississippi 55, 64, 102, 154
Missoula, MT 76, 89, 114, 115, 156, 177
Moccasin Mountain (Montana) 97
Modernism, Modernist 50
Momaday, N. Scott 4, 124, 128
Monette, Paul 113
Montaigne, Michel de 15
Montana 3, 4, 5, 6, 8, 24, 25, 26, 31, 35, 37, 47, 48, 50, 52, 53, 55, 58, 59, 61, 63, 64, 65, 75, 77, 78, 79, 80, 83, 84, 85, 86, 97, 119, 122, 128, 130, 131, 146, 154, 156, 160, 177, 179, 180, 183
Mormonism 30, 41, 45, 46, 51, 163, 165, 166, 167, 170, 171, 172
Moscow, ID 177
Mountain Meadows Massacre (1857) 30
Mourning Dove (Christine Quintasket) 125
Muir, John 51
Musselshell River 34, 35

Nalbantian, Suzanne 19
Natahki (Fine Shield Woman) 35
Nature Conservancy 93
Navajo Indian tribe 164
Neihardt, John G. 125
Nevada 137, 163, 177
Nevada Test Site 171
New Almaden, CA 44

New Orleans 148
New York 41, 44
New York City 44, 50, 56, 140, 147, 148
Nez Perce Indian tribe 9, 35, 37, 133, 141, 146
Non-Partisan League 42
Norris, Lisa 8
North Carolina 180
Northern Cheyenne Indian tribe 9
Northern Montana College, Montana State University-Northern (Havre) 79, 88, 130
Northwest College (Montana) 66
Northwest Indian College (Bellingham, WA) 144
Northwestern University 58, 63, 65
nostalgia 2, 7, 9, 21, 34, 50, 56, 61, 63, 74, 82, 91, 98, 102, 177

O'Connell, Nicholas 60, 61
O'Connor, Flannery 55, 65
Offutt, Chris 5, 113
Ogden, UT 6
Oglala Sioux Indians 139
Ohio 92
Oklahoma 24, 48, 105, 129
Olney, James 22
Olympic Peninsula (Washington) 85
Omak, WA 146
Ondaatje, Michael 4
Oregon 5, 9, 77, 137, 144, 146, 156, 180
Oregon City, OR 145
Oregon State University 160
Oregon Trail 31
Ott, Bill 65
Owning It All 43, 79, 157, 158, 174
Owyhee Mountains (Idaho) 155

Padget, Martin 73
Paiute Indian tribe 137
Palouse (Idaho) 113
Paris 41
Patchett, Anne 5
Paul, Rodman W. 44
Pennsylvania 83
Petersen, David 154–155
Philippines Insurrection 31
Phillips County (Montana) 113, 116, 121
photography 2, 25, 61, 62, 66, 68, 81–87, 89, 90, 94, 95–98, 142, 143, 145, 146
Piegan (Blackfeet) Indians 134
Pike, Zebulon 29
Pine Ridge Indian Reservation, SD 137, 139
Plath, Sylvia 20
Platte River (Nebraska) 154
Plummer, ID 140, 148, 177
Plutarch, *Lives of the Noble Grecians and Romans (Plutarch's Lives)* 1
Poe, Edgar Allan 18
Port Angeles, WA 85

Portland, OR 9, 89, 144, 145
Post Falls, ID 107
postmodern, postmodernism 2, 6, 7, 28, 50, 56, 118, 145
Powell, John Wesley 152–153
Powell, WY 66
Progressive Party 42
Proust, Marcel 20
Provo, UT 41, 46

Quammen, David 161

Rand, Ayn 92
Redford, Robert 65
Refuge 4, 9, 12, 22, 33, 156, 162–175, 180
Rember, John 12, 77, 155
Riding the White Horse Home 5, 12, 77–78, 88–99, 181
Riley, Jeanette E. 172, 173
Riverside, CA 139
Robertson, Frank C. 51, 53
Rocky Mountain National Park 31, 51
Roosevelt, Franklin Delano (F.D.R.) 42
Roosevelt, Theodore 52
Roripaugh, Robert 66
Rousseau, Jean Jacques 5, 19, 20
Rowbotham, Sheila 101
Ruckman, Jo Ann 43
Russell, Osborne 30, 34, 38
Ruxton, George Frederick 30

Saguache County, CO 40
Salish-Kootenai Community College (Montana) 146
Salt Lake City, UT 6, 31, 33, 52, 89, 90, 163
Sandburg, Carl 40
Sandoz, Mari 3, 61
San Francisco, CA 140, 144, 145, 180
Sarton, May 101–102
Schlegel, Friedrich 28
Schultz, James Willard 3, 30, 34–37, 38, 40, 42, 43, 45, 46, 48, 51, 53, 127
Seaman, Donna 140
Seattle, WA 7, 58, 112, 129, 144, 146, 177
Selway-Bitterroot Mountains (Idaho) 113, 155
Shakespeare, William 1, 40, 50, 168
Shelby, MT 129, 130, 131, 149–150
Sheridan, General Philip 145
Shoshone National Forest 65
Shoshone River (Wyoming) 67
Shoshone (Snake) Indian tribe 34, 36
Sierra Club 66
Silko, Leslie 127, 128, 132
Simonson, Harold P. 57, 180
Simpson, Elizabeth 58, 60, 61, 63, 64
Sixteenmile Creek (Montana) 59
Smith, Annick 3, 48, 160, 173; *Heartland*

(film) 3, 48; *Homestead* 24; *In This We Are Native* 24
Smith, Jedidiah 31
Smith, Joseph 30, 170
Smith, Sherry L. 140
Smith, Sidonie 12, 16, 19, 21, 22, 24, 27, 29, 32, 82, 100, 102, 116, 118, 123, 152
Smohalla 137
Snake River (Idaho) 51, 53
Snow, Eliza Roxcy 30
Snow, Lorenzo 166
Snowy Mountain (Montana) 97
The Solace of Open Spaces 5, 8, 25, 26, 27, 72, 74, 89, 155
solitude 7, 8, 32, 71, 74, 101, 121, 163, 169
Soto, Gary 91
South Dakota 12, 130, 137
South Moccasin Mountains (Montana) 81
Spacks, Patricia Meyer 101
Spanish-American War 31
Spengemann, William C. 19, 20
Spokane Indian tribe 7
Spokane, WA 107, 140
Spragg, Mark 1, 4, 16, 77, 90, 97, 98, 159, 177, 178, 179, 180, 182, 183; *Where Rivers Change Direction* 4, 11, 21, 55, 57–58, 65–76, 117, 181
Stafford, Kim 79
Stafford, William 55, 71
Stange, Mary Zeiss 114
Stegner, Wallace 3, 16, 44, 52, 53, 61, 91, 161, 165, 182
Stein, Bennett H. 35
Stein, Gertrude 5, 17
Steinbeck, John 55–56
Stevens, Wallace 167
Stewart, Clyde 48
Stewart, Elinore Pruitt 3, 44, 48–49, 51, 53, 54
Stewart, Rod 106
Stuttaford, Genevieve 131
Swann, Brian 124
Switzerland 168

Tacoma, WA 144
Taking Care 44
Tallmadge, John 171
Tanner, Annie Clark 44, 45–46, 47, 48, 49, 53
Tanner, Joseph Marion 45
Tanner, Obert 45
Taylor, Jeremy 183
Tetons 9
Texas, Texan 34, 154
This House of Sky 3, 11, 17, 44, 55–69, 73–76, 80, 84
Thomas, Dylan 111
Thoreau, Henry David 42, 52
Thornton, Deb 171

Tidyman, Frances Carson 62
Tijuana, Mexico 142
Tolstoy, Leo 149
Trippett, Frank 56, 60
Tsimshian Indian tribe 157
Tucson, AZ 129
Turner, Frederick Jackson 31
Turtle Mountain Chippewa Indian tribe 133
Twain, Mark 5, 30, 90
Two Medicine River (Montana) 75

University of Arizona 89, 128, 129, 130, 138
University of California–Berkeley 140
University of California–Davis 140
University of California–Santa Cruz 140
University of Colorado 40
University of Idaho 79, 102, 103
University of Iowa 160
University of Kansas 97
University of Minnesota 130, 136
University of Missouri 79
University of Montana 4, 25, 79, 89, 103, 114, 155, 156, 160
University of North Dakota 129, 130, 138
University of Oklahoma (Press) 81
University of Oregon 130, 140
University of Utah 89, 163
University of Utah Press 73
University of Washington 58, 64, 144
University of Wyoming 65, 66
Utah 5, 6, 8, 22, 23, 25, 30, 41, 45, 48, 51, 153, 154, 163, 164, 168, 169, 171, 175
Utah Museum of Natural History 162
Utah State University 154
Ute Indian tribe 9

Valier, MT 62
Vancouver, BC 140, 144, 148
Victoria, Queen 49
Vietnam 111
Vizenor, Gerald 127

Wagoner, David 91
Wallace, Margaret 41
Wanapum Indians 137
Wapato, WA 140, 143
Wapiti Valley (Montana) 67
Warner Valley (Oregon) 174
Washington 5, 91, 125, 144, 180
Washington State University (Pullman) 102
Watkins, Sam 17

Watson, Julia 6, 8, 12, 16, 19, 21, 22, 24, 27, 29, 49, 50, 82, 116, 141, 147, 150, 152
Weintraub, Karl Joachim 19
Welch, James 55, 127, 130, 131, 134, 161
Welty, Eudora 18, 102
Wendover, NV 168
Western Washington University (Bellingham) 142
Where Rivers Change Direction 4, 11, 21, 55, 57–58, 65–76, 117, 181
White Sulphur Springs, MT 58, 61, 62, 74, 79
Willamette Valley (Oregon) 156
Williams, Terry Tempest 1, 4, 9, 73, 177, 178, 179, 182, 183; *Refuge* 4, 9, 12, 22, 33, 156, 162–175, 180
Winnemucca, Sarah [Hopkins], 124, 125
Wister, Owen 90
Wolff, Geoffrey 5, 28, 150
Wolff, Tobias 4, 12, 66, 91, 129
Wong, Hertha D. 126, 127
Wood River (Idaho) 44
Woolf, Virginia 108, 116, 136
Wordsworth, William 14, 20
Work, James C. 30
work/workers 31, 40, 53, 62, 63, 68, 70, 71, 72, 91, 92, 93, 94, 95, 96, 114, 115, 117, 118, 119, 130, 145, 159, 160, 162, 173; *see also* labor
World War I 31, 42, 48, 61
World War II 32, 51
Wounded Knee, SD 137
Wovoka 137
Wright, Richard 5
Wrigley, Robert 102, 110
Writing Her Own Life: Imogene Welch, Western Rural Schoolteacher 2, 78, 85
Wulbert, Roland 98
Wyoming 5, 6, 8, 9, 21, 25, 26, 31, 48, 54, 55, 65, 69, 72, 75, 78, 89, 90, 92, 97, 98, 155, 180

Yaak Valley (Montana) 154
Yakama Indian Reservation, WA 140, 143
Yale University 89
Yeats, William Butler 64
Yellow Wolf 125
Yellowstone National Park 31, 65, 155
Young, Brigham 30, 166

Zinsser, William 15, 16, 47
Zion National Park 31
Zwinger, Ann 22, 23, 52, 152, 155, 162

www.ingramcontent.com/pod-product-compliance
Lightning Source LLC
Chambersburg PA
CBHW032056300426
44116CB00007B/761